RAGS to BONES

To the past, present and future generations of the Windle family

RAGS to BONES

A Child Murderer's Fate

from Arrest to Trial

in 1881 Derbyshire

LINDA GATTO

TAVERNICUS PUBLISHING

First published in 2014

Tavernicus Publishing, 11 Cavendish Lodge, Bath, BA1 2UD

Email: publishing@tavernicus.co.uk

www.ragstobones.co.uk

© Linda Gatto, 2014

The right of Linda Gatto to be identified as the Author of this work has been asserted in accordance with the Copyrights, Designs and Patents Act 1988

All rights reserved. No part of this book may be reprinted or reproduced or utilised in any form or by any electronic, mechanical or other means now known or hereafter invented including photocopying and recording, or in any information storage or retrieval system, without the permission in writing from the Publishers

British Library Cataloguing in Publication Data.

A catalogue record for this book is available from the British Library.

ISBN: 978-0-9564065-1-4

Typesetting and origination by Tavernicus Publishing.

Contents

Prologue-Tuesday 23rd August 1881- The Funeral of Eleanor Windle — 7

CHAPTERS

1 Saturday morning 20th August 1881-A Lost Girl — 15

2 Sunday 21st August -Discovery of a Body and an Arrest — 39

3 Monday 22nd August –The Prisoner before a Magistrate and the Opening of the Inquest — 61

4 Tuesday 23rd August –The Identification Parade and The Funeral — 109

5 Wednesday 24th August- Mansfield Tom and Mr Windle's only Interview — 123

6 Thursday 25th August-Further Identification Parades — 131

7 Friday 26th August-The Adjourned Inquest — 135

8 Saturday 27th August-An Interlude — 191

9 Sunday 28th August- Mayhem in Brimington — 199

10 Monday 29th August-The Adjourned Magistrates' Hearing — 203

11 Tuesday 30th August- Removal to Derby Gaol and Superintendent Carline's Career — 241

12 September and October 1881-On Remand in Derby Gaol — 257

13 Tuesday 1st November- Trial Preliminaries at the Assize Court at Leicester Castle — 285

14 Wednesday 2nd November- Gough's Trial Begins — 307

15 Thursday 3rd November-The Trial Continues — 367

16 Friday 4th November-The Condemned Cell — 397

17 Saturday 5th November-Gough's Early Police Career and Army Life — 401

18	Tuesday 8th November-Unfinished Business for the Trial Judge	411
19	Thursday 10th November- Gough's Letter to his Sister	413
20	Friday 11th November-Gough's Letters Again Appearing In Print	417
21	Saturday 12th November-Superintendent Carline's Thoughts on Gough	421
22	Monday 14th November-Life in the Condemned Cell	423
23	Tuesday 15th November-The Final Interview	427
24	Wednesday 16th November-The Publication of Gough's Letters by the Press	437
25	Thursday 17th November-Gough's Handcart	441
26	Friday 18th November-William Marwood	443
27	Saturday 19th November-Carline's Destruction of the Handcart	447
28	Sunday 20th November- Marwood Finally Arrives	449
29	Monday 21st November- The Hanging	455
	Postscript	471
	Bibliography	473
	List of Maps and Illustrations	485
	Acknowledgements	486
	Notes Regarding the Differing Fonts	488

PROLOGUE

TUESDAY 23RD AUGUST 1881

On Tuesday afternoon, amidst drenching rain and peals of thunder ever --- rumbling in the distance, the mortal remains of the poor child whose life was so cruelly taken on Saturday last, by a depraved, debased and inhuman being, were carried to their last resting place in Brimington Cemetery there to lie until the last great day. Under any circumstances a funeral cannot fail to be impressive and saddening but more especially is this the case when the body consigned to the grave is that of a girl in the springtide of life, who but one short week before was in the possession of health and strength, ------ and yet in one brief hour fell a victim to one of the most revolting crimes which can disgrace humanity. Words would fail to express the indignation which the outrage has created in Brimington and the neighbourhood and therefore it is not to be wondered at, that as the hour fixed for the funeral --- 5 o'clock ---- approaches large numbers of people gather in the vicinity of the house of the deceased's parents and also in proximity to the cemetery gates. The crowd though large is far from fashionable, it is a crowd -------- loud in the expression of their detestation of the tragedy which has taken a young child from their midst, which has thrown into mourning one of the most respected families in the village, which has turned a house of joy into a house of sorrow, which has robbed a mother of one of her youngest born and taken from a father one of those for whom it was his delight to toil. The crowd embraces the sturdy, rough spoken collier, the strong handed farm labourer, the able artisan, their wives, sweethearts.....and children, many of whom have been the playmates and companions of the child-------

The rain falls down pitilessly, ceaselessly and noiselessly, but the assembled multitude - though many of them are unprotected from it -heed it not. As the hour of interment approaches (the coffin is carried out of Mr Windle's house by two friends --- Calow and Wright. It is placed on a table near the door until the members of the bereaved family appear(ed), and whilst the coffin lays there it is covered with wreaths of flowers) the bell in the cemetery tower commences to toll in a doleful and mournful manner adding as it were to the solemnity of the occasion. The bell has not ceased its melancholy tolling 'ere the mourning procession leaves the house in Almond Terrace, and proceeds towards the cemetery which is situated some few hundred yards away. Plain and unpretentious is the mourning cortege, it includes neither hearse nor mourning coaches, but its very plainness lends an impress to the scene. Between the rows of villagers who line the road the procession proceeds with slow measured tread and the entrance gates of the cemetery are quickly reached. Here it is met by the Reverend Thomas Wilkinson, superintendent minister of the Chesterfield Wesleyan Circuit who has undertaken to perform the funeral ceremony. For Mr Windle and his family -------- are amongst the most regular attendants at Brimington Wesleyan Chapel, the deceased child having been also an attendant at the Wesleyan Sunday School.

As the procession nears the cemetery we note that at its head is Miss Hendrin, mistress of the Brimington National School, where the deceased received her education. (She was much attached to the murdered girl, for the child was one of her most engaging and intelligent scholars.) Miss Hendrin wears a white scarf and carries a beautiful wreath of stephanotis and cluster roses. Next come 13 scholars, members of the class with which the poor child was formerly associated. These are followed by 6 young women bearing the coffin, which is constructed of oak, and bears the simple inscription --------------

-"Eleanor Windle, born June 7th, 1875; died August 20th 1881". The young women are teachers in the Wesleyan Sunday School. ------Misses Bagley, Gibson, Larkworthy, Wharton, Astle, and Doughty (who wear white shoulder scarves across their black dresses and white tulle veils, and have each a bouquet) ---- Following close upon these come Mr. William Windle and Mrs. Harriett Windle, the parents of the deceased, the latter seeming overwhelmed and prostrate with grief. (She tottered in her walk, and had to be supported by her husband, on whose arm she leaned heavily) In close succession are Walter Windle (19yrs) the eldest son; and 5 other children, Frederick William (17yrs), Francis (16yrs), Alice (14yrs), Ernest Henry (10yrs), and Albert John (4yrs). Next are Mrs. Mary Windle, the girl's grandmother; and Mr. Francis Windle and Mrs. Mary Windle (uncle and aunt) of Newbold; Mr Joseph Windle and Mrs Elizabeth Windle (uncle and aunt) of Newbold, and many friends.

Prior to entering the cemetery Miss Hendrin and the scholars formed in two lines at the gates, and remained there until the mourners had passed on towards the mortuary chapel when they rejoined the procession and entered the building in which the first portion of the burial service was conducted. Mr Windle being a

Dissenter the first part of the funeral service is performed in the neat mortuary-chapel set apart for the use of Dissenters. The little edifice was quickly filled to its uttermost limits, hundreds of persons being compelled to remain outside. -------------- at (the ceremony's) close the procession reforms and slowly wends its way to the new made grave, which is situated in the Dissenters' part of the Cemetery (in the unconsecrated portion of the ground), some 35 yards distant from the mortuary chapel (about 50 yards from the cemetery gates and not far from the turnpike road. Undeterred by the rain, which continued to fall in torrents, the people crowded near the grave, ---some of whom found it difficult to retain their footing on the newly -turned soil, which became very miry with wet, and the trampling of many feet. The ground at the grave side was more like a morass than anything else, so incessant was the downpour...). Feelingly, touching and sympathetically, Mr Wilkinson performs the concluding part of the ceremony, and there is scarce a dry eye in the large concourse assembled round the grave as the coffin is lowered into the grave. Its lid is completely hidden by wreaths and flowers, amongst the former being one which deserves special mention. It is the gift of several of the deceased's companions, and it is composed of wild flowers, prominent amongst them being a sprig of the blackberry plant which the deceased and her playmates had set out to gather on the morning of the day which was to be her last on earth. These wreaths may be of somewhat rude construction, they may not embrace exotics and flowers of a rare description, but they are the freewill offering of friends and neighbours of the deceased's parents and, prompted by sympathy, their value is great. The rattle of earth on the coffin proclaims that all is over, and the poor mother who has with difficulty borne herself throughout the trying ordeal, now gives way to her grief, and, leaning her head on her husband's breast, sends up an agonising cry of "My child, my poor child" Gently and tenderly she is removed from the spot, the mourners take one farewell look into the grave of the child whose career on earth was so sadly terminated and then depart.------------------ so ends a scene which those who witnessed it can never forget. The rain still falls, the thunder peals, and the dusk of evening comes upon the scene, and beneath the sod in the hillside cemetery is left the body of Eleanor Windle,----------------------

As he made his way, rain- soaked yet again, back to town, Superintendent Elijah Carline was feeling all 42 years of his age. He shook his head in disbelief at the scene he had just witnessed and the turmoil one person could cause to so many people's lives in the space of just three days!

For an explanation of the different print styles which follow please refer to the "Notes" at the end of the book.

1. CHESTERFIELD AREA. 1880 ORDNANCE SURVEY MAP

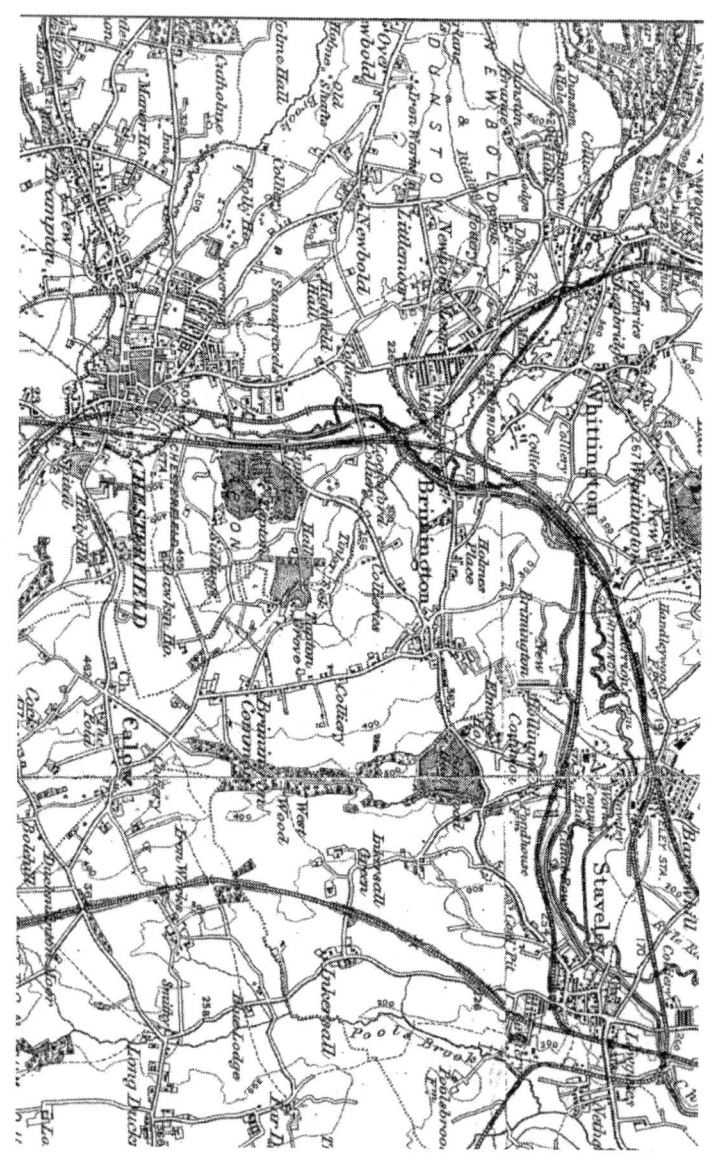

CHAPTER ONE

SATURDAY MORNING   20th AUGUST 1881

A LOST GIRL

Early morning and a beautiful day though Alfred Gough was in no mood to notice. He was still brooding over the previous evening's events. He was a hawker dealing in rags and bones with his own handcart (though this hadn't always been the case). He'd disposed of all his "toys" in his day's work and about half past six that Friday evening was passing the lodging house, that he had been billeted in for the past few days, in Church Lane run by William Stone.(A fairly central location in the bustling market town of Chesterfield).Next door to Stone's lodging house at number 10 lived a widow whose two daughters along with another playmate had caught sight of him and begun to follow for some distance. They had shyly spoken to him on previous occasions and were now emboldened to be more adventurous. He was heading west out of town and at some stage he offered or the girls asked if they could have a ride in his cart. He not being a family man with responsibilities thought nothing of it. However Hope Woodward, a young woman who knew the young sisters Annie and Ada and 7year old Annie Goodwin showed more concern. She hurried back to tell their parents what she had seen. John Goodwin, one of Annie's elder brothers went in search of her and when his luck ran out his younger brother Frank along with Miss Harriet Broomhead took up the quest. They found the girls opposite the Grouse Inn in Brampton nearly a mile from their homes guarding the cart whilst Alfred was in the pub getting a glass of beer. Seeing that the girls were being spoken to by this couple and being taken out of the cart Alfred came out and declared "Come along a little more dears, let us get a little further". Unfortunately for Alfred, John, the elder brother now appeared and after a short altercation he threatened that he had "serious intentions of giving him (Alfred) a good warming"! And that this was not the end of the matter. John Goodwin was going to return to this subject at a later point in time!

After the girls sulkily left with the three adults Alfred departed The Grouse. He pushed his handcart a short distance off the main Chatsworth Road and down the side street known as Hipper Street where Mr Thomas Newberry would be waiting to weigh his bounty of the day and provide more drinking money.

Alfred could have forgotten about his disagreement with young Mr Goodwin except for the fact that when he got back into town to his lodgings who was on the doorstep but the widow from next door! Annie and Ada's mother –Mrs Emma Todd (On the April census her family's surname was Jones).She confronted him with questions giving him "a good talk "on the subject.

"Don't you take them again. They're my children, and you had no business to interfere with them."

"Why, I've not done the little things any harm,"

"No, but at the same time I don't thank you or anyone else for taking my children away."

"They asked me to go, and I am so fond of little children that I could not refuse them."

Mrs Todd had already questioned the girls as to their actions and they had asked for the ride in his cart but that did NOT excuse him for what he did!

"You must know that it makes parents very anxious when children are away. You have had them much further from home now than they have ever been in their lives."

"I would give any child a ride that would ask me; bless the little dears! I love little children. You know I have done your children no harm."

"Well, now, let this be a warning to you never to take anybody's children again. You know we hear strange things these days, and I don't like the notion of little children going far from home at all."

"Yes, we do missis. I have read something to-day that perhaps you have not heard of...."

Alfred proceeded to tell Mrs Todd of an assault upon Sheffield girls in Rotherham one being only a little over 12 years of age but the anxious mother paid no heed to his ramblings.

"Well, master (probably pronounced "mester"), it is quite sufficient for me to know that you have had my children, and now take care that you don't take them again".

Following Mrs Todd to her own door Alfred protested that he had no intention of harming the children. He loved little girls!

"You will surely get yourself into trouble with this love for children if you take them away from home. In fact if the man had not come to say that my children were returning just at the time he did, I was going down to the Municipal Hall to get them to send a policeman after you."

(The Municipal Hall was only two streets away parallel to Church Lane but going south of the town in an east —west direction. It was a neat, modern stone building that housed the borough police force.)

Mrs Todd's remark of fetching a policeman unsettled Gough_____

"D___ the policemen. I would not care for 6 policemen, as I was doing no harm to the children".

After this outburst Alfred was very sorry for what he had done and left hoping Mrs Todd would not think ill of him.

Gough did not return to his lodgings immediately. There were plenty of drinking establishments in the town to drown his thoughts if he had a mind to and he did have a mind to! He returned much later with a bottle of rum, his intention being to stay up and drink it whilst smoking his pipe. Unfortunately his landlord thought otherwise. Words were said and Alfred took himself off to bed! Now Saturday dawned but his mood had not lifted. Whether his landlord

Mr Stone, had heard the goings on with Mrs Todd the night before or not Gough did not know but he was told in no uncertain terms that when he left the lodgings he would not be allowed back into the establishment. Stone's reasons were that Gough not only filled the whole house with the papers for making the toy parasols and windmills for his business but also because of his behaviour towards the other lodgers. These carryings-on Stone found objectionable and besides Gough, to his mind, was a very disagreeable person!

Alfred left the premises and without considering his breakfast headed straight to where he could drown his sorrows or fuel the feelings of injustice that were being heaped upon him. Fox's Vaults, then The Angel Vaults where in all he reportedly consumed 14 cups of rum and coffee! To quench his thirst he then called into The Crooked Spire Inn for 2 glasses of beer and all before 10 o'clock in the morning. Then fate took a hand. Originally he set out in a southerly direction out of the town with a view to doing business in Clay Cross or he could have gone to Brampton, Staveley or any of the town's surrounding neighbourhood but for some reason altered his mind at the last minute and headed north-east to Brimington. If only he had stuck to his original course of action all would hopefully have been well but instead……….

Eleanor Windle had been back at school for just a week after the Midsummer holidays. She loved school. The weekends got in the way of her learning and seeing Miss Handren, the teacher of "The Primitive and Methodist Infant Board School" of which she was one of 62 pupils. The 22 year old Miss Sarah Handren had only been at the school for a year but she was in charge, being the only certificated teacher there. Classroom help was provided by an even younger

Mary Palmer. Miss Handren had a soft spot for Eleanor. She knew something of the Windles from Mr Gregory whose family had taken her in as a boarder for Miss Handren was not local to the area. Mr Gregory worked at the nearby Iron Works where Eleanor's father was a foreman. Eleanor was recorded as being "a bright, intelligent child" despite an HM Inspector's report in August claiming the children were backwards in Reading, Writing and Arithmetic! The report continued by stating the children had been transferred to a room where in former times The National School was held. This was a forty year old single storey brick building on a site originally donated to the community by the then owner of the iron works, Mr G H Barrow. It was located just across the road from the church in Church Street right in the middle of the village. However, although the room had been improved the Inspector felt it was unsuitable for the infants and was only to be used temporarily. Indeed the local School Board was told in July that government funding was being withdrawn at the end of the school year unless there were signs of a building programme having commenced by the time of the Inspector's annual visit. It was now the new term and no mention is made of any building work at this point in time.

Eleanor was ignorant of reports and building works she just wanted to get back to school. She had risen early, she thought, but her father and three elder half-brothers had already left for work. She dressed herself quickly. She may be only six but she could put on her own soft flannel petticoat, "stuff" dress and white pinafore and she had no trouble pulling on her woollen stockings. She would put on her boots once she got downstairs. With those she still needed a bit of assistance. Mother did not like her clomping around the house if she could help it. Mother said there were enough big pairs of feet in the house without Eleanor adding to it! Alice, Eleanor's older half-sister and the only other female (apart from mother) in a house full of males, was helping with the two youngest children whilst Eleanor's mother busied herself at the brown earthenware sink in the backroom. There was no sign of Ernest! Eleanor wanted to talk of school again, she had been practising her capital and small letters on her slate yesterday and Miss Handren had said Eleanor had made an admirable effort! She could go on incessantly but Mrs Windle had other chores to attend to without someone constantly chattering in her ear. Eleanor was packed off to the shop on an errand and peace reigned in the household until she returned. She had even been promised a halfpenny if she was a good girl and didn't dawdle back.

Gough passed the Chesterfield Brewery with its intoxicating smells and the busy, brick-built, smoke-filled Midland Railway Station. (As a young man he too had worked for this railway company in Leeds as a porter but that was in another life.) Saturday was market day and this attracted many to the town. Over the river bridge and there on the right was the railway wagon works. The road hugs the railway lines to its right whereas the River Rother meanders along on the road's left to be joined further up for a short length by the Chesterfield Canal. This river was a mere trickle in comparison to some rivers he had crossed in his life. Bridges built of boats and rivers a mile wide or more!

Carrying on Gough passed the Malthouse and was dimly aware of the upcoming sound of the two weirs where the canal meets the river. Around here is the acrid smell of the chemical works and yet on the right beyond the railway lines is parkland and atop the hill- Tapton House, once the home of George Stephenson of "Rocket" fame. The road takes a sharp right turn over a railway bridge where to his left is the Tapton Junction signal-box. Fields to left and right are passed, along with a police constable though this does not register with Gough. Well why should it? A staggered crossroads is reached. To the right, the road leads up to Tapton House and further on, on the left – Lockoford Lane. Gough meanwhile continues on the road towards Brimington ahead.

Eleanor on her return from the shop met with Ellen Hadfield on the road. She was older than Eleanor and busy organising a group of girls all younger than she and all neighbours at Almond Place. They were off on an expedition blackberrying. Did she want to come too?

Eleanor said that she would have to ask if she could but she also needed to go and get a container for the blackberries. "Well hurry Nelly!"

Eleanor rushed through the door gabbling (so it seemed to her mother) about Ellen, containers, other girls and blackberries and she was in a hurry and was it alright?!Her mother was partial to blackberries, she could taste the pie already and it would mean Eleanor was occupied and the house would be quiet for a while longer whilst she saw to the men's dinner. "And take your straw hat with you it's going to be a lovely day for a change". Eleanor grabbed it and a "tin can" and was off "full of life and spirits".

Working along the stretch of road known as Tinkersick near to Lockoford Lane this morning was Charles Brown. He was a collector of tolls for the Chesterfield and Worksop Turnpike Road - the stretch between Chesterfield and Staveley, but he was not above having to mend the road as well. This Saturday morning he was breaking cinders at the side of the highway at the bottom of the hill leading up to Brimington. Brown had been at work since 8 o'clock and he thought it was around 9 or 10 o'clock when who should pass him but Alfred Gough pushing his hand-cart. The men knew each other by sight for Gough came into contact with Brown when he had to go through the toll bar at the other end of the village. Gough greeted Brown with a "Good Morning". Brown returned the compliment but then Gough went on his way. He was not much of a talker and so Brown continued his work.

A little further on at Peter's gate Ellen's group of children were blackberrying in the hedgerow on a bank alongside the road. Curious to see what toys Gough had, they peeped into his cart. He did not even have to blow his horn to attract their attention. His cart was full of brightly "fluttering paper banners", "little whirling windmills", parasols, small ware and "gaudy-coloured toys" of various descriptions. Some he had made himself, other items he purchased from makers in Sheffield. In fact, he was expecting a delivery today. The bright "baubles" he displayed would be exchanged for people's rags and bones and sometimes he would sell the toys if no rags were forthcoming.

When one of these children, a pretty little girl, saw the parasols, she was highly delighted, her eyes lit up and she was determined to have one. The one adorned with a pink ribbon.

"My ma has got a halfpenny of mine, and I will buy a parasol."

2. MAIN TURNPIKE ROAD LEADING TO BRIMINGTON

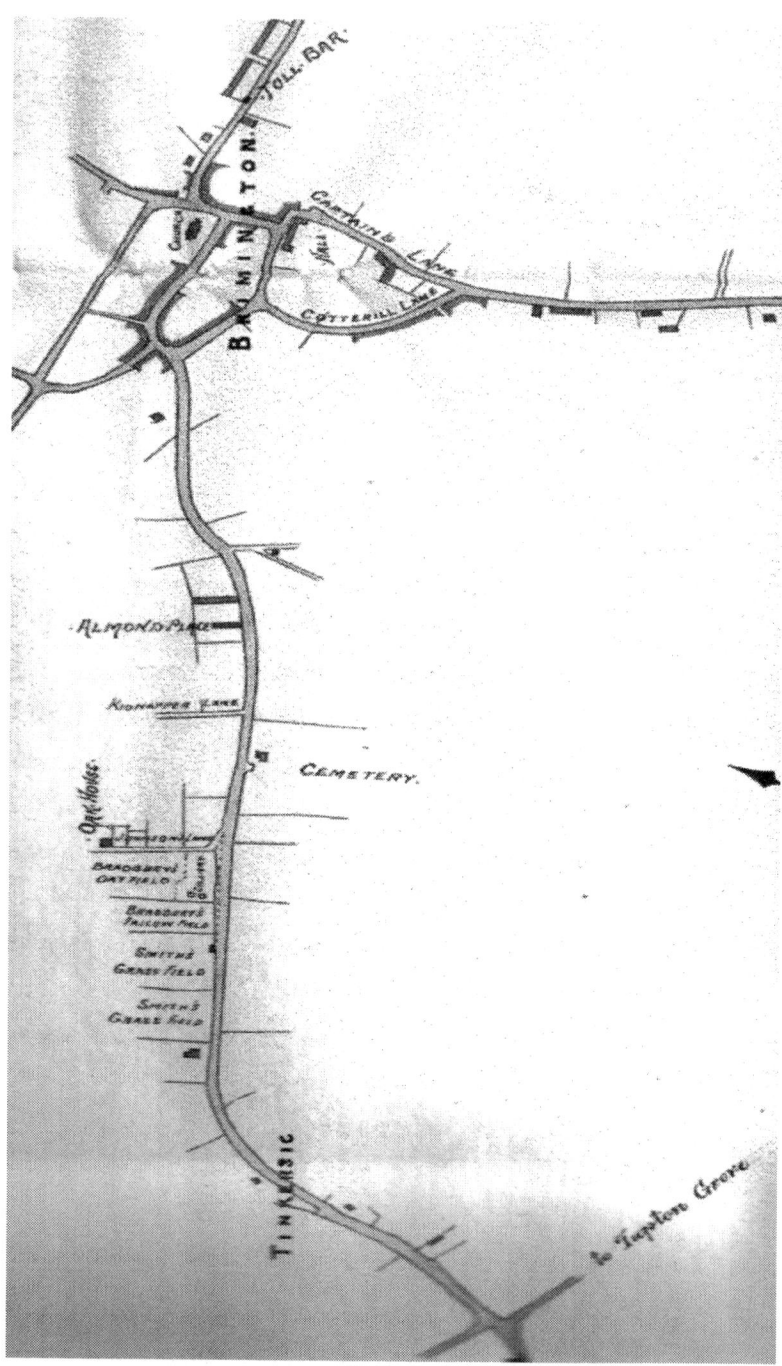

Ellen Hadfield had brought the young children down the hill to go blackberrying. She was uneasy with the situation but did not know why. In a phrase well known to children through the ages she called, "Come back, or I will not be friends with you," but "Nellie" refused to turn back to her friends. Her eyes were only on the prize she would get when she reached the top of the hill and home to get her money. Alfred did not care whether he sold a parasol or not but continued up the hill with this little six year old determined to keep up with him.

John Insley, a 56 year old local carrier, had left Chesterfield with his cart bound for Brimington about 10 o'clock that morning. He could see the children picking blackberries in the distance ahead of him and Eleanor Windle leave the group and follow quickly after Gough and then catch him up and walk alongside him. Mr Insley knew Eleanor, the two Jep(h)son girls and two or three of the Hawke's (Hawksworth's). All lived in Almond Place. He also recognised Gough as the hawker he had seen on the road before, pushing a handcart. He finally overtook them at the bottom of Johnson's lane where Gough had stopped his handcart. Eleanor was looking into the cart but nothing was said. Only that Gough looked upon her. About 20 yards past them Insley turned round and noticed only that Gough himself had moved closer to the lane but the cart and Eleanor were still where they had been when he passed them. Mr Insley had not turned round with any foreboding. He was just looking for someone who had also left Chesterfield and should be coming up behind him.

Gough was oblivious to Mr Insley's cart. He was hoping that the little girl peering longingly into his barrow might continue up the hill to her home and leave him to his thoughts. He thought if he spent some time in Johnson's lane collecting and cutting sticks to make new toys the child might get bored and move on. But she didn't!

SATURDAY AFTERNOON

The handle of the door turned and four hungry workers entered. Mrs Harriet Windle knew it must be about half past one and woe betide it if the men's dinner wasn't ready and on the table! All the family were assembled but Eleanor had still not returned. Where was she? It would not do for a mere child to keep her betters waiting. Harriet was anxious but William as head of the family was not prepared to wait and certainly would not be going out to enquire after her. He would speak sternly to her on her return. He had been working since early morning and nothing was going to keep him from his dinner!

He had been employed at Staveley Iron Works for near-on two decades and seen some changes in his time. William, now 41 years old, was a young married man in his 20's when he had started there. Then, it had been a private company run by the wealthy Mr Richard Barrow. He had run it and the mines successfully for his elder brother George for more than twenty years. In 1864, a year before Mr Richard Barrow died, the works and mines became a public company with a labour force then of 4,200 men. Eight times as many workers as when Mr Barrow first took over. Mr Barrow may not have "owned" the company outright but he was still one of the largest shareholders, was chairman of the board and had managed to poach his friend, Charles Markham, from the Midland Railway Company in Derby, to come and be his new Managing Director. Mr Markham was formidable. From contemplating getting rid of the obsolete iron works circumstances in the costs of pig iron made him do an about face and set-to, to rebuilding the two old furnaces. The late 1860's and early 1870's were boom years in the works casting iron pipes for the growing gas and water board companies. Some of the pipes were up to 56" in diameter! And, even though in 1881 William knew that generally the coal and iron trades had been in a depression for some years, at Staveley Mr Markham had continued to grow the business. Now there were six furnaces with an output in castings, the previous year, of 33,000 tons. More than double that of twenty years ago. Three of William's sons and his young nephew, Arthur on his wife's side, had found employment in the fettling department. Well, William was the foreman there and management encouraged the different generations of a family working alongside each other. It was a filthy job, "fettling", but youngsters had to start somewhere. Once the cast iron pipes had been broken out of their sand moulds it was up to the fettlers to clean up the castings. Their jobs were to remove the sand, the bits of extraneous iron and any other errors on the castings' surface and even look for any cracks in the castings. The air was thick with choking dust but William would rather he and his boys did this than go down the mines like his own father and two brothers had done. He never wanted to be a collier and he didn't want his sons to be either!

William glanced over to his wife and noticed she had hardly touched her food. She was genuinely worried about Eleanor's absence and although she knew better than to remonstrate with her husband now that he had finished his meal he did feel it was time to discover what was keeping her. Harriet had told William that Eleanor had gone out with her playmates blackberrying. She was probably at the home of one of her friends by now and was not aware of the time. Consequently, Ernest Henry, as the youngest responsible boy, was sent to see if she was at a friend's house. Meanwhile the plates were cleared, save for a place set for Eleanor, and Alice and her stepmother Harriet began to wash up in the sink whilst the men sat and relaxed. It was not long before Ernest Henry returned stating she was not there. William could see by his wife's face that she would not rest until she knew where Eleanor was so Ernest Henry was again dispatched to look in all the places where Eleanor was known to play. He returned around three but with no news. Harriet was now so worried that she took it upon herself to go and look for the child. Surely Ernest Henry had not been thorough enough!

Alfred Gough had spent the early afternoon going through the village of Brimington right down to the Common and back again. Initially, once he had got to the top of Brimington Hill he had called in at The Ark Tavern (referred to as The Oaks Tavern in the Derbyshire Courier though this is probably a mistake) and asked for a glass of beer (The Derbyshire Times claimed Gough was feeling ill). It was only when the drink had been poured that he told the landlady, Mrs Blower, he only had a penny to pay for it. She being kind-hearted and not wanting the beer to go to waste suggested she should have a flag for her daughter instead of the money. She even offered to go and fetch the flag from the cart herself or let her daughter choose. Alfred wouldn't hear of such a thing. He would go and fetch it himself!

He had done a little business here and there to put some money back into his pockets but then headed out towards Staveley. However, just before Ringwood Lodge he turned left down the private road that led to the iron works and on towards the village of Barrow Hill. By 3 o'clock he had passed the works and was pushing his cart under the railway bridge heading for that settlement where he would spend an hour or so trading his wares for rags.

Four o'clock and Harriet returned alone. She had no news of Eleanor at all except that she had been seen going along the lane with a man pushing a handcart. William could see the anguish on Harriet's face. (No mention is made at this point that Mrs Windle had spoken to a Miss Johnson who urged her to go to the police. Why was this? Was Mrs Windle in denial that anything awful could have happened to Eleanor? Surely she was only lost!)

However, this was not now the actions of a naughty wilful child. Something definitely was not right and, alarmed himself, William would now have to go looking for her. Thankfully his three eldest sons willingly agreed to help in the search. They all set out together and then William headed off through the village whilst his sons turned off right to go down towards Brimington Common and Calow.

The Windle brothers' quest was fruitless and so it was decided that someone should go to Chesterfield to get the bellman (town-crier) to "call" it through the town and in Brimington too. The covered wagonette pulled by two horses could be hired from The Ark Tavern just back up the road towards the main part of the village. It would be passing about 5 o'clock and again at 6. It cost 4d one way but time was of the essence and as many people as possible needed to know Eleanor's description and that she was missing.

Quarter to five and Alfred was retracing his steps back under the same railway bridge he had passed under nearly two hours earlier. He had done what business he could in Barrow Hill and was now heading back towards Brimington.

It would only have taken him about half an hour to return so the cart could have been heavy to push or he may have found more custom en route.

About 6pm and Gough was back in Brimington stood outside the little two- roomed toll house right on the side of the turnpike road heading back to Chesterfield. Before going through the tollbar gates he felt he had earned a drink. He parked his cart and bought himself a glass of ginger beer for a halfpenny from Charles Brown, the toll keeper. The door was open as the day had been beautifully dry for a change rather than what seemed to be the continuous rainfall experienced so far that month. Gough caught sight indoors of what to him was a familiar photograph. He had had such a photograph taken of himself. Gough stepped inside to take a closer look for the windows were small and the room seemed dimly lit. It was of one of Brown's sons, Charles, the youngest from his first marriage. Catherine was the second Mrs Brown. Charles was now 23 years old, a soldier and stationed with his regiment at York. A smile passed across Gough's face. He knew that uniform well. It was the 17th Regiment of Foot. He should know it he wore it for 9 years and 210 days! How smart the young man looked. That bright red jacket was certainly an "eye-turner" with the ladies! How smart Gough used to be. No less than the Commander in Chief of the Bombay Army and the Commander in Chief of India favourably commented on "the soldier-like appearance, dress and good conduct of the regiment" whilst on parade and the Brigadier General regretted their departure from Peshawur in 1876 stating that it was "such a fine and soldier-like regiment". What happened, as he glanced now at his shabby attire? - "His clothes were very old, and it was not possible to tell the original colour of his coat, which had grown dingy in its conflicts with the weather. His shoes were covered with dust"! Who would believe that he had once lived in India, batman to an officer and returned not long after the Prince of Wales' visit to that sub-continent? The Prince reached Portsmouth 11th May 1876 amidst celebrations and Alfred's troopship was in port a few hours earlier but probably protocol meant they had to wait for the royal disembarkation first. Was it really a mere 5- years ago? Alfred had returned from Bombay on the steamer- "Crocodile". The ship was primarily bringing back invalids - 653 of them but he was part of a group of 21 time-expired men and a couple of dozen or so soldiers from other corps along with wives and families. What was it, though, that he was coming back to? He surely did not expect it to be the life he was now leading?

His reverie was disturbed by a man's figure in the doorway. He was asking Gough a question. He stepped out to speak with the man. Had Gough seen a little girl when he came up to Brimington this morning?

"There are so many I did not notice. In our trade there are so many after us."
Mr Windle turned sharp on him and said "That is a lonely part of the road and you must know whether there was a child that came up with you or not."
Gough then said, "I did see a little girl; I remember there was a little girl that came with me from about the old machine house."
Mr Windle asked him where she left him, and he replied "She came up with me to the cottages just above the cemetery. The child wanted a parasol, and I told her that if she

would go and fetch some rags she should have one, and she went away. A lot more children got round, and I did not see any more of it." Mr Windle said to him, "It left you there", and he said, "Yes."

Gough asked Mr Windle if the child was his and when he replied in the affirmative Gough said,

"I am very sorry; it's a bad job."

William turned and walked back towards the village. Well, what else could he do? He only knew that Eleanor had been seen with a rag and bone man and nothing else at this point in time. As he headed towards the church he saw a short distance away the welcome outline of a policeman - PC Wright - and stopped him outside "The Three Horseshoes" pub to tell him that Eleanor was lost and that the hawker had seen her. Gough was following on behind William so that when he came upon him again PC Wright was stood waiting to speak to him.

"What about this child?"

Gough repeated what he had already said to William outside the toll-house. After asking after his trade PC Wright allowed Gough to go on his way.

"I hope it will soon be found. It's a bad job," called back Alfred as he headed towards Chesterfield.

William headed North West to Whittington on what was to be yet another fruitless search.

No doubt PC Wright jotted down the particulars in his notebook so that he could report back to his colleagues when he next met them at the "place of conference" on his beat. He

32

would have to arrive by the nearest turnpike road which he was already on or failing that the highway "but not diverge through lanes or fields"! The police constables and their sergeant would then wait at the designated meeting place for half an hour recording each other's arrival, how long they met for and the subjects discussed. This was a way of checking that the men were properly on their beat and not shirking their duties. A further check that the police were performing their duties correctly was "sergeants and constables will each day leave tickets at the house of some respectable person residing at the most distant point of that day's patrol, and also at the residence of any Magistrate or Clergyman or Gentleman by which they may pass. They will state in their diaries the names of the persons on whom tickets have been left. Should the parties called on have retired for the night the ticket must be inserted under the front door". (A History of Police in England and Wales 900-1966 by T.A.Critchley "Police Work" p. 157).

PC Wright looked on as the two men went their separate ways without a word.

It is to be presumed that once the police were informed of Eleanor missing they helped to organise a search in which many of the villagers participated though Mr Windle's immediate friends and neighbours would already have been mobilised. The impression was still that

"the child had wandered some distance from home, and had got lost."

On William's return from Whittington he had nothing to report except that he had spent nearly three hours searching and knew hardly anymore of Eleanor's movements than when he had set off! Home had more news to give him. A neighbour, retracing the steps of the young blackberry-pickers down Brimington hill, had gone up a lane opposite the cemetery. At the top of this narrow lane with fields to either side was Oak House where a Mr Johnson lived with his sister. The neighbour, Mr Jephson had already been given information that Eleanor had been seen near this lane and so walked slowly up it looking to left and right. He hoped that the Johnsons could shed some light on the child's whereabouts. He had knocked at the door and was met by Miss Johnson. Miss Johnson wasn't smiling! It was just after tea-time and she was not expecting visitors. This was a lonely spot and Miss Johnson, now in her 50's, would be reticent to open the door to a stranger. Her brother was in his 60's and there was no one else in the house. Edwin Jephson explained why he was there and that a little girl was missing. Miss Johnson said nothing but he felt sure she knew more than she was saying. He had gone back to the Windles' to report on what had happened but at that time William had not yet returned from his search. William could not have got back from Whittington if he had walked all the way to that village until gone 7 o'clock but as soon as he heard Jephson's story he was out the door in search of PC Wright to accompany him to Oak House and get some answers.

7pm and Gough was back, as he had been the previous night, in Hipper Street, Brampton to transact some business with the marine store dealer, Mr Newberry. (Such a curiously named profession consisted of buying and selling old rope, bunting, rags, timber and metal, sorting out the waste and mending sacking. Nothing it seems to do with the sea particularly as Chesterfield is more than 80 miles away from water in any direction!). Gough was paid 3 shillings for 5 stones (31kg 751g) of loose rags and bones. "Not so big a pile as usual" thought Mr Newberry for when the weather was fine Gough usually earned 6-7 shillings on average. Unusually Alfred asked Mr Newberry if he could leave his handcart with him in the yard? Mr Newberry had known Gough for about a year though he was a man of few words. He did not feel that he knew him at all though he called at his premises 2 or 3 times a week. Gough was always alone and said very little. However Mr Newberry found Gough to be a very diligent and industrious worker in the rag and bone trade and as this was the first time that Gough had wanted to leave his empty cart he willingly assented. The cart was placed in a warehouse and Gough walked out into the darkening night.

William Windle eventually found PC Wright and told Jephson's tale to him. "Dusk (had) deepened into darkness" and in the distance he could make out figures, highlighted by their lamps, candles, torches, twinkling lanterns and "anything that would afford illumination no matter how feeble", calling for Eleanor. So impressive but such a melancholy scene. Where was she?!

William and the young policeman (equipped with his issued oil lamp) slowly inched up the lane that led to Oak House. Any disturbance in the vegetation to left or right of them they noted. Any gaps in the hedge they noted though at this stage they did not know if it would be important or not. It was now around 8-8.30pm. When they reached the Johnsons' house PC Wright knocked at the door. Miss Johnson again came to see who could be outside at this time of night. When she saw a policeman stood before her she stepped out to hear what he had to say. PC Wright explained the situation though not that he was accompanied by Eleanor's father.

Could she shed any light on the girl's movements? Miss Johnson could. What she had to say must have made

William's blood run cold. She had seen a child in the morning in the company of a man. The man was being unseemly! It is doubtful Miss Johnson could bring herself to say exactly what that meant, be it to a stranger or a member of her family. It would be a coincidence if it was another child and not Eleanor. Miss Johnson could not say however that it was a rag and bone man for she never saw the cart. As far as she was concerned nothing had happened to the child at that point in time and when she had gone after them they just seem to have disappeared and that was that. William found it hard to believe that Miss Johnson told no one what had occurred. She made no effort to report it to the police or even tell Mr Jephson when he had called earlier even though she knew by then that a little girl was missing. Miss Johnson had been a teacher. Did she not feel obliged to take some responsibility for the child and check that she was safe?

When all was said Miss Johnson made to go back into the house. William could have sworn she muttered (no doubt under her breath) that they would never see the child alive again. But the door closed. Shocked by what he had heard William and the young constable walked back down the dark lane in deep thought.

William could not give up hope. He had to find Eleanor. He joined the growing number of searchers scouring the countryside with their lights ablaze way into the night.

What Alfred Gough did before going to his lodgings that night nobody knows or wants to tell. (The Leeds Mercury reported that he was seen the worse for drink in the town around 10 o'clock but this was not reported in any of the local papers.) However, when Gough finally reaches his night shelter the hour is late. There was still plenty of noise coming from the revellers in the town centre but not so

3. MAP OF JOHNSON'S LANE 1881

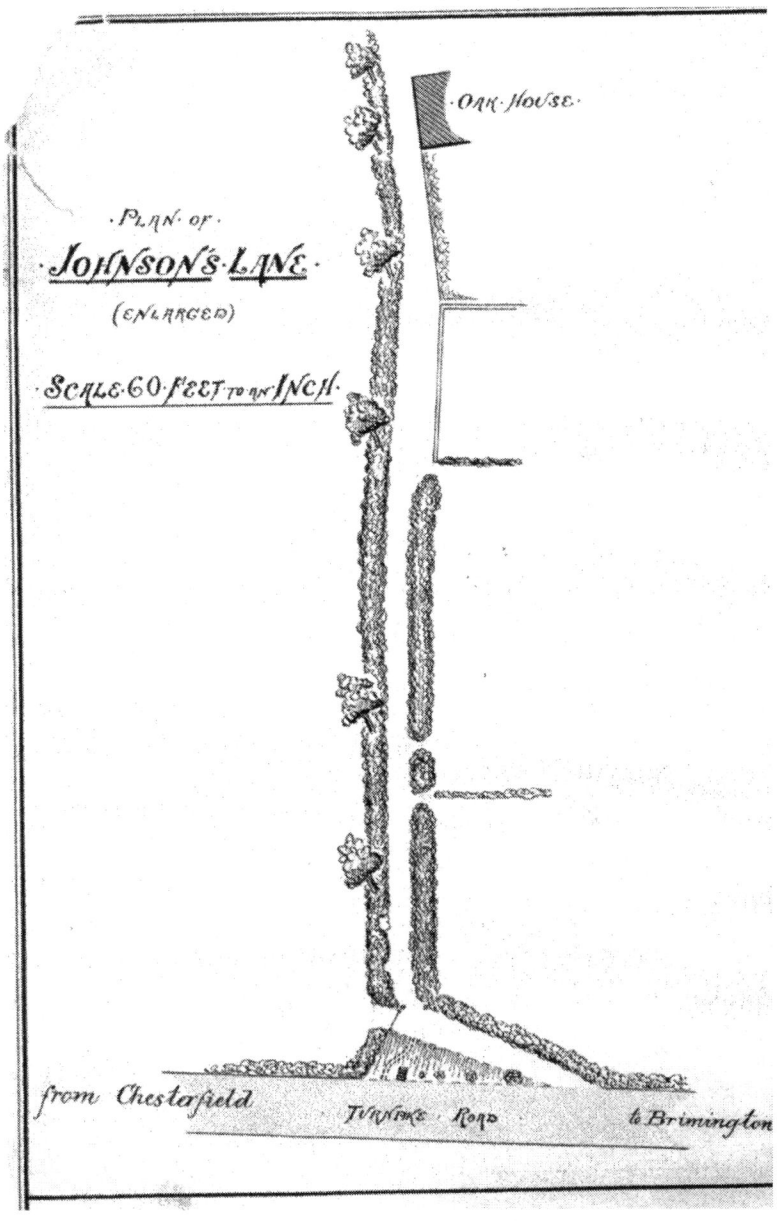

where he stood! The lights were already out! The Sheffield Daily Telegraph claimed it was between 11.30 and midnight and it was to Mr Spowage that Gough asked "if they could oblige him with a room for one man." He was unsure that they did have accommodation but when Gough said "he was poorly and would be glad to have a bed to himself" Mr Spowage relented and stated there was just one room vacant with a single bed but on the female side of the house. After paying 4d Gough was allowed in and probably Mrs Spowage escorted him to his room. She later informed the police that she saw nothing wrong in Gough's demeanour or appearance to suggest any horrible wrong-doing. Mr Spowage thought he was "quite fresh", in a "beery state" but quiet. Whereas Mrs Spowage did not have the impression at all that Gough had taken much drink and with the usual salutations she too was informed by Gough that he was slightly unwell but no-one could later confirm this. However, Mrs Spowage claimed he did seem unable to cut the twist tobacco for his pipe suggesting he was in a very nervous condition!

One presumed that Gough had arranged earlier in the day to stay the night here for he knew before he left the town that morning that he would not be welcomed back at Mr Stone's establishment. He must have also organised with someone to deliver to Spowages' some flags for his trade knowing that he would be staying there and in fact the Sheffield paper stated that a man had called that morning with a quantity of flags "and said he wanted lodgings for himself and his mate, and left the flags."

Gough may not have felt very well and suffered a restless night but at least he saw his bed. William on the other hand did not stop searching until about 2a.m. on the Sunday morning. He was exhausted but only rested for an hour then was back out looking for his daughter.

CHAPTER TWO

SUNDAY 21ST AUGUST 1881

DISCOVERY OF A BODY AND *AN ARREST*

The sun rose at 4.56 a.m. but clouds masked its brightness creating another dull start to an August day and still no sign of Eleanor although the search had continued throughout the night. William, friends, neighbours, family and indeed the whole community according to the Sheffield Independent had carefully gone over most of the fields in the neighbourhood, the lanes, brooks and all likely places but to no avail. What could the distraught William do now in his quest to find his lost daughter? Where could he go next? He certainly could not just go home and wait for tidings.

About half-past six on Sunday morning the news of the extraordinary disappearance of the child was brought -",

initially to the Chesterfield borough police station by two men. This is a supposition for Superintendent Carline states at the inquest that he received the information of Eleanor's disappearance about 9am on the Sunday morning. Such a discrepancy may mean that the two men first called at the borough police station in South Street. Finding, after they had told their story, that as the event had occurred in Brimington rather than in the town of Chesterfield itself they should probably redirect themselves to the county police station in Marsden Street. The borough police force had been set up in 1836 after the 1835 Municipal Corporations Act. A Watch Committee appointed by the borough corporation had the power to hire and fire its own policemen and in 1881 their Superintendent of Police was John Else. He was a local man who had been promoted from police inspector to head of the constables but only the constables of the borough! In 1879 Mr Else was in charge of 1 inspector, 2 sergeants and 14 constables but not Superintendent Elijah Carline. He worked for the county police force based at the other end of town. Carline was not answerable to Mr Else or to the local Watch Committee. His superior was the Chief Constable of Derbyshire and it was he who hired and fired the county police. Although the county force had not been operational for the same length of time as the borough police force Superintendent Carline brought to the job a professionalism that seemed lacking in the portly, middle-aged Superintendent Else. Both men lived "above the shop" of their respective premises but on a Sunday no doubt Else was pleased to pass on the case to Carline. Not that the police had Sundays off. In the 1870's they still worked 7 days a week and even in 1881 a constable might only have one day off in 4 to 6 weeks. The police were expected to attend church and the wearing of the uniform was, of course, compulsory. The uniform was to be worn at all times! Possibly Elijah was at his prayers when the two messengers of bad tidings arrived at Marsden Street.

"They stated the circumstances under which the child had been lost, and added that she had been seen last with a hawker, whose name they did not know, and of whom they could give but a very imperfect description. In consequence of the information Sergeant Radford (a 35 year old married man who was also quartered at the county police station) *accompanied the two men to the Chesterfield lodging-houses, but no traces---could be found.*

(In an interview given later in the week it appears William Windle must have been one of these two men as he claims he trawled round the lodging houses that morning with the police.) Two of the town's lodging houses gave scant clues as to the hawker's whereabouts. Mr Stone, a married man in his 50's, gave Sergeant Radford a description of a man of "very imperfect character" but this was no surprise after the events of Friday night at his establishment. Mr Spowage of the Beehive lodging house on Knifesmithgate denied seeing the man at all(even though Gough actually spent the night there).His premises, during the taking of the census, had room for at least 22 boarders, the majority of whom were single or widowed and not local to Chesterfield. So it could have been possible for the 51 year old Spowage to be unaware of all the guests that were under his roof even though he was the one that allowed Gough in the night before! It appears from The Sheffield Daily Telegraph that there may have been some confusion as to who the police were looking for. Mr Spowage claimed that they asked if he had taken in "a man with children's flags who had a little girl with him." They also had no name to give. Gough had arrived with neither flags (as his cart was with Mr Newberry) nor girl. Spowage went on to say he had been expecting an old soldier. That Saturday evening, (yet another newspaper version), a "short person" had called with some paper flags, the property of an old soldier who would arrive that day but as far as he knew the old soldier had not arrived! Mr Spowage did not know that Gough was the old soldier and there had been no mention of flags. The enquirers moved on, Sergeant Radford heading off to the lodging-houses of Brampton and Clay Cross with a like result. A lot of information was given to the police but of little value.

Several people had seen the hawker the previous evening but no-one knew where he had spent the night or knew of his whereabouts now. The only clue the police could get of Gough was that he had been seen on the railway bridge about 6 o'clock on the Saturday evening. (Even this information would be later discounted after hearing the evidence of PC Wright. He was speaking to Gough himself about 6 o'clock in Brimington village that Saturday evening and even at Gough's speed he could not have been on the railway bridge roughly one and a half miles away just after 6 pm.)

Meantime back in Brimington the searchers were dragging several ponds with no success. Charles Abney Hastings Brown decided to join the Brimington search around 11am, whilst Superintendent Carline back in Chesterfield followed another line of enquiry. It had been discovered that the hawker had at one time been doing business with a smallware dealer by the name of Marriott in Cavendish St. round the corner from the Beehive Lodging House. Carline called upon this dealer's manager, Mr J. Oliver to seek any further information. Luckily, Oliver knew the hawker, Gough, well and was able to furnish Carline with as good a description of him as he possibly could. Oliver even accompanied the Superintendent to numerous public houses in an attempt to find Gough throughout the morning. Though diligent in their searches it was as if the man was invisible!

The road labourer cum toll keeper Charles Brown took it upon himself to turn detective or had he another motive? William Windle with friends and neighbours had scoured every field and hedgerow with no success. They had searched throughout the night with the aid of torches and lanterns and found nothing. Now the 54 year old Mr Brown on his own proceeded to make enquiries as to Gough's route through the village on the Saturday. Did not the Windle family and friends think of this or were they hoping only to find a lost girl? Did they not want to face the awful conclusions as Saturday turned into Sunday? Rather than looking "the Chesterfield end" of the village Brown headed in the opposite direction towards Staveley. His wife, Mrs Brown had discovered from a neighbour, James Cropper that he had seen a cart parked by the side of what was known as Hoole's Plantation on the private works road the day before. James was going to go himself to have a look around but Mr Brown went instead. Why didn't they go together? Surely it would have been wiser to investigate in pairs so that if the girl was found someone could go for assistance whilst the other stayed with the child. She could have had an accident!

Brown may also have spoken to the Thorley household at "bottom lodge" near Ringwood Hall for Mrs Thorley had seen a hawker go by with a cart the previous day. He had passed down the private road towards the Staveley Works. Brown *"searched about the hedges in the neighbourhood first and then came into the private road, which is about half a mile from Brimington." "Upon this road he noticed the marks of wheels similar to those of the hawker's cart."*

(It is to be remembered that Brown had seen and spoken to Gough on at least two occasions the day before and Brown had been a toll-collector with over 20 years experience. He would be very familiar with various types of vehicles that would pass his way through the toll-bar). The wheel marks were outside a piece of rough raised and wooded ground,

4. MAP OF HOOLE'S PLANTATION

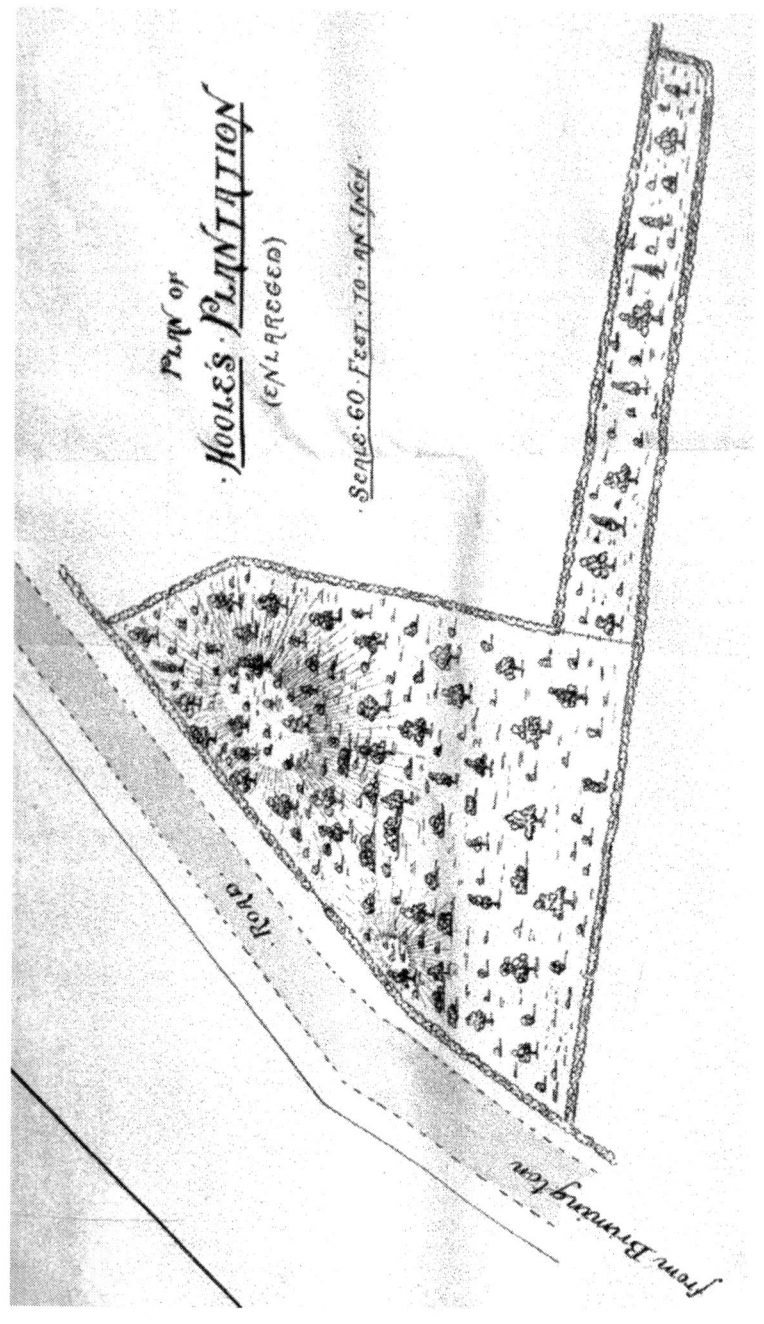

known as Hoole's Plantation, enclosed by a thorn hedge and post and rail fence at the side of the road. Brown would later testify that *"they were hand barrow wheel marks. The wheels were about two feet apart. It was evidently a hand-cart. The marks were quite plain. There were some cinders there which had been wet by the rain."*

It obviously rained at some time very early in the morning. *"The marks looked as if the barrow had been run up and down and then drawn close to the hedge."*

He saw no footmarks but still Brown climbed over the post and rail that "could easily be passed over" and followed the path that led through the plantation, turning some way in to his left. When he got 2 or 3 yards up the path he noticed a small bag or sack lying amongst some bushes that were growing on a bank. Brown examined it but found nothing remarkable except that the hem had been torn off. Without thinking, (or was he?) he picked it up and put it in his pocket! He then continued up to the top end and returned back on another section of the plantation. From here 18 or 19 yards down he saw a body or probably it was the straw hat which initially attracted his attention! Here was no footpath; the body was in the "underwood" which the "horrified" Brown had to negotiate. The corpse was lying beside an old nettle-covered spoil bank. (The waste material excavated from the mines and dumped at some time there to form a new landscape.) Eleanor was under a small tree amongst some tall grass. He went up to the body and saw that it was a girl. She had been placed on her back with her head reclining a little to the left. Her hands had been placed on her breast.

5. Sketch from Illustrated Police News 3rd September 1881

The dress was drawn up a little.

"One leg was drawn up. She was quite dead; cold and stiff. Her face was swollen, and so were her eyes. Her face was not much discoloured."

(Yet the Derbyshire Times reporter described the face as being "somewhat blackened"). Around her neck was a piece of sacking tied so tightly that her neck was quite swollen over it.

Only an hour of searching and Charles Brown had found the dead girl! It was now around mid-day. Brown claimed that he heard someone coming up the lane and on seeing that it was Edward Tulley called to him to come and look at the awful discovery. Brown then placed the straw hat over Eleanor's face and extracted the sack from his pocket in order to cover her body. As they both come out of the plantation lo and behold Brown then finds a piece of coloured wallpaper about 2 or 3 yards from the railings. Blue and red flowers upon a cream coloured background. The sort used for making toy parasols. The sort Gough would have used when making his toys! How is it Brown found this damning evidence? Why didn't Tulley see the wallpaper on entering the plantation? Surely he would have walked passed it to reach Brown if he was with the body? Would Gough really have left such incriminating evidence in the plantation?!

For now all Brown could do was seek out the local police and get word to Superintendent Carline in Chesterfield. It was Police constable Twigg of Barrow Hill who arrived first on the scene and hearing the sound of a pony and trap went to flag down the occupant. It was Mr Knighton, a familiar figure to him as he also lived in Barrow Hill though in one of the purpose built stone villas for the Staveley Works' managers. The 56 year old was the iron foundry manager of the Staveley Coal and Iron Company Works. On hearing that Eleanor had been found Mr Knighton did not hesitate to offer assistance. He had known the little girl's father William Windle for nearly 20 years. Ever since William had first come to work at the iron works as a labourer. Now he was a foreman in the fettling department. Mr Knighton had a respect for his workforce. He prided his ironworkers to have been "brought up on the place". William and his three sons were such an example and he himself had his own two sons follow him into the works. The miners may have outnumbered the skilled ironworkers by around 7 to 1 but they were the "foreign" element and always more difficult to handle. The ironworkers were nearly all recruited locally and trained on the job. Mr Knighton also had dealings with William other than work. He was a "Wesleyan sympathiser" and knew William to be a dedicated Wesleyan. William was a "class leader" being the spiritual guide on a regular basis to a like-minded group of people and was therefore well respected himself in the community. This terrible business with Eleanor would shake William's world. He knew that much and he wanted William to know he should not return to work until all matters had been dealt with.

Carefully the group of men, joined by Joseph Turner at some point according to his evidence, lifted Eleanor into the trap and Mr Knighton drove her through Brimington back to her home and parents.

"All the villagers turned out to see what little they could of the unfortunate victim."

Meantime, whilst Brown was making his awful discovery, back in Chesterfield at Spowage's lodging–house Alfred Gough had risen and was coming downstairs into the kitchen oblivious of all the goings-on. Miss Annie Elizabeth Clarke, the deputy of the establishment, glanced at the time. It was gone 12.30. Alfred greeted her with a "Morning" and she replied, with a hint of sarcasm, "Morning" back.

"Have you had any flags left here?"
"Yes, we have. Are you an old pensioner?"
"Yes."

Then completely changing the subject although in Annie's mind it was completely logical to go from flags to a pensioned off old soldier to the police, she remarked -"There have been five policemen looking for you this morning." This would have been Sgt Radford, the two men from Brimington (who were possibly mistaken for police) and probably two constables. They had spoken to Mr Spowage earlier, being the man of the house, but he had no idea that Gough was sleeping upstairs in his own abode! Obviously husband and wife did not communicate with each other as to why the police had called; for it is certain if they had worked it out they would not have allowed Gough to sleep in so late. Annie Clarke may have been told the police had called or perhaps she just heard them at the door but she knew no more. Gough queried "Have they got the man yet or the child?" but Annie had no answer to give. Gough initially showed no surprise that the police wanted to speak to him

"seeming to look upon it as a natural thing for them to do"

"Weren't the men talking about the child before I came down?"

"No one was talking about the child at all. The child was never mentioned till you named it to me."

What Annie did not know was that Gough had already been asked about the child the evening before and knew of Eleanor's disappearance. Gough then, according to The Derbyshire Courier, "exhibited signs of terror" as he went out across the road almost creeping in to the back of the Buck Inn. Feeling uneasy Annie followed him but waited outside near the railings against the "Crooked Spire" churchyard. In only a short time Gough came out of the pub and returned to the kitchen of the lodging-house. Annie made sure she was not seen. Gough was just stood with his back to the fire. (In Annie's deposition to the magistrate on Monday she would state that Gough "came back to the Lodging House and spoke to the man who had brought the flags and then he went back to the Buck." This would be natural enough that Alfred should want to speak to the person who had brought him a new supply of goods for his trade but it was not mentioned in any of the newspaper reports.) In just a short time Alfred returned to the pub and Annie according to The Sheffield Daily Telegraph sent off a person for the police whilst she "and some others whom she apprised" watched the pub from a safe distance.

A little before 1pm the awful news of Eleanor's murder and discovery of the body reached the Superintendent. He applied for assistance from the borough constabulary and wasting no time Elijah must have re-doubled his efforts in looking for the hawker for by quarter past one, acting on the tip-off, he was entering the Buck Inn in Holywell Street. In Annie's statement she claims when Gough left for the Buck Inn that was the last time she saw him except when he was being taken up the road (to the lock-up) by the police. Why would she have seen this if she was not expecting an arrest to happen? An arrest would only happen if she had told someone to notify the police of Gough's whereabouts!

6. Sketch from Illustrated Police News 3rd September 1881

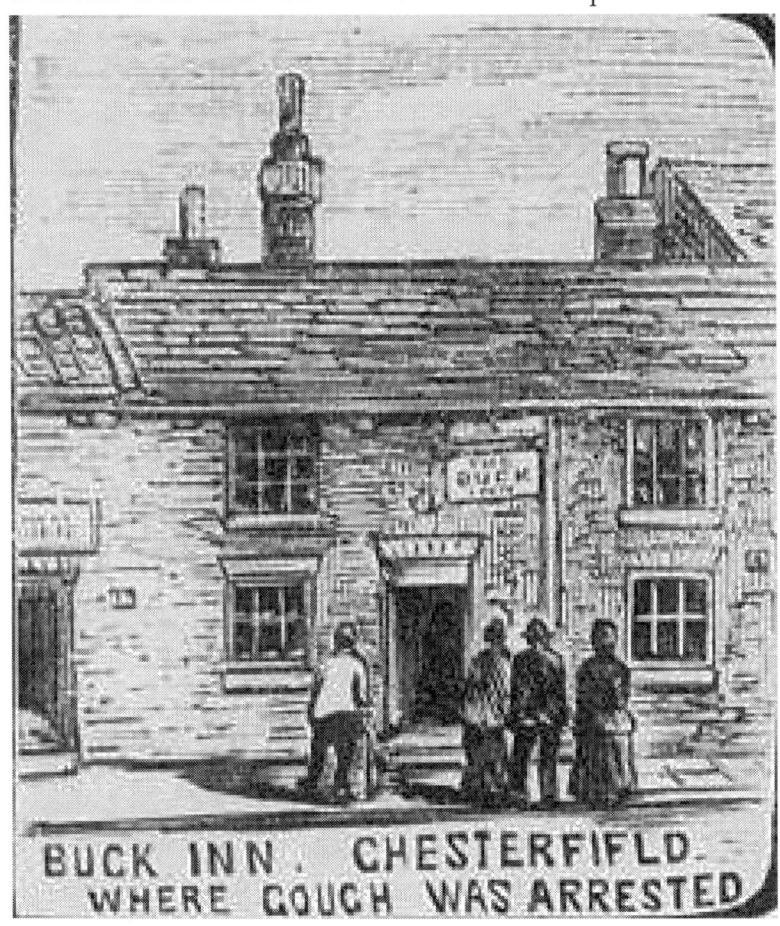

The Buck Inn was a drinking establishment right on one of the main thoroughfares through the town. It was run by George White and assisted by his children and new young wife. In one of the back rooms- the "bagatelle room" - Gough was seated, drinking a glass of beer. His head was bowed and was taking no notice of who was entering the room. Later witnesses remarked that when Gough entered the pub earlier his manner was strange and seemed to wish to avoid observation.

Carline went right up to him.

"I believe you were at Brimington yesterday."
A pockmarked face looked up:-
"Yes, I was."
"Then I want to speak to you"

Gough rose and went to the back door with Superintendent Carline. Elijah could see that they were roughly the same height though Gough was inclined to stoop. He could also tell that Gough had a somewhat military bearing even though he knew nothing about him at that moment, but his strong build and muscular physique gave that impression. Elijah continued:-

"I am a police officer; and I have come here to apprehend you on suspicion of having murdered a female child of the name of Eleanor Windle at Brimington, yesterday, and whose body has recently been found."
Gough, who did not appear to be at all frightened by the statement, mildly replied: *"I know nothing about the child."*
Other witnesses will say he turned "as white as death"!
"Mr Carline then handcuffed the man, and removed him to the police -station in Marsden Street."
Joseph Whitham, a workman at Staveley assisted Carline, according to a Sheffield reporter, by each man putting their arm through Gough's and marching him up the road. The Superintendent arranged for statements to be taken from the landlord, his family and those who were drinking in the pub at this time. Apparently Gough did not go to the bar where

other customers were being served but walked into a more quiet part of the pub where only two people were seated. Gough asked one of them, Chas Julian, to fetch him a pint of beer.

"The man thought it somewhat remarkable that he would not go to the bar for his own beer, but he willingly complied with the request."

Perhaps Gough offered to buy the man a drink for his trouble. Mr White's son, Arthur, served Chas who duly took the beer back to Gough and then returned to the bar with the correct money.

Gough *"did not drink his beer very readily, but seemed, according to the testimony of the two men, to labour under some suppressed feeling of excitement. He kept his head bent, but would cast rapid glances if any one moved about the door. All this seemed very mysterious to the men present, and observations to that effect passed between them. Before drinking his beer, Gough, having peeped at the company in the bar, walked into the backyard.*

Arthur White claimed he noticed "Gough come out of the bagatelle room several times and stoop down in the passage leading to the front door, as if he were trying to see the clock on the Parish Church, and in such a manner as gave one the idea that he was afraid of being seen by the people passing the open door leading into the street. Any person in the house can see the clock simply by walking along the passage to the front door, and the evident pains which Gough took by kneeling to see the clock without going to the door" gave

Arthur the impression Gough was afraid of something but he was only a 16 year old. Maria, the landlord's eldest daughter happened to be in the back yard when Gough left off his beer and he "gave her such a fierce look that she ran away and locked herself up in the washing-house, fearing that the man would do her an injury"! The landlord's 13 year old daughter Bertha passed him in the kitchen doorway. She claimed she was so struck by Gough's looks and general appearance that once he had gone she called out to Mrs White, the landlady, *"Oh my! What a fright that man is."*

The Sheffield Telegraph was even more graphic "Come, and look at this man. He would frighten anyone. He looks as if he would murder someone"!

Hindsight is a wonderful thing! Every glance, word or action from Gough was interpreted by the landlord's family and pub regulars as being sinister, odd and underhand. Mr White's establishment was going to be a popular drinking venue on the back of this even though Gough had never set foot in the pub before and the whole incident was over in no more than ten minutes! The increase in beer sales in exchange for lurid accounts of a murderer's arrest was "to give comfort to the heart of the landlord"!

The witnesses stated that Gough was out in the yard for only a few minutes but that could have been time enough for him to have gone back to the lodging house as Annie Clarke had claimed. Were Gough's thoughts in turmoil? He soon returned to the pub and strangely asked Chas to enquire of Mrs White if he could borrow a needle and thread to stitch the seam of his trousers! It was whilst she had gone to fetch these items that Superintendent Carline entered the Buck Inn and arrested "his man".

On arrival at the lock-up they entered the side gate, crossed the court yard and headed towards the central door that led into the charge office. There Gough was cautioned by Carline, *"I am going to arrest you now on a charge of wilfully murdering Eleanor Windle, at Brimington, yesterday. You need not say anything, but whatever you do say will be taken down and may be given in evidence against you."* Gough again denied all knowledge of Eleanor's fate replying *"I know nothing at all about the child except that I saw her against her own door on Saturday."* Gough *"did not offer to make any further explanation"* so was led to a door at the back of the room. Gough entered an inner lobby. To the right of him was a staircase which led up to the superintendent's office. The sign said so and he could read! Ahead of him was an opening that led into a corridor. He was now going left but for the moment his way was barred by a sliding iron door. He glanced behind him and saw that the corridor led to three cell doors. This must have been for the females - less security! The noise of the barred door hitting its buffer made Gough turn again. Ahead of him a corridor, lit by two barred windows to his right. To his left four cell doors. One of those doors was pulled open and he quietly entered the windowless room to sit upon the bed. Once Gough had been safely locked up Superintendent Carline headed off to Brimington and Sergeant Thomas Eyre (though stationed in Staveley, the other side of Brimington) was sent off to Brampton, completely in the other direction. There he was to pick–up and bring back to the police station Alfred Gough's handcart from the premises of Mr Newberry. This he did around 2pm. The Sheffield Daily Telegraph reported that when the police examined the cart they "found underneath some oil-casing, which lay on the bottom of the barrow, a quantity of grass and shreds just as if something which had been among the grass had been at one time, and that recently –for the grass was fresh – in the barrow." This was not reported in any other newspaper and sometimes it has to be remembered that the newspapers will print downright lies about Gough! The cart was empty of rags but there were two pieces of paper!

It is amazing how bad news travels fast for *"The excitement when the news spread that the body had been found in the wood was most intense, men, women and children ran out of their houses and down the road to the wood with a deep sorrow for the poor little girl."*

A report from the "Sheffield and Rotherham" newspaper on the Monday of the 22nd August stated that the village on hearing what had happened to Eleanor was thrown into a state of the "wildest excitement" and had Gough appeared amongst them he would certainly have been lynched!

Mr Knighton accompanied by Police Constable Twigg and Brown pulled up outside Almond Place. En route they would have passed the home of Dr Bradley. The constable possibly asked a passer-by to call at the doctor's to ask him to join them at the Windles' home. Carefully Eleanor was lifted out of the trap and Mr Knighton led the way along the bottom of the neighbours' gardens and up the path to one in the middle of the row of stone houses. Inside, the distraught family were in upheaval. For twenty four hours their world had been turned upside down. The "men" had been out searching the district since Saturday afternoon, through the night and all morning. Sunday was an important day for William. He was a staunch and highly respected Wesleyan who took a great interest in the welfare of his fellow believers. The children should have been at morning Sunday School. They should have had dinner though no-one could face that and at half past two they should be at the afternoon service or failing that the evening one. William was a leading light in the Wesleyan Movement and yet today his family pew would be unfamiliarly empty. What would his fellow chapel goers be thinking of the Windles right now?

The dreaded knock that the family was waiting for came to the door. At first William could not comprehend why Mr Knighton was standing before them. Had he come on works business? Was there something wrong at the foundry? Then Mr Knighton stepped forward to put his hand on William's shoulder. All eyes were upon him. The kindly gentleman, bringer of devastating news. Your daughter has been found. You must prepare for the worst. With this William dropped down insensible.

It was some time before William recovered and in that time Eleanor had been brought into the house and placed in the front room. William was attended to whilst young Dr Bradley gave a cursory examination of the body. Eleanor was still clothed, her dress was not in any way "disarranged or disfigured" though it was wet. The hem of the sack found in Hoole's plantation was tied tightly round the girl's neck. Not once but twice! This situation meant that Drs. Walker and his assistant Kerr were sent for from Chesterfield. A second opinion and a more experienced eye were needed. They arrived about 3pm, examined the body and gave their opinion "that an outrage had been committed, and that death resulted from strangulation". Dr Bradley concurred with the findings.

Superintendent Carline's main intention of being in Brimington was to hear from Charles Abney Hastings Brown how he had found the body and to recover the piece of wallpaper. No doubt he would have also spoken to Police Constable Twigg the local man on the ground, one or more of the doctors and called to view the body and offer condolences to the Windle family. However he probably did not want to intrude on their grief for too long. The wallpaper Brown had given to him was taken back to Chesterfield. This was to be a damning piece of evidence that Elijah would only discover when he returned to Marsden Street!

Back at the police station Gough *"was very reserved in his manner during the afternoon and evening"* but he did have a visitor. Late that afternoon Dr Walker called in to see the prisoner. Carline had managed to speak to him whilst in Brimington and asked if he could examine Gough and his clothing. The case interested Walker and he had no wife or family as such to get back to, only his spinster sister. However she was not his housekeeper. He had servants and a cook to look after him and his young assistant so all was well. Gough acceded to the intimate examination and removal of his clothes without a murmur. *"He made no reference whatever to the crime and, in fact, showed a decided disinclination to converse on any subject whatever. He was perfectly calm in his demeanour, and did not seem in any way to feel the very undesirable position in which he was placed."*

Dr Walker left with his findings. He would see Superintendent Carline the following day and let him know his opinion.

Sergeant Radford remained in Gough's cell for most of that night. Gough was not one for conversation, keeping up an indifferent demeanour towards his reluctant companion though he did divulge that he had passed the Saturday night at Mr Spowage's Beehive lodging-house. Well why not, the police would have found out eventually? Surprisingly that Sunday night Alfred slept well! Was it relief that the fate of his own life was now out of his hands? Since he had left the army his life had been spiralling out of control. Let somebody else do with it what they like!!

CHAPTER THREE

MONDAY MORNING 22nd AUGUST 1881

THE PRISONER BEFORE A MAGISTRATE

WITNESSES: MISS JOHNSON, MRS THORLEY, MASTER TURNER. MR BROWN

It was another dull, damp morning when Gough was brought before the magistrate, Mr Alfred Barnes MP. Proceedings were to begin about 10.30 at the offices of the justices' clerk, Mr J. Hallewell. Mr Barnes, now in his 50's, had become the parliamentary representative for Chesterfield the previous year. His family had been colliery owners and he continued that tradition. He was a prominent member of the local community and lived just a few miles to the west of Chesterfield. In fact, the solicitors' offices of Messrs. Shipton and Hallewell which today served as the County Police Court were on the right side of town for him. Their workplace on West Bars was a solid brick built Georgian house, well proportioned with steps leading up to a central door surmounted by an intricate "spider's web" fan light. Either side of the door were large square paned sash windows that usually only let the light in but today was different. The stone pillared gates, fronting the main street, opened onto a sweeping drive that led up to the front door and then swept off to the right of the building. It was set back from the busy thoroughfare that led into the town centre and was enclosed by a high brick wall to the right and iron railings upon a low stone capped wall to the left. Who would have expected this scene of calm gentility to be swamped by a seething mass of people curious and eager to get a glimpse of the man who committed (allegedly) such a heinous crime?

7. Painting: Alfred Barnes, Parliamentary Member for Chesterfield and Magistrate. Courtesy of The Chesterfield Museum and Art Gallery

The Sheffield Telegraph was the only newspaper to report that there was a slight hold up in proceedings as a Magistrate had to be found to try Gough that morning. Messengers were sent out from the police station to several local J.P.s "nearly all of whom were absent from home at the time of the messenger's call." However Mr Barnes was in the town that day and agreed to sit and hear the charge.

A little after 10 o'clock throngs of people started congregating outside the county police station in Marsden Street and the upper portion of Saltergate to see Gough being taken to the magistrates'.

"Each time the side door was opened to let in or out a policeman or anyone having business there the crowd crushed towards it, and a passage was rendered difficult."

It was usual to take a prisoner to the Magistrates' Clerk's office just handcuffed to a constable and on foot but...

"The crush near the (lock-up) gates was so great that it was decided to convey the prisoner in the cab...(It) arrived before half past 10 o'clock; and the prisoner, handcuffed, walked between Serg. Radford and Supt. Carline, towards the vehicle. He had to pass through the inquiry office, where some of the witnesses were seated, and as he did so he glanced round hurriedly, and played nervously with his scarf knot. There was no bravado in his manner. He had a crushed, melancholy, hopeless look upon his face: and was exceedingly unkempt" with his scanty beard and sandy coloured moustache. He looked "neglected in his appearance even for an itinerant windmill man.....He had a travel-stained, weary air, as if he had tramped about until he was tired."

The three men crossed the station yard. Once the iron-spiked large wooden gates were opened they hurriedly got into the cab amidst the jeers, groans and yells of the crowd. "Some epithets were used that don't look well in print!" Sgt Radford sat handcuffed to Gough whilst Superintendent Carline sat opposite, eyeing his charge, wondering if there was any emotion behind Gough's impassive expression. For safety's sake a couple of constables were to run in front of the cab whilst another sat on the box alongside the cab driver. The passengers were immediately driven down the cobbled streets- Saltergate, Soresby Street, through New Square and on to West Bars. A mere ten minute ride at the most, but the driver was struggling with the frightened horse and the mass of people were continuously closing in on the cab." Several times a rush was made for the cab, and there were determined efforts to stop the horse." The ride seemed to take an age. Hooting and jeering emanated from the following crowd with shouts of "Wretch" and "Kill him". Many women in no uncertain terms expressed "a wish that he might be let loose amongst them".

At last the cab turned into the gates of Shipton and Hallewell only to be confronted with yet more locals, "sturdy Amazonian women out of Castle Yard and the Dog Kennels (to the south side of the Market Place. The name tells all!), and righteously wrathful matrons from Brimington" outraged by the deed perpetrated on such a young girl. It was with great difficulty that Gough was safely gotten out of the cab for the crowd was out for blood but the driver made for the back entrance to the right of the building which meant the gap between the office and the wall was too narrow for the mob to follow.

On account of the limited capacity of the room where the proceedings were going to take place it was decided not to allow the public access. Therefore the public took it upon themselves to continually peer through the sash windows thus disrupting what was occurring inside.

"Time and time again did Mr Barnes, M.P., and Mr. Supt. Carline give orders for the low balcony in front of the window to be cleared of the anxious and noisy people who climbed to get a peep at the prisoner."

The police did try to hold them back but no doubt whoever was closest to the window at any one time would be relaying loudly what was being said inside! Mr Hallewell would probably have liked to close the shutters but with so many agitated people outside it was probably wiser not to upset them even more and so left well alone. "The open space in front of the office was crowded, and the walls, roofs, and other elevated positions were taken possession of" and nobody was thinking of dispersing until the proceedings had ended.

Mr Barnes considered why so many men were here and not at their place of work. However, he knew as a coal mine owner that it was a recurring problem getting the men to work on Mondays and Tuesdays. Even his friend, Charles Markham, the managing director of The Staveley Coal and Iron Company had calculated that he only got 260 working days out of his colliers and that didn't include any allowance for absenteeism! The men were usually still getting over the week-end's excesses! Today they had a better excuse!

Superintendent Carline conducted Alfred Gough into the room and he took his stand at the bar. Gough was no stranger to court proceedings but from this vantage point it was somewhat novel or was it? His demeanour appeared to all as one of utmost indifference seeming to be the least interested person present!

"He stood leaning both hands upon the rail, fidgeted about with his feet, and kept his eyes on the table, as if admiring the rapidity with which the depositions clerk took the evidence."

The remaining interested parties gained their composure as best they could in the circumstances and so the proceedings began. Mr Barnes asked Superintendent Carline what the charge was against the prisoner.

"He is charged with wilfully murdering a little girl, named Eleanor Windle, aged six years, at Brimington, on Saturday."
In answer to (Mr Smith), the Deputy Magistrate's Clerk, the prisoner said his name was Alfred Gough.
The charge against him was then read to the prisoner, but he made no reply.
Mr Barnes: "What evidence do you intend to bring, Mr Carline?"
Superintendent Carline: "I shall call witnesses to prove that the prisoner was seen with the child, and (witnesses for) the finding of the body; also to his apprehension yesterday."
Mr Barnes: "That is quite sufficient. Then you ask for a remand?"
"Yes. It is a case that will take a great deal of getting up, as there is so much circumstantial evidence. I don't think we can take it earlier than this day week."

WITNESS 1: HARRIETT JOHNSON

Harriett Johnson (the first of 4 witnesses) was then called, and was examined by Superintendent Carline. She stated that she was housekeeper to her brother, Alfred, and lived at Oak House, Brimington.
Mr Barnes: "Where is the house situated?"

Superintendent Carline: "It is up a narrow lane, and faces the cemetery."

Miss Johnson continuing stated: "I was in the lane on Saturday morning, between ten and half past."

Superintendent Carline: "You cannot fix the time nearer than half past ten?"

"No. This lane leads from the turnpike to our house."

"When you were in the lane did you notice anything?"

Miss Johnson: "I saw him (pointing to the prisoner) and the child just outside in the road, near the bottom entrance to the lane."

"Was it a male or female child?"

"Judging from the dress I should say it was a girl."

"Did you notice if the child had anything in its hand?"

"It had a blue piece of ribbon."

"Did you notice what the child was doing?"

"It seemed to be playing about at the time."

"You said you saw a man there. Was he near the child?"

"Yes. The child was playing about where he stood."

"Was he standing still?"

"He was."

"Did you notice anything particular about him then?"

"Not at the time."

"His dress appeared alright?"

"Yes at that time."
"I believe you went up home?"
"I went into the house."
"And how long were you in?"
"A very few minutes." ("I went out to see if the man was gone, as I did not like such men about")
"Did you return to the place where you saw him before?"
"I went lower down to see if he had gone."
"When you returned home did you return for some particular purpose?"
"Not when I went first"
"On coming out of the house the second time did you see anything of the man and girl?"
"I saw them both coming up the lane. The girl had a white pinafore on."
The Magistrate's Clerk: "You say you saw a man. Do you know who the man was?"
"I should say it was this man here (pointing to the prisoner)." ("But I cannot swear it.")
Superintendent Carline: "In what direction were the two going?"
"They were going straight up the middle of the lane towards our house."
"How far were they from the road at the time?"
"From five to six yards, or possibly more."
Mr Barnes: "How far is your house from the road?"
"I really don't know."

Mr Barnes suggested that a plan of the district should be prepared for the future hearing of the case.
Superintendent Carline (to witness): Did you notice if the child had anything in its hand?"
"Yes; it had a toy or something of that sort."
"Did you notice anything particularly about the man?"
"Yes; his dress was unfastened."

This caught Gough's attention, looking up quickly at the witness but just as soon his eyes were cast down again.

"Did you notice if he was exposing himself?"
"Most decidedly he was."
"Was he exposing himself to the child?"
"The child was very close to him and he had his hands in front of him."
"Did they still continue to walk towards you?"
"Yes but they did not see me."
"Did you speak to them?"
"No; I returned immediately into the house."
"Just tell the magistrate why you went into the house?"
"I went home to get a broom handle."
"Did you return at once?"
"Immediately, and ran down the lane again."
"What did you see?"
"They were much closer to the hedge. The child was standing on the other side of him. I fancy he must have heard me, for he went off very swiftly. That was the last I saw of him or

the child. I followed down the lane, but did not see them again."

Mr Barnes: *"How near did you go to him?"*
"Well, perhaps the length of this room (from 12 to 15 feet)."
Mr Barnes: *"Did you notice if the child's dress was disarranged?"*
"No. The child appeared just as it was when I saw it at first."
Superintendent Carline: *"How long do you think these events took?"*
"From my first seeing them to their disappearance I don't think ten minutes elapsed, I was very rapid in my movements."
The Magistrate's Clerk: *"You say they went very quickly either through the hedge or down to the turnpike?"*
(*"I cannot say whether he crushed through the hedge, as my eyesight is not very good. I only know that he disappeared suddenly."*) But *"My impression is that he went down the turnpike."*
Superintendent Carline: *"That is all I wish to ask the witness."*
Mr Barnes (to the prisoner): *"Do you wish to ask the witness any questions?"*
Prisoner: *"No sir, I have nothing to ask her."*

WITNESS 2: JOSEPH TURNER

Joseph Turner, a young labourer from Brimington was then called as a witness. He and his friend had been walking towards Chesterfield on the Saturday morning, just two days ago.

Superintendent Carline: "Now did you see anything of Eleanor Windle and this man?"

"I cannot say that I am certain of the girl, but I saw this chap (pointing to the prisoner) up the lane."

"Up what lane?"

"Up the lane known as Johnson's lane, opposite the cemetery"

Miss Johnson then interrupted: *"That is not the name of the lane. It is simply a private entrance to our place. People in the neighbourhood, however, generally, call it by that name."*

Superintendent Carline (returning *to the witness): "Where was the girl?"*

"She was beside the man in the lane."

"What time would that be?"

"About twenty minutes to eleven as near as I can guess."

"Now tell the magistrate as near as you can what they were doing?"

"The little girl stood beside the man, and he looked as if he had been getting sticks out of the hedge to make paper flags."

"Did you speak to them?"

"No. My companion and I stood to chat with an old woman for about 3 minutes. That was near the entrance to the lane."

"How do you know it was this man?"

"Why I have seen this man often for about three years. I could have_____"

Prisoner (interrupts the young man): "About two years."
"Well, say about that time, but I know you well."
Superintendent Carline: "You knew him previously?"
"Yes."
"Did you see the body of the deceased when it was found in Hoole's plantation, yesterday?"
"I saw it shortly after it was found."
"Do you know whether the body was that of the little girl you saw with the prisoner in Johnson lane on Saturday morning?"
"I think it was. The dress was alike, and also the Zulu hat."
Mr Barnes asked the prisoner if he had any questions to ask the witness.
Prisoner: "I don't think that I have anything (but turning to the witness) "Do you say you saw me?"
"Yes."
"The child went up the lane as far as the row of houses and I never saw her afterwards."
Mr Barnes (reminded Gough) "But have you anything else to ask the witness?"
"I don't think that I have."

WITNESS 3: MRS SARAH ANN THORLEY

A 41 year old married woman by the name of Sarah Ann Thorley was next to answer questions regarding Saturday. Her husband, Samuel, was described as an engine smith and later an engine-wright repairing engines and machinery but their living accommodation was given as the bottom lodge (a solid single storey stone building) at the corner of the private road leading from Ringwood Hall to Barrow Hill. That suggests that Sarah was possibly working up at the Hall though she had not been there for more than a few months. The stone built hall had been erected by Mr G. H. Barrow. He and later his younger brother Richard ran the local coal and iron works. It was the Staveley Coal and Iron Company that was situated down this private road that Sarah would be speaking of. Beyond the works was Barrow Hill, a model community built especially for the workers by Mr. Barrow. He needed to employ men in the mines (predominantly) and local workers and accommodation were both in short supply.

Superintendent Carline: "Were you at home on Saturday afternoon?"
Sarah Thorley: "I was."
"Did you see a man with a handcart and some children's toys in it?"
"Yes."
"What time would that be?"
"Very early in the afternoon. It must have been I think between 1 and 2 o'clock."
"Where was it you saw him?"
("I was standing near the door and") "He came past with a handcart and turned down the private road."
Mr Barnes: "Did you know who the man was?"
"It was the prisoner. I did not see the child with him."

Superintendent Carline: "Which direction did he take?"
"He went towards Barrow Hill."
"In going that way would he be passing Hoole's Plantation?"
"Yes"
Mr Barnes (to the prisoner): "Have you any question to ask the witness?"
Gough: "No."
Mr Barnes: "She says she saw you" ("pass")
"Yes." ("Sir. I did go down that way to Barrow Hill")

WITNESS 4: MR BROWN

Mr. Brown, the 54 year old tollgate keeper at Brimington, was the last witness to be questioned that morning. He had earlier identified Gough as the man in question and now related all of the day's events on Saturday and Sunday for he was the one who found Eleanor's body. He had not been the toll collector at Brimington above two years but he had been a keeper of turnpike roads for over 20 years, though previously in the Nottinghamshire area and his native Leicestershire.

On the Saturday morning he had been working on the road between Chesterfield and Brimington, close to an area known as Tinkersick. ("Sick" means a small stream.) Superintendent Carline started the questioning:

"Did you see the prisoner that morning?"

"Yes, sir. It was between 9 and 10 o'clock, and he was coming from Chesterfield to Brimington. He had with him a little handcart with some paper toys in it."
"Did you see him again that day?"
"Yes, about 6 o'clock in the evening. He called at my house to have a glass of ginger beer."
"Had you any conversation with him?"
"Yes."
"Was it general conversation, or about this child?"
"There was nothing said about the child till the father came."
"When did the child's father come?"
"When the prisoner was in my house."
"Will you tell the magistrate as nearly as you can what was said between the father and the prisoner in your hearing?"
"The father asked him how far the child walked up the road with him that morning. The prisoner said that he had seen the child, but as there were so many children about, he could not say anything of it. The father was very severe with him - spoke very sharp with him. He said: "Well there was a child that followed me from the old building where the machinery used to be." "Where did it follow you to?" asked the father. "To the little house this side of the cemetery." (Meaning Almond Place) replied the prisoner. He said he remembered this child as it wanted one of his parasols. He said also that he told the child to go and get

some rags and bones and then he would give her the article she wanted."

(Mr Smith, the Deputy Magistrates' Clerk queried: "Did he say "this child"?"

"There was no other that followed him."

Supt. Carline: "Did he give any reason for knowing the child?"

"Not at all."

Mr Smith: "I suppose he remembered the child following him up?"

"Yes, sir.")

Mr Barnes now queried: "Did he say that he remembered "this child (of Windle's)" or "a child"?"

"He remembered a child. I don't think he said this child."

Mr Smith: "And the father asked him where he left her?"

"Yes, sir."

Supt. Carline: "What did he say about the rags?"

"He said that he told the child to go and get some rags, and it should have one of the toys.")

Superintendent Carline then continued: "How far did he say the child followed him?"

"From the old building to the cottages."

"Did he say anything more?"

"He said the child went away and he did not see anything more of it. He said there were so many children about that he did not notice it."

76

(Did you go out in search of this lost child on Saturday night?"
"No, sir; but I went on Sunday morning.")
"Now, in the course of your search did you go to this private road that leads from Ringwood to Barrow Hill?"
"Yes, I did."
"What time did you get there?"
"A little after 12 o'clock at noon yesterday."
"Now, will you tell the magistrate what you noticed in the lane?"
("I did not go straight from my house to the lane—"
"Never mind, you got into the lane. What did you notice?")
"I noticed the marks of wheels against the gap that leads into the plantation."

Mr Barnes sought clarification: "As if the cart had been backed up to it?"
"Not exactly backed up to it, but running close to the side."
Superintendent Carline continued: ("Can you tell the magistrates what sort of wheels?"
"According to my idea, wheels about this width (indicating about 2 inches)."
"What was the gauge? How far were they fixed apart?"
"Not more than that (measuring with his hands outstretched about 2 feet)."
Mr Barnes: "A two-feet gauge?"
"Yes, sir")

The Clerk asks: "You say this was opposite a gap in the hedge?"

"It is not really a gap, as there are some railings there."

(Supt. Carline: "Was it the fence to Hoole's plantation?"

"Yes."

"Between the plantation and the road?"

"Yes, sir.")

Mr Barnes: "Judging from the marks, how many wheels do you think the vehicle had?"

"Two."

("A two-wheeled conveyance, with about two-feet gauge?"

"Yes, sir.")

Superintendent Carline: "Now when you noticed these marks what did you do?"

"I went over into the wood to search."

"Just tell the magistrates what you saw."

"I turned up the wood to the left hand along a little footpath which goes between two banks. I turned round the bank to the left, and when I had proceeded 2 or 3 yards I found a sack. Coming to the other side I saw the child close by the bank under a little tree."

"Did you notice anything about the child?"

"I noticed that it was lying on its back."

"Did you see anything about its neck or head?"

"There was a piece of an old bag stuff tied round its neck. That must have strangled it.

The bagging was about the width of my two fingers."

Mr Barnes: *"Was the child wet?"*

"Yes."

"And appeared as if it had been there some time?"

"Yes."

Mr Barnes then spoke to Superintendent Carline to see if there were to be any more witnesses?

"No, no more today."

Mr Brown piped up that he had helped to remove the child to its home but there was to be no more questioning from those in the room. Only Gough had one question to ask the witness:

"Did you see any child with me when I came through the tollbar?"

"No."

Afterwards Mr Barnes asked Gough: *"Have you anything to say why you should not be remanded?"*

"All I have to say is that I only saw the child. That is all I have to say. I don't know anything more."

"You are remanded to 11 o'clock on Monday next," (29th August). The same office unless the magistrates were to decide otherwise.

The morning's proceedings having come to an end Gough was removed into custody. He was taken into the ante-room where he was allowed to sit on a bench and where he quietly submitted to being handcuffed by Sergeant Radford, an Irish man similar in age to himself. The two were sharing the same living accommodation at present. Radford along with his family were at 37, Marsden St, Chesterfield as so too was

Alfred Gough. Except that Gough was in one of the four cells allocated to male offenders! The Sheffield Independent reported that Gough now

"had to make an effort to keep back his tears. He sat with his hands folded listlessly, and with his deeply lined face, and low-spirited bearing, was a picture of misery. The little window at the back of the building was darkened by people who flattened their noses against the glass rather than miss anything. They could see nothing except his boots."

The cab was fetched and the door to the solicitors' office was opened. For a split second the sight greeting Gough unnerved him. Quailing perceptibly he glanced at Radford and Carline then stepped out to a "thunder of groans and hisses from the assembled crowd." The front "yard" and the main road beyond were a sea of bodies and it was with difficulty that the cab drew up to the building. From nowhere a cordon of police cleared a short distance to the door and down the steps struggled Radford and his charge. In turn this caused "a great rush" and renewed excitement from those close by. "Groans and hisses (rang) in the air while those on the outside of the crowd vainly though roughly struggled to get a glance of the prisoner's face." The courageous and determined driver of the cab had in his own interest as well as that of the prisoner to drive quickly though it was a struggle. The mob was out to drag Gough out of the cab and in going down the yard leading from the office, a boy named John Malloy was pushed between its wheels and the office wall." It was first feared that the boy had broken his leg but the cab could not afford to stop in such a situation. He was carried to the local hospital at the other end of town and

80

was examined by a Dr. Rose. Luckily the injury was a graze and the boy was not seriously hurt at all and could return home to Long Court Yard. By then the excitement outside the solicitors' would be over for the boy but the afternoon would see a new drama unfold at a new location....

MONDAY AFTERNOON 22nd AUGUST 1881

OPENING OF THE INQUEST

WITNESSES: MR WINDLE, DR. WALKER, MR BROWN

Two miles North-East of Chesterfield Railway Station and 153 miles from London was the parish of Brimington. Classed as a township it had an array of shops for day to day living, public houses, a Victorian church, various non-conformist chapels and schools, but to the locals it was a village. There were farms in the area, the chief crops being wheat and oats but this was a village whose residents were, for the majority, employed at the Staveley Iron Works or in the mines. Coal and ironstone were found "in abundance" in this area and Brimington was one of the outlying villages that provided the Works and mines with its labour. As the industrial enterprise grew so did the village. In 1871 there were 2,403 souls. In 1881 this had grown by nearly half again to 3,457. The town of Chesterfield itself in 1881 had a population of 12,221 so it is understandable why Brimington was thought of as simply a village!

The Red Lion Inn on the main turnpike road running through the village of Brimington was chosen for the location of the inquest. (It was not unusual in this period to hold such events in a public house). It was on the Chesterfield side of the village, a mere 2 miles north-east of the town and Christopher Preston was the landlord, a 45year old married man. The stone built property was not the only pub in the village but it was one of the nearest licensed houses to Mr and Mrs Windle's home. Not that they would ever have set foot in such an establishment William being a staunch nonconformist!

Superintendent Carline had managed to grab a bite to eat after the morning session with the magistrate. He was informed Mr Newberry had brought round to the police station some rags (pieces of a cotton handkerchief?) from Gough's haul of Saturday night that might be of interest. These were sent on for Dr Walker to examine. Sergeant Eyre had something interesting to show him but he did not have the time to wait. Elijah was now in Brimington ready to start proceedings with the coroner. He was still smiling over Sergeant Radford's words to Gough as the cab got back to the lock-up-"Old boy-that has been a fine crush" A slight understatement! "Yes", says the prisoner, "I'm glad we're here."As if the two had returned to the safety of their home!

It was decided that rather than have yet another disturbance Elijah would leave Gough in his cell. His men had struggled to keep order at the magistrates' in the town where he could call on the borough police if necessary. Out at Brimington Carline and his men would be on their own and there was no telling what would happen. They certainly could not guarantee Alfred's safety and he was innocent 'til proved guilty at least in Carline's book!

The women of Brimington thought otherwise, according to The Sheffield Telegraph, they were meeting in groups, regretting the law did not allow them to have Gough in their clutches for just "one sweet half hour". "Magesterial

8. COMPLETE MAP OF BRIMINGTON AREA IN 1881

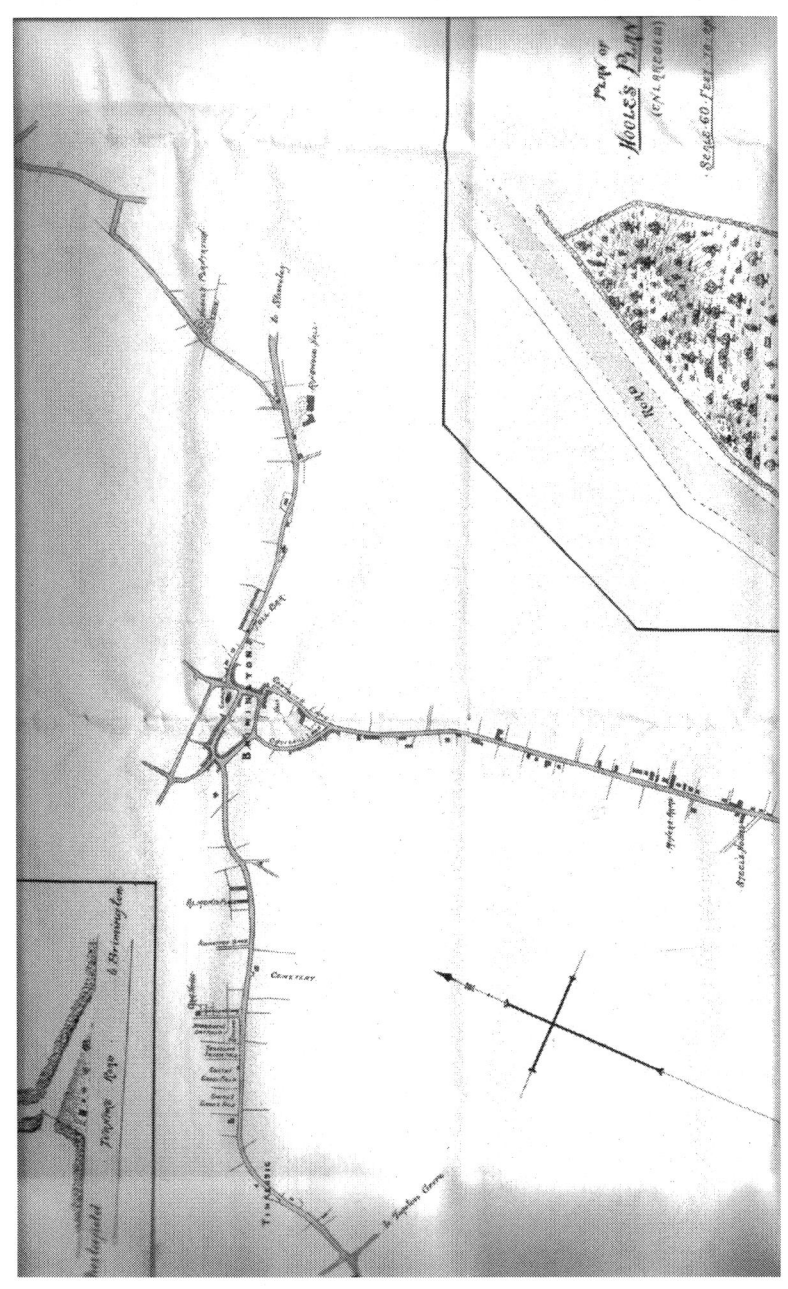

inquiries" and "crowner's quests" "are to them tiresome proceedings, necessary perhaps, but very uninteresting. They do not trouble to ascertain what the law says as to evidence, personal, absolute, or circumstantial. They know a foul outrage has been committed upon a little girl, a pet and favourite of the village; they know that that little one has been murdered cruelly and horribly; they know that they have in their midst a weeping mother and a well-nigh brokenhearted father; they also know that lying in the lock-up at Chesterfield is a man accused of the foul deeds which bring a blush to the face when spoken of; and this to them is sufficient."

These women were part of the local crowd of all ages now surrounding the Red Lion Inn. But, as Gough was not in attendance, the mood was initially less heated. The chief topic of conversation was naturally the murder of poor Eleanor. She was well known to many of them and it seemed incomprehensible that this should happen to such a young child.

Mr Charles George Busby, 30 year old solicitor in the firm of Busby and Son in town, was the coroner. He was following in his father's footsteps and as late as 1879 Mr Busby senior was still listed in the local directory as the coroner for the 100 of Scarsdale (an administrative area of Derbyshire). Now it was his turn. Charles had gone away on holiday to Filey but when he heard the news of this tragic event he rushed back home in order not to delay matters. So around 3.00pm he duly opened the inquest.

First was the matter of the swearing in of a jury. All 12 were local men though it was not unknown to have as many as 23 men in a jury at this time- John Wakefield (grocer and beer retailer), Joseph Cropper (mason, builder and contractor), John Hazard (grocer and postmaster), Thomas Haywood (farmer), Henry Turton (rate and tax collector and estate agent), John Calow (wheelwright) and friend of William Windle! John Lakin (grocer and draper), James Cook (shopkeeper), John Ashmore (butcher), Thomas Drake(pork butcher), James Baker and John Lingard (farmer). This would be the typical makeup of a jury in the 19th century – tradesmen and farmers.

Mr Lingard was elected foreman of the jury and then Mr Busby informed them that *"their first duty would be to see the dead body, and they, headed by himself and Superintendent Carline ....accordingly proceeded to the house of Mr Windle, followed by a number of women and children. The house* ,(the fourth in a row of neat but plain cottages was a surprise to some - neatly furnished "and considerably above the average of men in" William's position according to The Sheffield Telegraph,) was *one of a row named Almond Terrace, about 200 yards from the inn* (going back towards Chesterfield). It *was soon reached; but upon entering it* (the house) *at the back the Coroner was informed that Dr. Walker, whom he had instructed to make a post-mortem examination of the body, had not quite finished his task."*

Dr Walker had already been at the Windles' for at least an hour or two. It is unclear whether he had brought along his young assistant, Joshua Law Kerr but in later years it was thought best practise that an assistant was needed at an autopsy in order to take the notes. No protective gloves were worn at this time and when undertaking dissection the hands were soon covered in blood and tissue. This meant that if the doctor was working alone he would have to continually stop to wash and wipe his hands in order to record his findings. It was not thought satisfactory at all to record findings after the autopsy was completed and so this may well be the reason why Dr Walker was not quite ready for the jurors' inspection of the body. It was not unusual at this time for autopsies to be conducted in private houses in some light and airy room. Daylight was a necessity for colour changes to a body are often invisible in artificial light .It was recommended that if the room's windows were small the windows were to be thrown wide open! This must have been an ordeal for any family whose house configuration meant that they were only in the next room.

On Dr Walker's arrival he had requested from Mr and Mrs Windle certain items- a couple of wash-hand basins, two buckets, clean rags, a number of newspapers, three or four sponges, a piece of soap, several towels and a plentiful supply of hot and cold water. They provided what they could. At one stage Dr Walker was to commandeer the kitchen table but as the body was not that of an adult he felt the small table Eleanor was lying on would probably be sufficient covered with stout Mackintosh, (a rubberised waterproof cotton fabric). Otherwise they could take a door off its hinges and support it with two chairs! What was the good doctor going to be doing? Nobody wanted to know!

G. Sims Woodhead wrote a manual for medical students and practitioners entitled "Practical Pathology". The first chapter describes how a post- mortem examination should be conducted in detail from start to finish and although this was not published until two years after Eleanor's murder the procedures were based upon the work of a German physician named Virchow who introduced a standardised technique for conducting autopsies in 1874. From the way Dr Walker conducted his autopsy he appears to have covered all the procedures described by Woodhead. Start at the head and examine all the cavities of the body! This was to help in prosecution cases in order that defence counsel could not state generally that a victim could have died by some other cause. If all the organs had not been examined it could mean a second examination having to be carried out. However, it is doubtful this argument could have been used in Eleanor's case.

It had been dinnertime for the Windle household but with the smells of turpentine and carbolic oil, the sounds of sawing and the replenishing of blood stained water nobody had an appetite. Their imagination was in over drive as to what was going on in the next room- adult and child alike!

At least fourteen men were standing in the Windles' back room and although the house was of a modest size there were only two rooms downstairs and one contained the child's body! It was all becoming too cramped. As the weather had brightened up since the morning it was suggested that some of the jurors should make their way further down the main road (in the direction of the town and away from the Red Lion) to view Johnson's Lane- the place where it was alleged Gough murdered Eleanor.

By the time of their return to the house the little body had been stitched up, and was viewed by the jury. It lay in the front room, (upon a small table) and *presented a somewhat sickening appearance. Upon the lower part of the nude body lay the sheet, while on the head were the bandages, placed there by the doctor after opening it to examine the brain. The lips were purple, and separated, thus showing the clenched teeth of the child, while the eyelids were slightly open. The disagreeable duty of the jurors having been fulfilled, a return was made to the inn for the purpose of hearing the evidence as to how and by what means Eleanor Windle came by her death."*

Once the jurors and interested parties had settled themselves into the low, dark club room as best they could(for the crowd were getting noisy outside) and the configuration of the room was inconvenient, Mr Busby began:-

"Gentlemen, this is a case which will require a great deal of careful attention on your part, involving as it may do from the evidence, a charge of murder against somebody. A great deal of evidence, as far as we can tell, will be laid before you but it will be entirely circumstantial, and I want you to dismiss from your minds any reports you may have heard, and to be guided in arriving at your verdict solely by the evidence laid before you, and to give your verdict without fear, favour, or affection, or any feelings of malice, hatred, or ill-will against anyone."

A tall order for local business men and residents of Brimington to fulfil. Outside was a crowd of people who had already decided on the verdict!

For a good hour, whilst the Coroner was attempting to record in writing the depositions or sworn statements of the three witnesses, he was contending with the "great noise outside" emanating from the people. Constant talking and laughing!

"The noise was unpleasantly increased by the shouting of children playing, and the crying of children in arms."

It was unfortunate that the Red Lion was more or less on the main road and proceedings were held in one of the rooms at the front of the pub. All the general public had to do was listen and look in at the small-paned windows and no doubt give their opinions too! At one stage Superintendent Carline had to send out one of his men to try and quell the disorder."

WITNESS 1: WILLIAM WINDLE

William Windle, the girl's father was the first to be called. After giving his address as Almond Place rather than Terrace, his occupation and place of work he confirmed that the body seen by the jury was that of his daughter.

Mr Busby as Coroner then proceeded to begin questioning Mr Windle:

"When did she die?"
"On Saturday the 20th."
"How old was she?"
"Six last June, sir."
"Did you see her at all yourself on the Saturday morning?"
"I did not."
"Were you away at your work?"
"Yes, sir."
"What time did you return?"
"About half past one I believe, sir."
"In the afternoon?"
"Yes, sir."
"Was the child at home when you got there?"
"No, sir"
"Were your family anxious at her absence?"
"Yes, sir, when I got home, because she was not there."
"What is your dinner time?"
"Half past one on Saturday."

"*Did you wait for her at all?*"
"*No, sir.*"
"*Did you begin dinner?*"
"*Yes, sir*" ("*but felt very anxious when she did not return, and my wife could scarcely eat any dinner.*")
"*When did you last see her?*"
"*She went away with some other girls.*"
"*But you don't know that of your own knowledge?*"
"*No, sir.*"
"*Well, we can't have that. When did you first miss her?*"
"*Directly after dinner my wife began to get anxious.*"
"*When did you first make inquiries?*"
"*Just after dinner.*"
"*At what time?*"
"*About half past two.*" ("*Two o'clock*")
"*Where did you make inquiries?*"
"*Not suspecting anything and thinking that she was with her playmates we sent a boy of mine aged 11 years to a neighbour's in Brimington, and he came back and said she was not there.*" (This would have been Ernest Henry. It is interesting to note that William called Ernest Henry "a boy of mine" as this is a child from his first marriage.
Eleanor was the first born of his second marriage!)
"*Did you go out yourself?*"
"*No, not then. We despatched him off a second time to all the places where we knew that the girl went to play.*"

"*At what time did he come back?*"
"*Well, sir, I should think it would be about three. Then the mother went in search all about the place.*"
"*Did she come back?*"
"*Yes, sir. She was away perhaps something like an hour, and then me and my three sons started off. My wife returned, saying that she had no tidings. My sons' names are Walter* (the eldest at 19years), *Frederick* (17years) *and Francis* (16years). ("I went towards Brimington tollbar* (the other end of the village going towards Staveley eastwards and away from Chesterfield) *and the others Calow way* (directly south from the centre of Brimington).

"*I suppose you were unsuccessful?*"
"*Yes.*"
"*Where did you look?*"
"*I went through the town* (meaning Brimington, which is a village) *up to the tollbar. I met a person named Gibson near to the tollbar, and asked her if she had seen anything of our little girl, whom she knew well, and told her that the last tidings we had were that she was seen going along the lane with a man with a handbarrow. I was at Mrs Gibson's two or three minutes.*(Mrs Gibson lived on Staveley Road next to the Methodist Chapel at the other end of the village to where the Windles' lived quite close to the tollbar.) "*While I was speaking to her Mr Gibson* (a railway porter) *came up, and he said that he had overtaken the man with the hand-cart, and that we should see him directly.* Mr Windle then stated that he left the

10. MAP OF ALMOND PLACE TO THE TOLLBAR

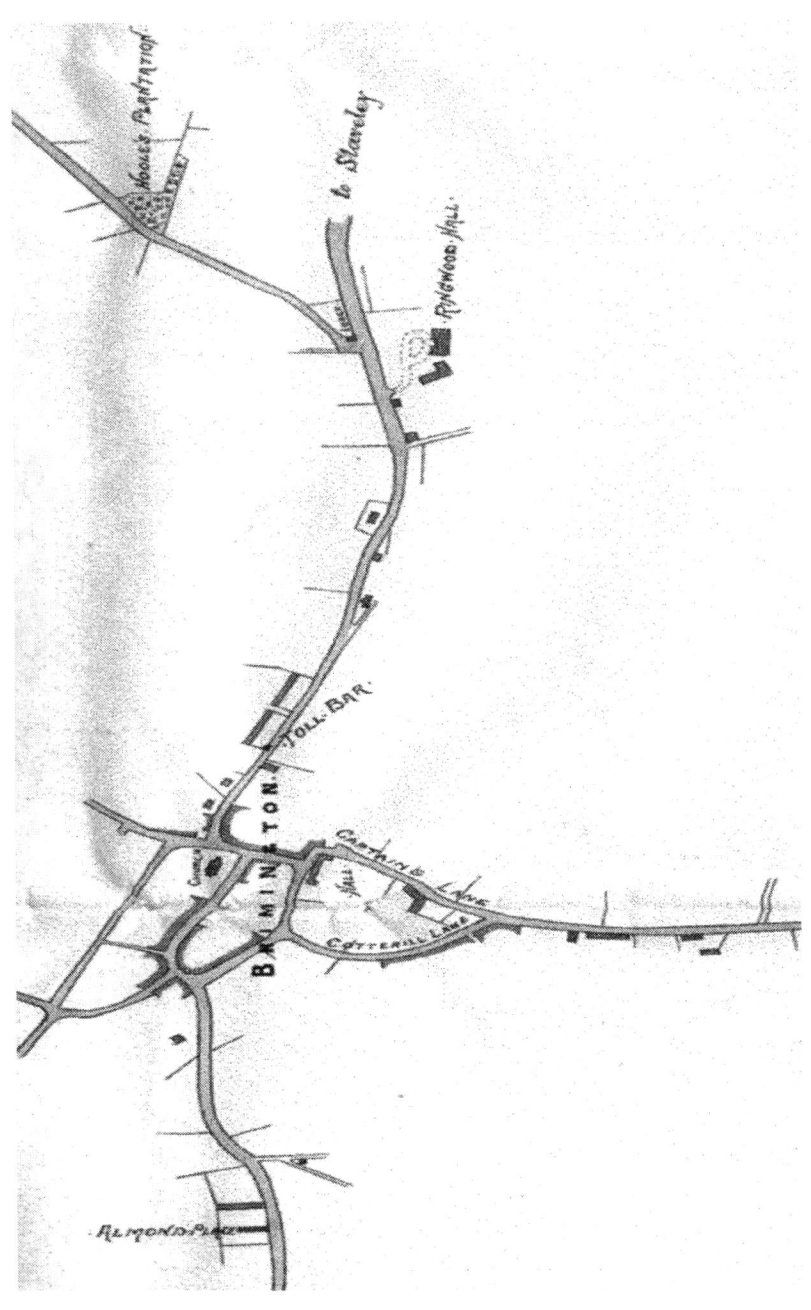

Gibson's house, crossing over the road and walked along to the tollbar in the direction of Staveley and met a man with a hand-cart that contained a quantity of rags, bones and flags. The man wheeled his cart through the tollbar onto the Brimington side.

"You have not seen the man since, have you?"

"No"

"You don't know him?"

"No, sir."

Mr Busby then stated: *"It is purely a question of identification, and I think it would be better for this witness' evidence to stand over until the adjourned inquest, when I understand that the man will be present, and it will give him an opportunity of identifying him as the man with the cart."* This was more an aside to Superintendent Carline who nodded knowingly to the Coroner. However so far there had been no time to bring Mr Windle before the man being held in the cells in town.

"When was your daughter's body brought home?"

"On Sunday, sir."

"In what condition was the body?"

"I never saw it, sir. Not until this afternoon."

"Can you describe the man?"

"He was about my own height - about 5 feet 8 inches, or something like that."

"How was he dressed?"

"I believe he had light corduroy trousers."

"Are you certain?"

"I will not swear, but I thought from general observation that he had, and a sort of an old heavy blue pilot jacket." (Broad lapelled, double-breasted often with large wooden or metal buttons and slash pockets.)

"Did you speak to the man?"

"I went up straight to him and said "What sort of_____"

The Coroner immediately interrupted with another question: "But first what kind of a looking man was he? What sort of a face?"

"Rather long features, sir."

"Sallow?"

"Yes, not very pointed at the chin, which was middling square. I believe he had a little pock mark about the face, not much."

"What did you say to him?"

"Hearing that there were more handcarts than one that had been seen in Brimington ("I had also heard that another man had been seen in Brimington with a similar cart") it induced me to ask him what sort of a girl it was that came up the hill with him. At once he said "About so high," showing me with his hand, and he described her exact height. How was she dressed, I asked him, and he said that she had a light ("pinner") pinafore on. "What sort of a hat had she on?" He said "I cannot tell exactly." He said he believed that she had an old straw hat on, but he would not be sure because there were so many children following him. Then I said to him, "You had not many children following you

there, you had only one." I also said that he could not walk with a girl at his side all up that hill ········ meaning the hill near Brimington. Then I said to him, "If you brought her to the top of the hill, how is it she has not got home, when she followed you for the purpose of purchasing one of your things?"
About this point in Mr Windle's account, according to The Sheffield Telegraph "the noise of the people outside became disgraceful, the shouting and laughing very loud and much out of place". So much so that Superintendent Carline went out himself and asked them to behave themselves "but his request was not heeded for long"! "... and (William continued) then he replied that he did not know; was it my girl? Then he says, "I am very sorry; it is a bad job." By that time he was going on, and I had no more to say to him. He passed on amidst a crowd of children, not doing any business with them, on the way to Chesterfield. I walked on faster than him and when I got to the Three Horse Shoes Inn I met Police-constable Wright, and told him what business I was on. While I was telling him my business the man with the cart came up again. Then I believe the officer spoke to him about the girl. I believe he said "What about this girl?" and he said it was a bad job, or something to that effect."
"Are you quite sure?"
"Yes, sir. Of course we had no suspicion of anything wrong, and he started on his way, and I went on to Brimington."

"Did he go on his way to Chesterfield?"

"No, sir, down what they call Cow Lane." (This was off to the north of Brimington, down the back of the village heading towards New Whittington though how Mr Windle would know this is hard to imagine. The Derbyshire Courier reports that the man did go on his way to Chesterfield and that Mr Windle went to Whittington in search of his daughter. (The original deposition of William actually states that Gough went "towards Chesterfield down Cow Lane and I went to Whittington".) The Derbyshire Times reporter just mis-heard the facts.

"Were you searching all Saturday night?"

"Yes, except for one hour, from 2 to 3."

"You had her cried by the bellman at Chesterfield?" (This was Mr Evans, the town crier who would go around the streets of the town ringing his bell to attract the attention of listeners with the news of the missing girl)

"Yes, sir,"

"At what time was the body brought home?"

"On Sunday."

"About what time?"

"3 o'clock I think. I was not thinking about the time. I saw it this afternoon, and identified it."

Mr Busby then told Mr Windle that an opportunity would be provided for him to visit the man held in custody to see if he was the man with the hand-cart. William was going to Chesterfield that evening and asked if he could see the man then? Superintendent Carline remarked that he should be at home that evening by about half past six and Mr Windle could call into the police station to make the identification.

Elijah Carline was also living under the same roof as Gough! (The original deposition given before Mr Busby has a note written at the bottom of the page dated 22nd August, signed by William and countersigned by Mr Busby. "I saw him at the Chesterfield lock-up on Monday." It will be seen later that this official document poses something of a problem to the narrative of events as the story unfolds!)

As an afterthought Mr Busby asked just one more question:

"What age was the man?"

"To all appearances I should judge him to be about 40 years of age."

WITNESS 2: Dr. WALKER

Two medical men were present at the inquest. One, (a young married Irishman and father to a baby boy,) was the 26 year old Dr. David Bradley who had graduated from Queen's University in Ireland and was now working in Brimington. In fact he was the next-door neighbour of Mr and Mrs Preston, the landlord and lady of the Red Lion! The second doctor was slightly older and more experienced. Thirty-five year old William Abraham Walker M.D. MRCS. He was a local Chesterfield man, single, living with his older spinster sister, his young assistant and four servants. He had trained in Aberdeen, worked in London but was now employed back in his local town. His was the job of performing the post mortem on Eleanor Windle.

Dr. Walker began his deposition by stating:

"I was called in yesterday (Sunday) to examine the body, which I saw about 3 o'clock in the afternoon (all the clothing was

wet as if from a rain shower). It was in the house of the father, at Almond-place. The deceased was fully clothed. She had on an ordinary stuff dress, flannel petticoat, cotton drawers, woollen stockings, and boots. There was no hat on the head. I found the face deeply turgid (swollen) *and purple.*

Not surprisingly around this time Mr Windle stood up and left the room. He was greatly shocked and horrified at his daughter's fate. He could not look upon her as a corpse and he certainly did not want to hear how Dr Walker had ravaged her further in his examination.

Frothy blood was oozing from the mouth and nostrils, the eyes were open and the "white" of the eye reddened. (This occurs when the blood flow from the head is obstructed.) *There was a slight scratch on the right cheek, as if by the puncture of a thorn. I found round the neck a deep impression, as if a cord had been tightly bound round it. The skin was here and there abraded* (rubbed away) *by the force of the pressure, and on the left side of the neck there was a portion of skin nipped, showing that the ligature had been twice round the neck (once would not produce that result). There were extensive, deep, purple discolourations over the shoulders and neck generally, more than would naturally occur in the time (before the post-mortem examination).* (This implies these injuries were caused before strangulation but whether they are bruises it is difficult to tell.) *She appeared to have been dead at least 24 hours.*

The whole of the clothing were damp, but the drawers were quite wet. The wetness was apparently caused by rain, and the outer clothing had been partially dried by the heat of the day. I found the drawers marked with blood stains."

Dr. Walker continued to give details on how he removed the child's dress and examined the lower parts of her body but this information was withheld by the newspapers. Obviously this was too sensitive a matter for 19th century sensibilities although nothing else seems to have been left out of the doctor's findings! Proof was conclusive that Eleanor had been indecently assaulted.

Continuing Dr. Walker said: *"I examined the whole body carefully for broken bones, but found none, and no wound on the head. I noticed that the fingers and nails on both hands were deeply discoloured. This (Monday) afternoon I made a post-mortem examination of the body, which was that of a female child, evidently about six or eight years old, well nourished and well grown. I examined the surface of the body more thoroughly, but found no further bruises or signs of injury. The depression of the ligature extended completely round the neck. The front part of the ligature had evidently fitted over the upper edge of the thyroid cartilage, which is a most fatal situation to apply pressure to. The ligature extended in an even line with this point, showing that death could not possibly have occurred from hanging, but from direct compression. Very great pressure must have been used (for the neck was very much narrowed). The mark was such as was likely to be produced by the narrow piece of sacking produced. I opened the head, and found the surface of the brain congested, but the whole brain, in other particulars, normal. The sinuses of the skull were filled with venous blood.* (The blood that flows through the veins on its way back to the heart and lungs.) *There was nothing in the head to account for death. I opened the chest and examined the heart, the right side of which I found to be filled with venous blood, and the left side completely empty.* (These comments of the findings in the brain, heart and lungs all fit with strangulation. The blood remains in the brain because the veins carrying the blood are compressed and so the outflow of the blood is obstructed.) *The lungs were charged with impure blood. I extended my examination up to the neck. On exposing the windpipe and opening it, I found it free from laceration, but the internal membrane was congested. I traced the line under the skin with the ligature, and found signs of it continued in the tissue below the skin. There was no dislocation or fracture of the spinal column. I opened the abdomen. The liver and kidneys presented a congested appearance, but the stomach was normal, and contained a small portion* ("three parts of a tea cup-ful") *of partially digested food. The bladder was empty and otherwise natural.*

101

The Coroner: "*Then as to the cause of actual death?*"

"*I am of opinion that the deceased died from asphyxia occasioned by strangulation with a cord or ligature of some kind.*"

"*And what do you base your opinion on?*"

"*Upon the internal appearance of the body which coincided with the external marks of violence.*"

However Dr. Walker could not state positively whether the child had been actually outraged by her assailant, but it was evident that she had been violently assaulted before being murdered. "Outraged" was the term used at this time by the press for rape,(in fact the term "rapist" was only first used, two years later, in 1883 in an article in the National Police Gazette).Some doctors who had to appear before the courts were more comfortable in suggesting an indecent assault had occurred rather than a "rape". Even though roughly 30 years earlier Dr. Alfred SwaineTaylor had published "Elements of Medical Jurisprudence" and in it was able to quote case law that "it is now…an admitted principle that a sufficient degree of penetration to constitute rape in law may take place without necessarily rupturing the hymen." In practise, "penetration was almost universally seen as essential". At this point in time Dr Walker preferred to find that a violent assault had taken place. This would have been a sexual assault for Eleanor's drawers were blood stained. Dr Walker also examined the lower parts of her body. Rape had been likely either full-blown or by use of an assailant's fingers. However, perhaps he was mindful of the crowd outside and what their reactions might be to his words.

WITNESS 3: CHARLES ABNEY HASTINGS BROWN

Charles Abney-Hastings Brown was the final witness to be called that afternoon. Towards half past four "the crowd began to diminish". Had they heard all the "juicy bits" by then? After all they had probably been loitering outside for a good two hours and some would have been in Chesterfield in the morning outside the solicitors' office trying to catch a glimpse of Gough. It had been a long day!
Still, there was the evidence of the toll-bar keeper, Mr Brown.
After Mr Brown's deposition the inquiry was drawing to a close.
It was nearly 6.30 pm and by this time there were only *"a few knots of people in the road conversing,"* the majority of the crowd having started to disperse a couple of hours earlier. The Coroner remarked to the jury: *"That is all the evidence that I shall be able to put before you today. I shall now be obliged to adjourn the inquest till a later date. I think Friday will probably be the day to which I shall adjourn it, and you gentlemen, will have to attend at half-past nine o'clock."* Mr Busby felt sure Friday was going to be a long sitting!
A juror asked if the inquest could not be adjourned until Thursday, as that day would suit, he believed, the majority of the jury better. The tradesmen probably thought their businesses would suffer less this day than on a Friday. However Superintendent Carline said *he should be happy to oblige the jury if he could, but really there was such a large amount of evidence which would require sifting that it*

would be impossible to get it ready in a tangible form fit for the jury in that time. Witnesses were cropping up every hour, and though the evidence was short it was important. Mr. Busby remarked that this was a case where other things had to be put to one side. *It was a case of emergency, and he must request the jury to assemble on Friday morning at the hour named.*

And if Mr Busby had not made it clear enough, each member of the jury would be paying a fine of £10 each if they did not appear! Proceedings were then concluded having lasted over 3 hours and 40 minutes. An enquiry, to Mr Busby's mind, "conducted under very unpleasant circumstances"! Once the jury had left the clubroom the coroner handed the certificate of burial to William, at the same time sympathising with him at the loss of his child. William desired to bury Eleanor on the Wednesday "but for sanitary reasons it had to be fixed for" the next day. Some jurors probably stayed on for a well-earned drink in one of the other rooms in the pub. These had been tolerably well filled by the public during the afternoon with just one topic of conversation. Other jury members just wanted to get home and back to their families. Superintendent Carline would not be making it back to town for 6.30 to set up an identification parade for Mr Windle. That time had already passed and due to the lateness of the hour Elijah took the father to one side suggesting it could be dealt with in the morning. This was agreed for although tomorrow would be the funeral and there was much to do William wanted to get the identity of the rag and bone man dealt with out of the way.

Elijah had been hoping to remove Gough to the county gaol in Derby until the following Monday when the magistrates' proceedings would re-commence. He was not comfortable having this man under the same roof as his wife, Elizabeth and their four children:-11 year old George, his eldest and the three younger children born in the town - five year old Reginald Henry, Annie Elizabeth Mary who was 2 years old and 1 year old Frank Eustace. Elijah knew his wife could cope. Throughout their 14 year marriage she had proved herself a "real help mate". She probably did not know it when she first met Elijah but as a policeman's wife she would be called upon to act as gaoler and matron when female miscreants were taken into custody. Sometimes even dealing with murderesses! However there was also Sgt. Radford's family of four young daughters on the premises. One the same age as Eleanor Windle. He was not unsympathetic to his sergeant's feelings. The day's events showed that the removal to Derby might even de-fuse the situation but this idea had to be abandoned. Gough would just have to stay as "house-guest" in the Carline establishment; the brick built "county lock-up" built twenty-one years earlier in 1860 at a cost of £1,300. A lock-up that could, at a push, accommodate 14 prisoners in its seven cells. To the right of the centrally located charge office was the Superintendent's accommodation-a parlour, dining room and kitchen and upstairs ample bedrooms for the family. To the left of the charge office was Sergeant Radford's less commodious living quarters. A scullery and kitchen leading up to three bedrooms.

Whilst in Brimington, that Monday, Carline's men had been approached by those in the crowd who had seen Gough on the Saturday and wanted to help by saying what they had seen. Indeed it seemed the inhabitants themselves were anxious to take on the role of "amateur police officer for the collection of evidence against the accused". After an elderly villager departed from sitting on the steps at the bottom of Johnson's Lane other locals alleged they saw Gough come down that lane

"and wheeled the handcart to another lane about two hundred yards further up the hill. This second lane (the aptly named Kidnapper Lane) *runs parallel with that up which he took the girl. They are divided by several fields, and a high and well-foliaged hedge runs along the whole length of the fields. Near to this hedge in Johnson's -lane , is rather a wide gap, caused by the clearing away of the bushes, and it is stated that he pushed the body of the child through this gap and carried it along the higher side of the hedge and deposited it in the second lane while he went for his barrow. It is stated positively that he took the barrow up this lane and came down again shortly afterwards. It would be in this manner, if the child was murdered in Johnson's-lane, that it could be taken to the second lane, and placed in the sack without being observed."* Another observer claimed Gough passed by Cropper's Buildings near the tollbar later and he was asked if he had any flags to sell? *"He did not appear to notice the remark but proceeded quickly on his way"*! Fresh witnesses were continually coming forward. Fresh theories were being discussed:- *"the murderer before outraging and murdering the child must have gagged*

her. Miss Johnson, who lives close to the place of the outrage, did not hear the child scream. Mr Platts, the registrar of the Cemetery, was only fifty yards off, and he did not hear the slightest noise of a suspicious nature, and some workmen who were painting some iron rails close to the lane state that they must have heard a scream or a shout" but did not. Did Gough wash himself and scrub his clothes after the crime and before his arrest?

Superintendent Carline had to evaluate all the information that was being presented to him and then witnesses would have to see if they could identify Gough as the man. It just was not feasible to have the prisoner 29 miles away in the south of the county. He needed to speak to his sergeant about getting up a rota. The prisoner would have to be watched. Sergeant Radford had already taken his turn in the cell with Gough on Sunday night. He wanted to be sure Gough was not going anywhere whilst his daughters were asleep upstairs! This duty would need to be shared with the constables Curtis, Davis and James Mc Gillivray. Young PC William Davis, a Somerset man, was single and lodging at the police station along with Radford so that was not a problem but McGillivray was a married man living at another police station on the Sheffield Road and Curtis was married and living in Brampton. Policemen's wives had a lot to put up with! Most of the county police forces insisted on "approving" prospective wives but rather preferred their recruits to be single. However once married it was required that wives should not work. God-fearing, domestic respectability was expected at all times. Police men knew they had rigorous rules to abide by or suffer severe discipline: - no drinking, gambling or smoking in public. Attendance at fairs, pubs or race meetings was prohibited except in the capacity of doing one's job but these rules seemed to spill into family life as well. It made it difficult for policemen's families to fit into community life particularly as a constable could expect to move several times in the early stages of his job as Elijah himself had done and, though working class themselves, their men- folk were policing their own group of society that enjoyed the amusements forbidden to police officers.

CHAPTER FOUR

TUESDAY 23rd AUGUST 1881 – NOON

THE IDENTIFICATION PARADE

William Windle turned into the glistening narrow cobbled street that led down to the County Police Station. Behind it towered the workhouse shimmering through the rain. A constant reminder that hard work would keep you and your loved ones from those gates, God willing. He did not want to do what he was about to do but it was better than being at home. So many sympathisers, so many funeral arrangements, so many tears. William was a private man but his life was now in the public domain whether he liked it or not. Representatives of both the "National School" and the Wesleyan Chapel, that Eleanor attended, had called at the house. They all were as shocked as the family. They wanted in some way to show through action how much they cared for Eleanor. Could they participate in the funeral in some way? William left it to his wife, Harriet, to deal with such matters. Much had already been attended to whilst he had been at the inquest. He had had to obtain the death certificate, for without it he could not apply to the Superintendent at the cemetery lodge for a grave. The cemetery had only been completed three years earlier. William's first wife, Ann, had died in 1873 and was buried in the local churchyard of St. Michael. The same church where William married his second wife, Harriet, nearly 14 months later. Now parishioners were buried on the outskirts of the village. 9s 6d for a plot for an 8year old- sized child but that included the fees for the Board (the administrators of the cemetery), the Sexton (who dug the graves and tended the burial grounds), the Minister (though William would be organising Reverend Wilkinson to officiate), the registering and the tolling of the passing bell better known as the death knell and the ringing of the funeral bell for a full 15 minutes! Board rules were that a good 2 days clear notice should be given before a burial could take place but these were exceptional circumstances. Mr Lingard, a juror at the inquest had been president of the burial board and knew that this rule could be dispensed with provided it was certified by a medical man. All that was needed was one more Board member to agree the dispensation and that could easily be found. Indeed, the death certificate was not actually registered until 1st September. Local feeling was not going to calm down yet, possibly a funeral might help matters?

Through the side pedestrian gate William Windle quickly crossed the courtyard and opened the door to the charge office and out of the pouring rain. He was soaking wet! Where was everybody? Not a soul about. Suddenly a door opened and in walked Sergeant Radford. Seeing how drenched William was he ushered him into his own house beyond the official area and sat him down in front of the kitchen fire to dry off. The sergeant apologised for his senior officer not being there to meet with Mr Windle but Superintendent Carline was spending the wet morning alongside his police officers busily questioning the residents of Brimington to find out who had seen Eleanor alive before she had disappeared on the Saturday and who had seen Gough after the time he had supposedly committed the murder. The investigations were going well but they still needed witnesses to place Gough at the scene of the Plantation.

Once William was settled the sergeant had to take his leave for he had some matters to attend to. William suspected he was preparing for the identification parade. After all that was why William was there.

It was now mid-day. Mr Windle was correct in his assumptions. In the 19th century an identity parade usually consisted of 8-10 persons. However, quite often the general public were understandably reticent about taking part and so numbers had to be made up using the local policemen. There was no obligation for the police to assemble a group of men who resembled or dressed as the suspect but if they were policemen at least they would be in plain clothes. Eight years earlier instructions had been issued that police should only be used as a last resort and out of uniform. The fallibility of identification evidence was well understood in the 19th century and in 1874 this unfairness was supposedly addressed but there were still instances of blatant injustice. Now Gough was brought from his cell, the one he had occupied since Sunday, and was placed amongst a group of other men waiting in the corridor. Sergeant Radford had only managed a line-up of six men but this would have to do. A constable was then sent to fetch Mr Windle from the sergeant's house and he entered. He had been told not to speak to the prisoner. Gough shifted about uneasily not daring to look up. (It was later stated that Gough appeared very depressed in Mr Windle's presence.) He refused to consider his circumstances it was nothing to do with him! Without the slightest hesitation William pointed out Gough as the man with whom he had conversed at the toll-keeper's house in Brimington on Saturday. Suddenly and without warning

William cried, **"You wretch"** and lunged at Gough as if to do him harm. The rage at the thought of Gough's attack upon his daughter welled up inside him. His Christian beliefs were in tatters, he could not forgive this "depraved, debased and inhuman being"! Sergeant Radford restrained Mr Windle gently and prayed him to be calmer. Gough, shaken, was quickly removed to his cell and Mr Windle was led out of the corridor. He regained his composure and apologised for attempting to break the prison rules. Radford looked upon him sympathetically, one father to another, but could not condone William's action. William was beyond caring. He knew it was his duty to show regret but he was out of control in the presence of the man who was likely to have been the murderer of Eleanor.

For now, William parted company with the Sergeant who assured him Superintendent Carline and his men would be on hand in Brimington later that day. It would be William and his family taking centre stage and the police in the wings. The funeral was fixed for 5 o'clock.

TUESDAY AFTERNOON

THE FUNERAL

When William got back to Brimington and Almond Place he was met by his 63 year old mother, Mary. His father had died two years earlier and William was thankful for that. The shame he had put upon his whole family would be hard to explain. As it was, he was head of the extended Windle family and would keep his explanations to himself and his Maker. William's two younger brothers had brought their mother and their wives from Newbold. A village larger than

Brimington, about 2 miles North West of Chesterfield. In other words Newbold was one side of town and Brimington was on the other side. The whole Windle family had been born and brought up in Newbold. William had even started married life there. His eldest son, Walter had been born there. Yet William, rather than be a miner like his father and brothers, found a job at Staveley Iron Works as a labourer in the foundry. Could William's moving away from Newbold have caused friction with the other family members? It was possible. William's first wife, Hannah (Ann) was originally from London. She may not have fitted into the tight-knit Derbyshire community. Later when William's two younger brothers married it was to two sisters but William's first wife, Hannah (Ann) was more than 10 years their senior. However, by then William and Hannah had already moved to Brimington and were living on the Common (south of the village) with their growing family Walter, Frederick William and Francis. The Common literally was that 40 years previously, covered in gorse and broom but with the enclosure a straightened road had been created and dwellings were being built along its edge. Indeed the growth of the village was linked to the growth of the mines and Iron Works. Since 1871 the village had grown by a thousand souls and with that came more housing, new schools, a cemetery and even a much waited- for brand new Wesleyan Sunday School now under construction.

Whilst living on the Common William came into contact with two of these new souls - the Pass brothers. They all worked at Staveley Works, the brothers were furnace labourers and William was a foundry fitter. John Pass was the same age as William. Robert Pass was a couple of years younger. They had originally been brought up in Lincolnshire and both had spent some time working as carters - John in Nottinghamshire and Robert in Cheshire. However, it was the younger brother Robert, along with his Lincolnshire wife, who came to Brimington first and he probably persuaded John to come and work alongside him. Wages in the foundry would be more than John could earn working the land. John had moved to the area around 1870 with his wife. Their first child was born in the same year as William's fourth son, Ernest Henry. William and Ann's only daughter, Alice was born in 1867 four years earlier.

It was July of 1873 when tragedy first knocked at William's door. His 37 year old wife Ann was struck down with gastro-enteritis. Vomiting and diarrhoea preceded her demise on the 20th July. Now William was left with a young family of five children with ages ranging from 12 to 3 years old. Not an unusual situation at that time. He had no extended family around him; they were all still living in Newbold. His brothers each had three children and his parents were in their mid to late fifties. Old by Victorian standards when the average life expectancy was in the 40's! A solution needed to be found and the Pass brothers had the answer. Their 27year old unmarried sister, Harriet!

At the time of William becoming a widower at the age of 33, Harriet was probably still working as a domestic servant in Nottingham. She had been employed by a draper and silk mercer (dealer) along with one other domestic servant to look after a household consisting of the draper's wife, eight children, a governess, an aunt and four boarders! Taking on a widower with five children would be child's play but she had to meet William first. No doubt her eldest brother John made the introductions. She could visit her two brothers and their families easily by train from Nottingham to

114

Chesterfield. John knew William well enough to suggest he should be thinking about re-marrying for the sake of the children. He would need someone proficient in the keeping of a house and John's sister, the "charming" Harriet fitted the bill. On the 8th September 1874 at the local parish church in Brimington William married Harriet witnessed by John and his wife Martha Pass. And nine months later, on 7th June 1875, baby Eleanor was born. Now six years later, on 23rd August 1881, he was about to bury her.

William had had to steel himself to enter his home. Almond Place had been a step up in the world from living on the Common. It even had its own stone plaque high up on the end wall facing the main turnpike road: - "Almond Place AD1852". Such a grand plaque. The wording placed upon a shield surrounded by bold acanthus leaves was supported by a tapering bracket. The row of six neat, honey- coloured stone houses stood end on to the road and so were quite private. A stone wall ran the length of the first house's front garden parallel to the road but William lived in the middle of the row (the fourth), and was not bothered by the flow of traffic outside. Today there were rain-soaked people milling outside in the road, in his front garden and even in the house. He did not want to be here. He should be at work. He was the foreman of the fettling department and he was letting his men down. But, more than likely his men were stood outside in the road or at the cemetery gates waiting for him to pass by with his family and Eleanor.

As the afternoon wore on William's mother and his sisters-in-law busied themselves in the back room making tea on the range and washing up tea things in the brown earthenware sink. They needed to busy themselves. They couldn't cope with Harriet's grief except in a practical way. The Windle way!

11. Sketch from Illustrated Police News 3rd September 1881

The coffin bearers had arrived. All Sunday school teachers at the Wesleyan Chapel that Eleanor had attended:-Alice Doughty and Carrie Larkworthy were both 15years old. The two eldest girls were Thirsa Wharton and Miss Bagley. The youngest was 13 year old Mary Gibson (whose mother had spoken to Mr Windle when he was out looking for Eleanor on the Saturday evening) and Miss Astle. All dressed in black with white shoulder scarves and all veiled in white tulle. "Miss Hendrin" (actually Sarah N Handren) the young mistress of the "The Primitive Methodist Infants' School" housed temporarily in the National School opposite the church had arrived with 13 children, all Eleanor's classmates. Rather than bring all the children indoors they waited patiently outside in the rain for there was not enough room for everybody. Miss Handren took William aside, for Eleanor's death had been a particular shock to her. Eleanor had been a popular girl, obedient and one of the most intelligent in the school. She wanted to give Mr and Mrs Windle something as a keepsake- Eleanor's slate *"on which the deceased wrote the last time she was at school"*. It had Eleanor's name on the top of the slate and was covered in capital and small letters. Hand-writing that was excellent for a child so young. William was very touched by Miss Handren's gift but did not show it to Harriet. She had been strong organising and dealing with the sympathisers but now that the funeral was at hand she was beginning to crumble. It was William's turn to be strong.

William's children kept to their rooms upstairs. Walter, Frederick and Francis, the three eldest teenage boys were up on the top floor looking out at the crowds assembling outside. Their rooms had aspects to Brimington at the back and Chesterfield to the front but through the incessant rain it was hard to distinguish the Crooked Spire today, that famous landmark of the town, and anyway their attention was taken by the people standing quietly along the roadside and down to the cemetery. Alice and Ernest were on the first floor in their parents' bedroom trying to keep the two youngest Windle children quiet and amused. Albert was 4years old and Alfred was just a baby born the previous year. It was not seemly to make too much noise in the circumstances.

Eleanor was on a small table in the front downstairs room. She was now resting in an oak coffin, waiting.

Through the pelting rain could be heard the muffled sound of a mournful bell calling Eleanor to her new resting place. All but the immediate family left to take up their places. William's friends Mr Wright and Mr Calow left the family in the backroom and quietly entered the front room to gather up Eleanor. They gently carried her outside into the downpour and placed her upon a table near to the front door. Immediately it was covered with 8 or 9 wreaths of flowers sent by friends and neighbours in the district. Flowers that had been recently growing in their little gardens and had now been picked to make up these tokens of remembrance- geranium, fuchsia, stock, marigold and sweet "jessamine" (jasmine).

The Windle children having heard the bell put on their outdoor clothes and standing on the staircase waited for the adults to process out of the door. All were to attend except baby Alfred. He was to remain at home with a neighbour.

Miss Handren took the lead in the procession. There was to be no hearse. The friends and family would walk to the cemetery with their heads held high. The schoolmistress wore a white scarf and carried a wreath of cluster roses and stephanotis. Behind her walked "Nellie's" 13 classmates. Nellie was never called Eleanor by her friends! The children had been taken out of school at 3.30pm by Miss Handren. The remainder of the school was left in the charge (for half an hour) of Mary Palmer, a local teenager who assisted Miss Handren. The entry in the school log book simply states that the children's absence was "to attend the funeral of their late school friend Eleanor Windle."

Mr Calow and Mr Wright helped the 6 Sunday School teachers to carefully lift the small flower bedecked coffin for they were to be the pall bearers. Each girl carried a bouquet. They slowly set off behind the children through the front garden, along the little path that ran along the bottom of the row of houses and stepped out onto the turnpike road and a sea of faces standing either side of the highway. Faces, some of whom had come a great distance to pay their respects. Tears mingled with the incessant rain and the bell tolled and the thunder clapped. Mr and Mrs Windle followed their daughter. The sight of the little coffin had completely unnerved Harriet. William thought she would faint and held onto her to prevent her from collapsing. This short walk down to the cemetery was such an ordeal. They were going to leave their daughter alone in a graveyard, in this weather and in the dark! How could this be?

Silently followed grandmother, aunts and uncles, Eleanor's siblings and many friends of the family.

On reaching the cemetery's large iron gates Miss Handren and her pupils formed into two lines to let the coffin and mourners pass. They had been well rehearsed! Waiting patiently was Mr John Platts, the registrar of the cemetery who lived on site with his family and the Reverend Thomas Wilkinson, a 56 year old Lancashire man. He lived in Chesterfield but Brimington was in his "parish" as he was Superintendent Minister of the Chesterfield Wesleyan Circuit. He had been in the area for less than three years but on his first visit to Brimington he had been welcomed into the community by William who was "one of the class leaders in the Wesleyan Society". It was only just over a month back that he was laying a foundation stone on behalf of the Sunday school children for the new Wesleyan chapel in Heywood

Street and Eleanor had been there with her family smiling and curious as to what he was doing. Now, though he found the situation hard to believe, it was his turn to be there for William and offer what comfort he could. As the cortege passed through the gates to the left of them stood the substantial stone built lodge with the commodious Board Room attached. All the buildings and walls were constructed of Dunford Bridge stone from Yorkshire. Solid brick-shaped blocks in the old English style. Nothing fanciful but solid, upright and typically Victorian. Up the path and ahead of them was a massive stone archway tapering to a point and near its summit was the mournful bell. Still tolling! Either side of the archway was a red-tiled "Gothic" mortuary chapel. The mourners entered the chapel to their right followed by the children. *"Although the crowd in the cemetery, near the porch, was a very large one there was no unseemly crushing, and the behaviour of the villagers was very reverent."* In the plain mortuary chapel the coffin was placed on a trestle near the doorway whilst the family mourners occupied the seats to the right of the reading- desk -open forms with backs instead of pews. The children, Miss Handren, the pall bearers and *"such spectators as could be accommodated"* sat on benches on the opposite side. Far more people would have entered the chapel but the reverend had to state that only a limited number was allowed inside. Mr Platts informed the doorkeeper that no more were to be admitted and duly the arched double doors were then closed leaving many out in the rain which continued to fall ceaselessly. Whilst the mourners waited for the Reverend to begin some were avidly studying the architecture of the building –the polished oak of the roof's Gothic arches, the large circular window flanked by two lancet-shaped windows. Anywhere but look at the coffin!

Thomas Wilkinson read the service very impressively the congregation unable to with-hold their tears. Afterwards the doors were reopened to allow that final journey to a spot in unconsecrated ground. (Eleanor was a Nonconformist and there was a specific area in the cemetery for those of that persuasion.)The cortege followed Reverend Wilkinson back out into the crowd, through the torrential rain, down the path a short distance and then turned off to the right. The ground was completely sodden due to so much rainfall and so many feet had made it worse. Near the grave side where the earth had been disturbed, ready for Eleanor, the ground had become a morass. So much so that some of the mourners found it hard to keep their footing. Reverend Wilkinson concluded the burial service with much feeling and great sympathy. When the oak coffin was lowered into the ground it had become a mass of flowers. Not sophisticated wreaths containing exotic flowers but ones of "rude" construction though no less heartfelt in their intentions. In particular was a wreath of wild flowers and prominent amongst them was a sprig of the blackberry plant. No-one could fail to understand the significance when it was realised that this was a presentation from Eleanor's companions. There was scarcely a dry eye around the graveside. The Reverend approached Harriet with words of consolation but the rattle of the earth upon the coffin signalling all was over caused her to let out an agonising cry. *"My child, my poor child."* She had borne herself with difficulty throughout but now her head was against William's chest sobbing piteously. The sight and sounds of this scene must have unnerved many in the crowd and particularly the children. It was not helped by the continuous onslaught of rain, the rumbling thunder and the dwindling daylight, even though it was August. To some, God was certainly not happy in his heaven and the world did not seem to be alright!

William gently led his distraught wife away from the onlookers and back through the iron cemetery gates. He had shown a dignified calm throughout this ordeal though inside he was screaming. Turning right the family wended up the hill crossing the turnpike road to find sanctuary in their house. Superintendent Elijah Carline watched as the mourners disappeared behind the solid stone wall and up the steps that led passed their neighbours' homes. A solid, upright family that lived in a solid upright house. Carline had seen enough of the scene gave a nod of acknowledgement to his men stationed amongst the crowd and made his way back the 2 miles to the local town of Chesterfield. Back to the county police station in Marsden Street, home to his family and the "depraved, debased and inhuman being" whose encounter with the child's father earlier had made Gough very restless and uneasy causing him to lose his composure!

CHAPTER FIVE

WEDNESDAY 24th AUGUST 1881

MANSFIELD TOM AND MR WINDLE'S ONLY INTERVIEW

The Derbyshire Times began its reports of the murder today. Its opening paragraph stated:-

"That a young girl of but six summers should be outraged and then cruelly strangled by a man who has done service under Her Majesty's colours appears almost incredible, but such, however is the charge. ....Circumstantial evidence of the most convincing description is forthcoming to bear out these simple yet most revolting facts, and if they should be proved in evidence there can be but little doubt that 'ere many months are past the man—if man he can be called—now incarcerated in the County Police station at Chesterfield, will have paid the highest penalty of the law, that of death, for the crime which has been committed. According to our English law a man is considered innocent of any crime laid to his charge until his guilt is established. But certainly in this case there seems but little room for doubt, and although we trust the man in custody will have a fair trial, the evidence proves that there is some man amongst us whose instincts are so brutal as to

lead him to take away the life of an innocent child, and not only to take away that poor child's life but to outrage her before so doing. We can scarcely conceive of a more disgusting and villainous crime and glad we are that this county is as a general thing so free from such tragedies."

Nothing like the press being unbiased then!

As was claimed, the evidence is all circumstantial but the reporter has "but little room for doubt" although it was to be hoped a fair trial was to be had. The following day The Sheffield Telegraph claimed the people of Brimington already knew who it was and "grow angry at the law's delay." They wanted to administer "rough justice" –"as primitive as the village of Brimington itself"! Gough living one more day meant one more opportunity for him to escape! If Gough was reading the papers he must have felt his fate was already sealed.

On Saturday 27th August The Derbyshire Times reported "A Strange Story" which first started circulating on the Wednesday. Thomas Holmes, known as "Mansfield Tom" gave his address as Spowage's Lodging House the same abode Alfred stayed in on Saturday the 20th. However "Mansfield" had not been there that night. He was a cattle drover, though not by trade, and had been going to Brimington on the Saturday evening to Mr Lingard's- "He had been driving some beasts, and was now going to get the money for delivering them." Mr Lingard lived in Church Street in the centre of the village but farmed 54 acres in the locale. "Mansfield" claimed that he had been out of the area since Saturday and had not known about the little girl's murder or

Gough's apprehension. However on his return he heard of nothing else! Mr Lingard, who was the foreman of the Inquest jury, may even have spoken to "Mansfield" graphically about the inquest and murder. As a jury member he had seen the state of the little girl's body and knew as a local what an upright family the Windles were and what evidence had so far been gleaned. Could "Mansfield" have taken it upon himself to say he had seen Gough also? If he could clinch the final piece of the puzzle instead of the evidence being wholly circumstantial what a hero he would be! He claimed to know something about that day's events and like a dutiful citizen went to the police with information that would be damning to Gough!

That evening there was a knock on the door at Almond Place and amazingly a reporter from The Sheffield Daily Telegraph was admitted to interview William Windle. It seems odd that such private grief would want to be shared but this was the only interview William gave as far as can be seen and not to the Chesterfield newspapers either. It is possible that the "Telegraph" with its Conservative leanings was more favoured by William. This was another Sheffield daily newspaper and William may have already been spoken to by their reporter in the course of the week and the identity parade was something William wanted to talk about. William was sitting resting by the fire, surrounded by his family, when the journalist entered. William's wife was "busying herself at the table" "bearing the dreadful infliction as best she could". Harriett was a great knitter and Wednesday evening was probably the first opportunity for her to once again pick up her knitting. She had had no desire before then. That afternoon William had gone out of the house for the first time of his own volition rather than having

125

to go because of some "heart-revolting errand" he had had to attend to or deal with. He walked as far as his place of work- Staveley Works- just to see that he could. He felt he must get back to some kind of normality, he had a responsibility to his fettlers, he had to wake up from the nightmare. It was not helping that he had eaten nothing since Saturday tea time. It was small wonder that he collapsed when Eleanor was brought home on the Sunday. He had spent most of the night looking for her and then the next day in Chesterfield looking for Gough until 1 o'clock returning home in "a state of complete prostration"! His family were very supportive but they had said all that was going to be said and they could not just continue looking at each other. Nothing was going to bring back Eleanor! But, on William's return from his walk he found all his strength had been sapped. What was once a strong and healthy man, sinewy of muscles and a good and powerful constitution was now rendered someone feeble and weary. By the evening William had rallied round enough to be interviewed by the reporter. "He readily gave an account of his visit to the police station", meeting Sergeant Radford and what occurred during the identity parade. "I merely went to see that the person they had in custody was the same I had an interview with at the tollbar house on Saturday." However, William continued recounting his first meeting with Gough at Mr Brown's little house where he had stood in the doorway looking at Gough through the gloom at the far end of the room, "looking as if he were a familiar friend of the occupant's." "At that time I had not the least suspicion of him. But there came over me such a feeling at the very moment I set my foot on the door-step that I could have gone and clutched him. I do not know what possessed me. I just felt I could have collared him, but after asking him about my child, and knowing nothing of the frightful tragedy, I left him. It afterwards struck me as very strange that without any previous thought or suspicion to cause it, such a strong feeling should seize me on seeing him. You see I had heard that there had been two men with barrows through the place that day, and I just went to see if this man had seen my child. That feeling came over me instantly I set eyes on him, and I just felt as if I could clutch him."

It appears William just could not stop himself now, "The trouble (his mental anguish) won't admit of my eating food, and what with trouble and want of food I feel quite exhausted. I do not know how I can get under or over the trouble. It is so fearful to think of." Poor William everywhere the family turned there were reminders of that fateful day! "We cannot look from our sitting-room window without seeing the spot where the tragedy took place. (The house is only separated from the lane by a small field, and Miss Johnson's house is in view.) We cannot look from our bedroom window without being confronted by the same spot. We shall have to quit here." (Interestingly, in October's "The Brimington Quarterly Messenger"- a Non-conformist pamphlet-there is a house to let in Almond Place for 4/3d per week. Could this have been the Windle's home?)

Agonisingly William continued, "When the child was up in the bedroom she would cry, "Mother, let me look at your face." Her mother would then peep round the door to have a look, and then the child would say, "Come and let me kiss you." If I happened to go up stairs, noticing the different footstep she would say "Father, is that you?" and then say, "Come and let me kiss you." "Ah," proceeded the father, almost overcome with emotion, "out of full glee, without a

127

moment's notice; nobody can conceive what a horrid heart-rending it is."

In the room where the interview was taking place above the mantelpiece was a recent photograph in a large frame of the whole Windle family – William, Harriett, the six boys and two girls. William carefully took it down to show to the reporter and in "a very tender manner" pointed out Eleanor – a bright and cheerful child. The interview was nearing its end, William was tiring and the reporter had got more than enough exclusivity for the story he would write.

However, it was not just the newspaper reporters who were circling like vultures to get tasty morsels of information. Apparently the Sheffield Telegraph knew of an "enterprising photographer" who "has managed to obtain a photograph of the little girl, and this he is using in a business manner." How can that be?! Another "has taken photographs of the cemetery, the house where the child lived, the scene of the outrage, and the plantation." Then there was the "enterprising artist" from Sheffield who actually applied to the Police Court in Chesterfield for permission to take a sketch of the prisoner. He claimed he represented "a certain illustrated paper published in London, sold at one penny, and remarkable more for the audaciousness and vigour of its pictures than regard for accuracy." Obviously the Sheffield Telegraph did not rate this London paper very highly and neither did the Chesterfield magistrates as they refused the artist's application. No one was permitted to visit the prisoner or even converse with him!

"The Illustrated Police News" of 3rd September, (amongst sketches of other events on their front page,) did actually carry some drawings of scenes from Eleanor's murder that the newspaper itself commissioned! Almond Place, The Red

Lion, The Buck Inn, Mr Scott's lodging house in Sheffield, Hoole's Plantation, a scene where Eleanor first meets Gough and a profile of Alfred opposite a profile of Charles Abney Hastings Brown! (These drawings can be found within this book.) How accurate the sketches are is difficult to judge but Almond Place and the Red Lion look as if the artist did actually see these buildings or at least have a photograph of them to copy from.

CHAPTER SIX

THURSDAY 25th AUGUST 1881

FURTHER IDENTIFICATION PARADES

Superintendent Carline assisted by two of his most able men both destined for future promotion - 32 year old Sergeant Eyre and the young 24 year old PC Wright were "constantly labouring, early and late, at the unpleasant but necessary task" of gathering, sifting and preparing the evidence. Since Sunday they had spoken to many potential witnesses. Their chief difficulty was that of obtaining the evidence "required to supply the missing links in the chain which must be completed and presented to an impartial jury before a conviction can be obtained". That jury was going to reassemble on Friday. A mere twenty four hours away.

That Thursday evening, after yet another wet day, young Mrs Neal came from Brimington to the lock-up to see if she could identify Gough as the man she had seen on the previous Saturday wheeling his cart through the village. The line-up including Gough only consisted of 5 men. It was a difficulty for Superintendent Carline to find enough volunteers particularly as he had gathered so many witnesses now. Including himself he had over 20, each one having to attend the county police station in order to hopefully recognise Gough from a line-up.

"It must not be supposed that all the witnesses who today identified the prisoner......simply went to the cell and pointing to the man, said, "That's him." Full care was taken that the identification was real and genuine. Four or five men were taken at haphazard from the market place and arranged in a line in the corridor of the cells and the prisoner having placed himself among them where he thought proper, the witnesses were admitted one by one, and each person....without a single exception, identified "Gough." Nothing of the slightest nature was done to influence or guide the witnesses in their identification of the man."

Half a dozen witnesses, according to The Sheffield Telegraph, including Ellen Hadfield had gone to Marsden Street for that purpose that morning (but that could have meant the Wednesday morning). The report also gave some insight into Superintendent Carline's reasoning for choosing the various witnesses. Elderly witnesses were not pursued but young Ellen was "selected" as she was the oldest of the group of girls blackberrying; she was intimately acquainted with Eleanor and lived but a few doors away from the Windle family. Carline found there were no witnesses wanting who had seen Gough go in the direction of the Plantation all stating that he had not made a "single rest". But if Superintendent Carline did not feel it necessary to use them, these witnesses could always relate their stories to the waiting press. One such person was Mr Cheetham, a 50 year old shopkeeper who lived at the "Hole in the Wall", the other side of The Red Lion in Brimington. According to Mr Cheetham it was Gough's custom (which seems to imply that Gough was a regular to Brimington) to come to a standstill near The Red Lion and blow his horn to attract the children.

"When they came he would allow them to peer into the cart and see the toys contained therein, and even to push it along for a short distance."

On the Saturday (the day of the murder) he neither stopped nor blew his horn. This was noticed by both Mr and Mrs Cheetham who also observed "something bulky in the cart" that was being pushed along "with difficulty" .Then, that same night when Gough returned through the village on his way back to Chesterfield Mr Cheetham saw him again and noticed that the cart still contained toys giving the impression that Gough had made no effort to get rid of them.

Mr Cheetham "thought it extremely singular that the cart should be so well filled with them that he remarked to his companion that Gough had not tried to do any business."

"He little knew then of the horrible and fatal business which had been transacted within a comparatively short distance of his house."

Poetic license, I believe, from the reporter at The Derbyshire Courier!

Mrs Blower, the landlady of The Ark Tavern, also reported to the press that when she had seen Gough earlier in the day *"he seemed very desirous that no one should go near it* (the cart) *but himself. He would not allow her or the child to go to it."*

An elderly man by the name of Ashmore spoke to Gough on Brimington Common. He told Gough he would need new wheels if he kept carrying the loads he appeared to have in the cart! Gough supposedly replied

"I shall have to get some" then proceeded on his way *"till within about 50 yards from an old unused pit belonging to Mr Black; here he stopped and put his hand-cart against the end of the house, he then approached a little*

133

nearer, watching that no one interfered with it, but appeared disappointed at finding the entrance barred by a gate which is securely locked."

This may have been Brimington Colliery (although there is also an old coal pit marked on the 1877 Ordnance Survey map a field away from the recreation ground opposite The Miners' Arms) which would have been on Gough's left walking back up into Brimington village. However, if he was supposedly looking for somewhere to dump a body would he not have noticed the gate was locked on his way down to the Common? An elderly lady by the name of Mrs Carrington with her neighbour also supposedly witnessed Gough trying the locked gate to Mr Black's disused pit but left because "he perceived the women watching him"!

CHAPTER SEVEN

FRIDAY 26th AUGUST 1881

THE ADJOURNED INQUEST

Superintendent Carline had advised the Coroner, Mr Busby that feelings were running so high in Brimington over the girl's murder that it would be unwise to continue the inquest in The Red Lion. The local women, "one and all", were vowing that if they could get near enough to Gough he would not be taken back to Chesterfield or anywhere else alive. Phrases such as "he ought to be cut up into mincemeat" and "hanging's too good for the villain" abounded. It would be better to have the inquiry away from the neighbourhood where the murder was committed. He could not guarantee the safety of Gough. Monday's hearing in Chesterfield was fraught with problems and it was only with difficulty that Carline got his man back to Marsden Street "lock-up". Since then, although The Sheffield and Rotherham Independent and The Sheffield Telegraph scooped the local papers with the story on Monday 22nd August (as did The Leeds Mercury, The Birmingham Daily Post, The Glasgow Herald and the Pall Mall Gazette!) word of mouth must have played a powerful part in whipping up the populace. The Derbyshire Times made up for lost time when it published on the Wednesday. With a weekly circulation of 14,000 copies at a cost of 1d it is to be imagined that the citizenry could not get enough of the shocking story. And the paper together with The Derbyshire Courier (which did not publish until a week after the murder) gave its readers a day by day, hour by hour and minute by minute account of all that had happened since

Eleanor's disappearance on the 20th. Those who could not read due to infirmity, poverty or illiteracy could be read to aloud by those with some education in the local drinking establishments so that all could give their opinions as to the goings-on. Even Gough would be permitted access to a newspaper in gaol.

Mr Busby concurred with Superintendent Carline's views as to security. The threats to Gough's person by the local inhabitants of Brimington would have made it impossible to protect him. The Manchester Times claimed that "The colliers in the district left work nearly in a body, intending it is believed, to molest the prisoner and great excitement prevailed." This sort of behaviour could not be allowed. Yet the inquest still re-commenced in The Red Lion Inn at the appointed time of 9.30am on Friday the 26th. Outside the pub were the colliers, who had given themselves a holiday in the hope of seeing the prisoner (any excuse!) alongside many women and children.

"It had leaked out that the prisoner would be present at the inquest, and a rush was made towards every vehicle that stopped at the door of the Red Lion, and the Coroner, the reporters, and Superintendent Carline all received some of the attention meant for the accused"!

On realising that inside Mr Busby had merely got the jurymen to answer to their names and had just adjourned proceedings to the Municipal Hall in Chesterfield the crowd "expressed their disappointment very forcibly, shouting, "Where's Gough?" "You daren't bring him." "We should have made him black and blue."

And even after the Coroner and the jury had long left for Chesterfield some of the villagers waited near the public house "thinking perhaps that by some miracle the prisoner would yet appear amongst them."

Little did they know that Carline had given orders to wake Gough early that morning so that they could remove the prisoner by cab to the Municipal Hall when very few people were "astir". Gough "seemed surprised at being roused from sleep, but accompanied the officers unresistingly. Under the care of Supt. Carline and Sergeant Radford" they left the Marsden Street police station and at the end of the short road turned left along Saltergate then right down Glumangate and into the large cobbled Market Place. Skirting the left of the square the cab drove left passed the chemist's shop on the corner into Low Pavement and then turned right, down into South Street. Here, opposite Beetwell Street was tucked away on the right the Municipal Hall. This "neat modern building" was built of stone some 32 years earlier with four large windows to the side of the hall overlooking a medieval bowling green. It was the court house for the weekly borough and county petty sessions. It also contained the offices of the Borough Police and had cells adjoining the Municipal Hall. It was to here at 6.30 am that Carline and Radford brought Gough. Police officer Nicholls was already on duty in the charge office and after the formalities Gough was escorted to a cell and with him stayed three constables: - Udale, or possibly Udall a young 19 year old Irishman, Thomas Dooley, another Irishman, 26 years old and unattached and the eldest of the three, 33 year old John Curtis who had already spent time keeping watch over Gough at the "lock-up".

Whoever were "our own reporters" in The Sheffield and Rotherham Independent seemed to find out the most intimate of details. Neither of the Chesterfield papers recorded that "Gough, on entering the cell, noticed a very uncomplimentary expression written near the door, probably by some former prisoner, and the language, more emphatic than polite, made him laugh with apparent heartiness." This would make him seem human and that was not how they were portraying Gough.

The jury and witnesses arrived at the Municipal Hall shortly after 10.00 so that by 10.30am Mr Busby, the Coroner took his seat on the bench near to the Mayor of Chesterfield, Alderman J. Brown Esquire, and opened up proceedings to a packed house. The news that the inquest was to be held in the town rather than Brimington spread like wild fire, even though steps had been taken to keep the alteration in location as quiet as possible, and before proceedings opened *"the usual complement of idlers who have their regular seats in the Court were seeking admission, but the greater part of them were unsuccessful, as the police wisely only admitted sufficient to comfortably fill the seats of the Court, and excluded those of the rowdy element who were likely to cause any disturbance or trouble."* Indeed these public seats which only filled a small portion of the court were principally filled by Brimington residents "many of whom had trudged hurriedly" after the jury.

"The hall was not large enough, however, to accommodate the whole of the people who desired to attend the inquiry, and the doors had to be closed lest the court should become overcrowded."

The town's Mayor only stayed to hear part of the proceedings but seated on the bench near to Mr Busby also, was Mr John Middleton, a young 26 year old local solicitor of the firm of Jones and Middleton. He was appearing on behalf of Mr and Mrs Windle. Superintendent Carline was there on behalf of the police." The 12 jurymen sat at the solicitors' table whilst the witnesses took their seats behind them. William Windle was there looking "exceedingly ill" and "jaded"."His daughter's dreadful end has thoroughly unnerved him." He sat next to Miss Johnson and near to the dock. 23 witnesses were assembled in all! Superintendent Carline, his sergeants and constables had been exceedingly diligent in their investigations.

The prisoner, Gough was brought into court by several police officers, presumably Udale, Dooley and Curtis. The Derby and Chesterfield Reporter claimed that Gough did not look any the worse *"for his week's confinement. On the contrary, the enforced ablutions and the compulsory temperate life which he has led during his week's incarceration seem to have brightened him up in appearance considerably"*!

However, whilst the Coroner addressed the jury Gough stood in the dock "nervously glancing" at the Royal Coat of Arms positioned behind the judge's bench even as it is today. Mr Busby enlightened the jury as to why he had taken the step of reconvening the inquest in the larger premises of the Municipal Hall. "The prisoner himself, who from the evidence appears to be connected with the serious crime, might have an opportunity of attending and hearing the evidence that will be given at this inquest today; and from the reports of the police it was considered that it would hardly be safe to have him taken up as far as Brimington." That said Gough took his seat, which was provided for him, in the dock facing the Coroner and witnesses but with his back to the public and Mr Busby commenced to take the evidence of the first witness.

WITNESS 1   ELLEN HADFIELD

Ellen was the 9 year old daughter of George Hadfield and neighbour of the Windle family in Almond Place. Mr Hadfield was a bricklayer's labourer who in April had been a boarder with the Hawksworth family in Almond Place but by the August had secured a house there for himself and his family. On the Saturday (20th), Ellen, Eleanor Windle and possibly 4 other companions had walked down the hill from their homes along the main turnpike road in the direction of Chesterfield. They would have passed the cemetery on their left and continued on past fields to left and right of them with the odd building either side. At Peter's gate just before Tinkersick they came upon the hawker with his brightly coloured windmills and toys. Ellen told the court what Eleanor had said about her mother having a halfpenny of hers and that she would buy a parasol. Ellen had told her not to go and that she would not be friends with her if she did. Eleanor did not listen and when the girls saw that" Nellie" was leaving with the "windmill" man they continued their blackberrying up the lane to Lockoford.

Mr Busby, pointing at Gough asked Ellen *"Is that the man?"*

"Yes sir."

Ellen thought that she had gone out that morning about 10 o'clock as: - "We had breakfast late that morning" according to the words written in her original deposition.

WITNESS 2   JOHN INSLEY

A carrier of Brock-hill, Brimington, said:
"*I left Chesterfield, with my cart, about 10 o'clock last Saturday morning. I was going to Brimington. When I got to Tinkersick farm I saw several little girls apparently blackberrying near to Bradberry's hedge. There seemed to be six or seven of them. I knew the little girl, Windle, perfectly well. The man Gough, whom I had also seen many times previously, came along the road from the direction of Chesterfield wheeling his barrow. He got past the girls 50 or 60 yards, and then Eleanor Windle left the others, and overtook him, walking by the side of his barrow. The man and the girl stopped at the bottom of Miss Johnson's lane, and I passed them both while they were standing there. The girl appeared to be looking at the toys in the barrow, but I did not hear any conversation. After I had gone 20 yards past them, I turned round to see if a man* ("another greengrocer") *who had left Chesterfield at the same time that I did was coming, but I could not see him. I, however, noticed that Gough had moved a little towards Miss Johnson's lane, but that the barrow remained in the same place and the girl was still standing beside it.*"

According to Mr Insley he could not say what time it was. It was, however after 10.00 and probably not yet half past.

Questions were then fielded by a juryman and then Mr Middleton for the Windle family:-

"What kind of toys were there in the barrow?"
"They appeared to be sunshades of a very dark pattern."
"Was the barrow full of them?"
"Yes, pretty full."
"You did not notice exactly how many children there were?"
"I should say six or seven."
"Did you notice anything else in the barrow besides the sunshades?"
"No, sir, I did not notice anything else."

Mr Insley according to his original deposition for the coroner could "not remember seeing John Cook." (A witness who would give evidence later.)

WITNESS 3   JOSEPH TURNER

The young illiterate bricklayer's labourer from Brimington who had already given his evidence on Monday before the magistrate was deposed next. (A deposition is a statement made on oath before a magistrate or other court official, i.e. the coroner, by a witness and recorded in writing.) :

"I was coming to Chesterfield on Saturday morning last, about 20 minutes to 11. I know the time, because the mate I was with (Henry Witham) had to be at Chesterfield at 11 o'clock."

Twenty-three year old Henry Witham happened to be the son of William Windle's neighbour living in Almond Place.

"About 5 yards from the top of Johnson's Lane a hand-cart stood on the road, with no one in charge of it."

The entrance to Johnson's lane itself is actually on higher ground than the main turnpike road but Joseph probably means that the cart was 5 yards passed the lane and closer to Brimington. Later, Joseph will say he saw the cart and then passed the bottom of the lane on his way to Chesterfield.

"It was a two-wheeled cart, full of paper umbrellas and things- "as full as it could stick." There was no one near it except a woman, who was walking towards Brimington from the direction of Chesterfield. I did not look in it at all. It was standing close to the road, on the right-hand side looking from Brimington. I stood talking to the old woman two or three minutes, but no one came up to the cart. We started towards Chesterfield, and as I passed the end of Johnson's lane, I looked up it, and saw a man and a little girl there. They were standing close together, and the little girl appeared to be looking up at him."

Mr Busby then asked: *"Do you know the man?"*

"Yes, that's the gentleman across there (pointing to the prisoner.) "The "gentleman across there" did not seem to relish Turner's observation, and pulled his thin beard rather nervously."

I have known him for some time, (2 or 3 years) and am quite certain that it was he. I did not know the little girl, but I noticed that she appeared to have a "lightish" dress on, and also a "Zulu" hat. I saw the body on Sunday, soon after it was found, and before it was removed from the plantation. It was the size and appearance of the girl I saw in Johnson's lane. She had a "Zulu" hat on, same as I saw in the lane. When I saw the two in the lane, the man appeared to have been cutting sticks—short ones like flag sticks, and the girl was watching him." The Sheffield newspaper indicated that Joseph thought Eleanor seemed pleased with the windmill man looking up into his face whilst he was cutting the sticks. "The Derby and Chesterfield Reporter" added that Gough "whittled a small stick which he held partly under his left arm and partly in his left hand". *"That was all I saw, and I then went on towards Chesterfield. They would be 10 or 12 yards up the lane. I saw the man's face distinctly."*

WITNESS 4   HARRIOT JOHNSON

Miss Johnson was next to give her deposition. She too had already given evidence before the magistrate on Monday. She lived at the top of what was known as Johnson's lane at Oak House. She kept house for her 64 year old bachelor brother, Alfred but in the past she had worked as a governess and schoolmistress. She too was unmarried and at the age of 53 marriage was not to be a likely prospect. Alfred had lived there with his sister for over 20 years. He had been an iron fitter at the iron works but was now retired. He seems to have kept a low profile in all these proceedings.

Those assembled in the Hall were about to listen to her evidence with "considerable interest". Miss Johnson "appeared rather perturbed"; still she told the Coroner "with much dignity" that her name was "Harriot" not "Harriet" Johnson. A probable dig at The Derbyshire Times for misspelling her name!

"I am a retired schoolmistress. Our house is situated at the end of what they call "Johnson's-lane." I cannot tell the distance it is from the turnpike road, but it may be 100 yards. (According to the measurements provided at the time for the court proceedings it was 133 yards.) *Between 10 and half past, last Saturday morning, I went out, and looked down the lane. I saw a man and the child outside the lane, standing on the bank at the side of the turnpike road.* (The embankment is some 5 or 6 feet high) *The man was standing still, and the child was moving about. I could not see any hand cart. The child seemed to have in her hand a piece of ribbon or paper, which she was waving about, and which was apparently of a "pinkish" colour (but I cannot say for certainty).* (On Monday it had been blue according to the Derbyshire Times!) *I could not distinguish the man's face at all. He had a dark coat on, and was rather tall. I went back into the house, and remained in a very few minutes --- not above 3 or 4. I then went out again, and walking about 30 yards down the lane, I saw the same man and child coming up in the direction of our house.*

(Could Gough not have been coming up the lane to see if he

could do any business at Oak House? He could not have brought his cart up the lane as he probably could not have got it up the embankment.) *The child was rather in advance of the man, and they were walking quietly. I could not distinguish the man's face. They would be about 25 yards from the turnpike. (They were not half way up the lane.)* (That is still about 80 yards distance between them.) *I noticed that the man's trousers were unbuttoned, and that he was exposing himself as they walked along. I am not aware that they saw me. I did not stand watching them two seconds, but turned round immediately and went in the house to fetch a broom handle to drive the man off. I did not know the child at all. (I know very little of the Brimington children.* And did not want to know them for knowing she was a good deal alone they would run up the lane just to tease her!*) I was in the house but a very short time---merely the time it took me to get the broom handle. As soon as I had got it, I ran down the lane as quickly as I could go. The man and child were a yard or two higher up the lane than they were before, and nearer the hedge on the left side, as I was going down. The man was in about the same position, and he was still exposed; the child standing by his side. (I believe that (pointing to the prisoner) to be the man. I am scarcely sure about it.) I did not get near to them, for the man either heard or saw me, and disappeared so suddenly that I could not see* which way he went. Of course he must have started running down the lane. I did not see the girl at all. The man must have had her in the front by some means or other, for I neither saw man nor child afterwards. I went down to the bottom of the lane. I noticed the place where they were standing last, for I looked through the hedge to see if there was anyone in the field. There was a gap in the hedge a little higher up than where they were standing, but none lower down. (They might have got through the gap, but it is almost impossible, for the man would have to turn in a different direction.) I looked through it to see if the man or child were anywhere about. The lane is rather narrow, there being only just room for a cart to get up. There is a good deal of undergrowth at the sides of the lane, but I think not sufficient for anyone to hide in. I did not examine the undergrowth at all, as I did not think there was any necessity for it. I was not away long, as I ran down the lane, and walked slowly back at once. I returned into the house, but came out again several times to see if I could see anything of them. I was in and out frequently between half past 10 and (half past) 2."

The Coroner, Mr Busby, then asked Miss Johnson some searching questions and the "interest in the inquiry increased greatly at this point":

"Did you go at once and tell the police what you had seen?"

"No sir."

"Why not?"
"Because such things are by no means uncommon in our neighbourhood."
"Very well; if it is a common occurrence, your best way to put a stop to it was to inform the police at once, when you had seen it yourself."
"The police would have been at Chesterfield."
"Do you know that?"
"Yes, of course, because I saw him (the police constable) go down."
"Could you not have gone down to Chesterfield?"
"I did not go down."
"But you might have done?"
"But I did not think of it. Such things are quite common." ("Men will come up the lane, followed by a parcel of children. I have seen them many times do so.") (Men will come up the lane for convenience. I have seen many a decent man come up the lane.)
"That does not say much for the morals of the neighbourhood."
"I don't consider that I am to blame for what occurred. I have had quite enough of it."
"It was your duty to have at once informed the police," rebuked the Coroner.
"I have done my duty." "She angrily retorted with some asperity."
At this point Mr Busby changed tack in order to calm down what was becoming an overheated argument between himself and the ferocious Miss Johnson!

To his new questioning Miss Johnson replied: *"When I went down the lane I did not see a handcart. I saw no one but a man passing in a trap, drawn by a grey horse. The child had a light dress on."* ("A holland or very light print")(Holland is a type of coarse linen fabric that is sometimes mixed with cotton.) *I did not notice her hat. She seemed a tall, thin child."* (The Sheffield news report stated that Eleanor was shorter than Ellen Hadfield.) *"I did not notice the man's face. It all occurred in such a short time that it was impossible."*

"There might have been a difficulty but it was not impossible."

"I have seen the prisoner at the lock-up, and also before the magistrates. (On the Monday) *I believe him to be the same man I saw in the lane, but, as I told you before, I should not like to swear it."*

She was not nearly so confident in her statement as she was on the Monday!

One of the jurymen then presumed to tackle Miss Johnson: "Did you notice if the man was carrying anything before him out of the lane?"

"I don't know."

"You don't know whether he was carrying the child?"

"No."

"Did you look around when you got to the bottom of the lane?"

"Of course I did. Do you suppose I did otherwise?"

Coroner: "Never mind about supposing."

"Was it possible for you to miss the man provided he stood there?"

"I do not know."
"Did you go right down to the turnpike?"
"No."
"Would you have seen him if he stood by the bank side?"
"Possibly. I saw no cart."
The young solicitor for the Windle family, Mr Middleton, then asked similar questions to try and establish what had happened to Eleanor. She could not have vanished into thin air! She must have been somewhere about the lane.
"I could not state the nearest distance I was from the man that morning. It might have been 7 or 8 yards. I could see the turnpike from where I stood as the lane was perfectly straight. The child's clothes were not disarranged when I saw it. I cannot say where the child went to."
"You say you rushed down the lane? Did you pass the child?"
"No."
"You say the road was straight, and that these two people stood between you and the road, now do you mean to tell me that you do not know where the child went?"
"If the child ran before the man I could not see it."
"Did the man run fast?"
"Of course he ran fast."
"Did you see the child running?"
"No."
"Did you see it being carried?"
"No."
"Could it have gone through the hedge?"
"It might have gone."

"Was there any gap near?"
"There was."
"A newly made gap?"
"No, an old one."
"If the child had gone through this gap would you have seen it?"
"Certainly, when I returned."
"Well, did it go through the gap?"
"I don't know."

Miss Johnson's answers "were so vague that one might have supposed Eleanor Windle had been spirited away by some demon, so suddenly did she disappear"!

Mr Busby, the Coroner queried:" Why must you have seen the child if it had gone through the gap?"
"Because I looked into the field."
"But she might have run alongside the hedge."
"Yes, of course."

Mr Middleton: "You are sure the man did not go through the gap?"
"He went down the lane; he must have done."
"Did you see him?"
"Of course I saw him."
"You saw him run into the roadway?"
"I did."

Mr Busby re-read Miss Johnson's earlier deposition. Her evidence then was that she had stated that the man turned so quickly that she did not know where he went to!

Miss Johnson retorted: "I don't know which way he turned when he got to the end of the lane."
"Oh, he ran down to the end of the lane?"
"Certainly."

Mr Middleton: "You followed this man down as quickly as you could to the roadway?"

"I didn't go into the turnpike."
"But you went where you could see the turnpike?"
"Yes; I went as far as the embankment."
"Did you look up towards Brimington?"
"Yes."
"And you didn't see him?"
"No."
"And you didn't see any cart or barrow on the road?"
"No, I didn't."
"Did you look towards Chesterfield?"
"No."
"Why?"
"Because I could not see so well one way as the other."
"But why didn't you go where you could?"
"Because I have told you such things are by no means uncommon there."
The Coroner:" Oh, yes, yes."
Miss Johnson "appeared very much annoyed at Mr Middleton's questions, and evidently thought she was an injured woman."
Mr Middleton then asked Miss Johnson when she had heard about a lost child.
"I heard--------- after tea time, a man named *Jephson* ---telling me." (Gibson, Hudson or Judson are given as the possible man's name in the Sheffield and local papers. I suggest Jephson, as he is a neighbour of the Windle family in Almond Place, has daughters about a similar age to Eleanor and was probably called upon to help in the search. *"I did not tell him what I had seen. The deceased's father afterwards came up to my house"* accompanied by P.C. Wright. Miss Johnson did not know

that Mr. Windle was Eleanor's father. She only found out later that he was.

The young Mr Middleton then put to Miss Johnson: "I will ask you a question, but you need not answer it without the Coroner tells you to do so. Did you tell the father that whenever the child was found it would be dead?" William Windle had told The Sheffield Telegraph reporter this on Wednesday evening and it had been reported the following day.

"No; certainly not." The Derbyshire Times states Miss Johnson spoke "warmly", *"decidedly not. The policeman came up with him.* (Mr Windle)"

Mr Busby stated that she need not have answered the question and decided not to place it in her deposition. However everyone in court had heard what seemed to be a heartless statement to make to the worried child's father. All the local papers reported it and even though Miss Johnson denied it, rumours would abound and repercussions would follow!

WITNESS 5 JOHN COOK (E)

John Cooke was described as an old man living in Brimington and working on the highways as a labourer. That Saturday morning he was sitting on the steps that cut into the embankment by the side of the main turnpike road and at the bottom of Johnson's lane, smoking his pipe and watching the world go by. He was now 72 years old and living with his daughter and her family in Church Street, right in the centre of the village. His son-in law ran a greengrocer's there and now that Mr Cook was a widower he liked to get away from the hustle and bustle of the shop life. It was not for him.

He'd never been much into schooling and education, he liked to be outdoors. He arrived according to three different newspapers from 10.20, 10.30, and 10.40 up to 10.45. but definitely remained there until 11.30 or even a little later. In time to walk back up the hill for his dinner.

"When I got there I saw a hand-cart containing paper umbrellas and parasols. (I don't know what they call them.) It was 8 or 9 yards nearer Brimington than where I was sitting, and on the same side of the road. There was no one with the cart. I had seen the cart frequently, and knew the man who used to bring it. I did not know his name, but knew him well by sight."

"Stand up and let me see you," Cook said, addressing Gough in the dock; "and the prisoner "stood up" promptly," Is this the old soldier in him? "and gazed at the witness with great unconcern."

"After I had smoked my first pipe, I got up, and looked up the lane, but saw nothing, although I stood nearly a minute looking. I then walked up to the hand-cart, and looked into it. I saw a bag----or there might be two----lying on the side of the cart-a thin one something like an onion or a potato bag. There were also a lot of split deal sticks, as if they were to be used for the toy windmills and parasols. They were at the front of the cart-the side next the handles. At the back was a hamper, containing a large number of toys made of coloured paper. (I pulled one out and examined it. The sack I saw was exactly the same sort of stuff as the one produced by Supt. Carline, but it was not so clean as that. There was also a very large number of "windmills".) A good piece of the cart bottom was bare. The cart would be about 2 feet wide, and a foot deep. After I had examined the cart I went and sat down again on the steps. After waiting about 10 minutes I filled another pipe of tobacco, and smoked that, and then sat for about a quarter- of -an- hour longer. After I had finished the second pipe I got up, and looked up the lane again, but there was not a soul about, although there were plenty of persons passing on the turnpike-road.

I then went to a field near, to look for mushrooms, but I could not see Johnson's lane from the field. I was there from 10 minutes to quarter-of-an-hour, and then went back to Brimington.

The cart was then gone.

While I was sitting on the bank I did not hear anyone run down the lane. No one came out of the lane. I don't think anyone could come down without me seeing or hearing them, I did not see Miss Johnson at all."

Cook was later reported in the Sheffield Independent as stating "he neither heard a noise of scuffling nor saw Gough, and he supposes that he was watched by him, and that when he left the accused put the child's body in the cart and then went into the village." But this is only his supposition.

At the Inquest Mr Busby questioned: *"You say you know the man who used to drive this cart about. Have you seen him lately?"*
"Yes, sir, I think I have."
"Can you point him out?"
"Yes, sir, that's the man (pointing to the prisoner.)" ("He has been in the habit of coming to Brimington every week.")

Mr Middleton queried John Cook as to his own whereabouts and whether he had seen Mr Insley, the carrier on the road that morning.

"I went from Brimington to the steps where I sat. I believe I did meet Insley coming up the hill with his cart." (Between Brimington village itself and the steps.)

Gough's cart he felt was removed whilst he was looking for mushrooms in Mr Bradberry's field, which was in the direction of Chesterfield. The next witness Mrs Cantrill must have passed by the steps whilst John Cook was still in this field and when Gough came back for his cart.

WITNESS 6   SARAH CANTRILL

Sarah was the 26 year old wife of James, ten years her senior. They lived in Heywood Street at the back of what was the main village. Handy for James as he worked as a furnace labourer in the Iron Works as did a number of his immediate neighbours. The same workplace as William Windle. On that Saturday Mrs Cantrill had left home to go to Chesterfield and around 11.30 she was passing near to the bottom of Johnson's lane just as Alfred Gough was preparing to wheel away his cart.

Her account is somewhat melodramatic but all the events and wild rumours could have coloured Sarah's evidence:

"When I got to Miss Johnson's lane, I saw a handcart, containing a large number of parasols. The prisoner Gough was standing by it."

The Coroner asked "You are quite sure it was Gough?"

"Yes, I am." Her next remark according to The Nottinghamshire Guardian made the prisoner smile.

"I was very much afraid of him, as he looked so vicious at me. He was placing some rags or bags, (something dark coloured) on the top of the cart, which appeared quite full. There were some toys lying at the top not made up. The cart was a little higher up than Miss Johnson's lane, and one of the wheels was in the ditch. He was just in the act of moving it as I had got a few yards past, I turned round to look. He appeared to have difficulty in getting the wheel out of the ditch. It seemed to be very heavy, and I wondered at it, for such a small cart. I did not speak to him at all.

WITNESS 7   ERNEST HENRY WINDLE

Ernest was the youngest child of William's first marriage. He was 10 years old and a bit of a loner. His three elder brothers all worked as iron fettlers alongside their father at the Staveley Iron Works. His sister, Alice was 14 years old but she didn't have any time for him these days. His step-mother had produced three more offspring-Eleanor who was 6 and only a girl (and anyway she'd already gone off with a gang of girls blackberrying!) and his two half-brothers who were only 4 and 1. You couldn't really have any fun with them! That Saturday morning Ernest was at a loose end. He was sat on the bank at the side of the main turnpike road close to his house at Almond Place. From his vantage point he could see down the hill towards Chesterfield.

"I was sitting on the bank at the side of the road near our house, about …12." According to Ernest's original deposition "I remember the time because my mother had nearly finished her work in the house. She finishes at 12."

"I saw a man come up with a handcart, with paper parasols in it. There was no one with him when I saw him. I have seen the man since at the lock-up. I identify Gough as the same man I saw coming up the hill. There were other men present at the lock-up, but I recognised Gough at once. I did not notice whether his barrow was empty or full. The man went on towards Brimington. He was walking very fast and did not stay at any of the houses."

"My sister Eleanor went out of the house about a quarter to 10 that morning. I saw her go. She went on an errand into Brimington, returned home, and went out again about 10 o'clock with a number of other girls, her intention being to go blackberrying."

WITNESS 8   ELIZABETH NEAL (E)

Mrs Neal, a young woman of 21, who could only produce a cross for her signature, lived on Brimington Common with her husband, Jacob and their 2 young children. Jacob was 26 and a miner like many of their neighbours, but he was still living at home with his widowed mother and young 12 year old sister.

"Our house is at the top of Cotterill Lane (but not in it) *which leads from Brimington village towards the Common. About quarter past 12 last Saturday morning I was going down the street, (towards Cottrell Lane) when I met a man wheeling a hand cart, with paper toys in it, towards Brimington Common, from the direction of Captain's Lane.* (It was also from the direction of the Three Horse Shoes Inn which is situated set back from the main turnpike road diagonally opposite the church in the village. This is not to say that Gough was coming from as far up as the pub just that he was coming from that direction.)

I turned back (to my house) *and fetched some rags to buy my little girl* (2 year old Sarah) *a parasol. The man would not have stopped, but I called out "Stop, master, and let me have one for this little girl."* (Again "master" in the Derbyshire dialect would be pronounced "mester" meaning "mister" not the seemingly grand title of "master".)(I handed him the rags and chose a toy.) *I stood close by the side of the cart while he sold me one. I looked into it, and saw that the front part was filled with something about three parts up and 2 onion*

159

12. MAP OF VILLAGE CENTRE TO MINERS' ARMS

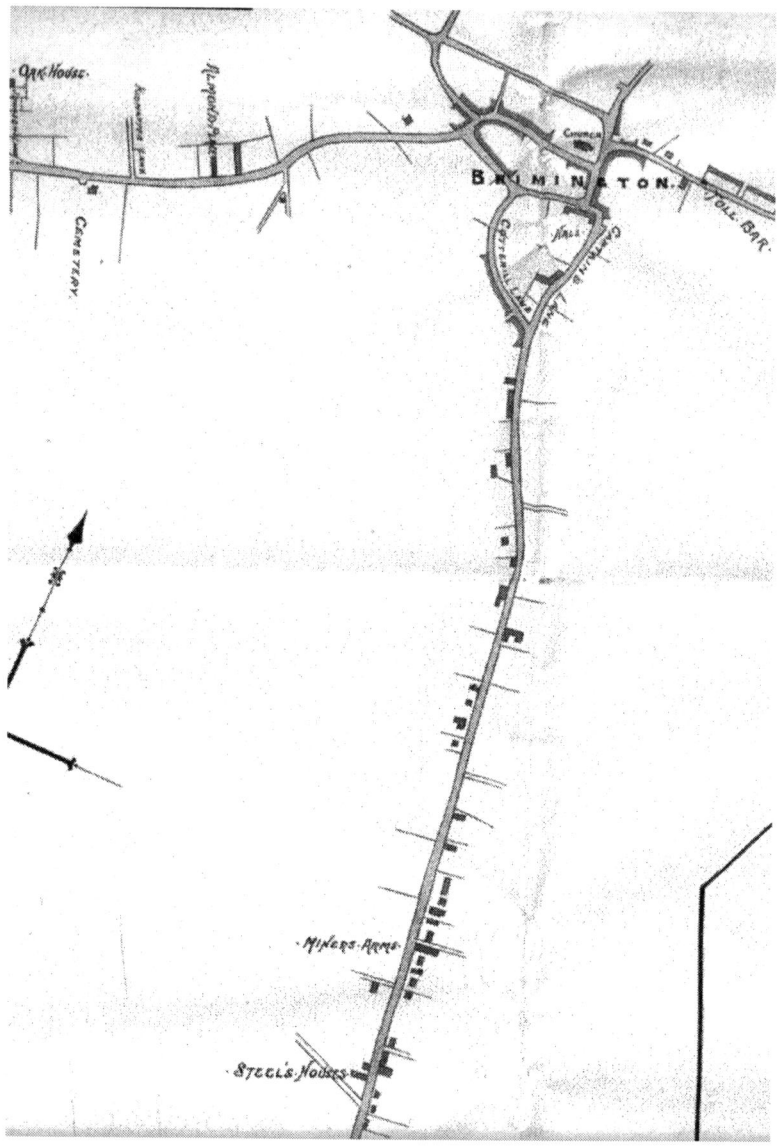

bags were laid flat on the top." Mr Busby, the Coroner then asked "Could you see what was below them?"

(No, Sir. There was a hamper of toys against the side that the man pushed from and in the middle there was a little bundle, which

looked to be about a quarter of a stone in weight.(This is about 3 and a half pounds or 1kg 587g in weight.) *It was wrapped in black cloth."*) (The Sheffield and Rotherham Independent states the weight as a stone- (14lbs. or 6kg 350g.).This still would not be the weight of a 6year old child!)

The Sheffield newspaper reports with more colour that:

"This witness caused some amusement, by stating that the prisoner's handcart contained a parcel the size of the Mayor of Chesterfield's hat, which was hanging on the chair in which Mr Busby was seated." Whether Alderman Brown was still in the Hall or had already left without his hat is not recorded! *"There was a large number of "umbrellas" in the front portion of the cart leaning over the cart.*

I said to the man "What a many umbrellas you have this morning" and he said "Yes." I remarked "You have not got many rags," to which he replied "No; but I have not come very far yet, you know." At the same time he picked up his horn, and pretended to blow it twice, but it made no noise." "Under the influence of dread"! according to the Sheffield newspaper.(The horn was the way Alfred advertised his presence in the neighbourhood just like today's ice cream men play a tune from their vans in the streets to attract the children.)

"I then left him, and went on to Brimington. He went right forward towards the common. I was away in Brimington a little over an hour, and as I was going back home about 20 minutes past 1, I met the man returning.

He was a little nearer Brimington than when I first saw him, (between my house and the Prince of Wales Inn kept by the 42year old Liverpudlian *Mrs Hall) ---he was going (very fast) towards Captain's Lane in the direction of the Three Horse Shoes.*
I did not speak to him, but I noticed that (he was in his shirtsleeves,) *he had taken his coat off, and thrown it over the bags.*
I identified the man last night at the Chesterfield lock-up, as the prisoner Gough. There were four other men present when I recognised him.

A juror then queried what Mrs Neal had seen under the bags in the cart and where Gough went to, after she had seen him the second time to which she replied:

"I had no idea what was in the cart. I said that there were very few bags in. He did not turn down Cotterill Lane."

At this point in the inquest proceedings Mr Busby allowed 20 minutes for all parties to partake of luncheon. He knew from Superintendent Carline that there were still a good many witnesses to get through and he needed to finish all the depositions today.

The afternoon's evidence began with:-

WITNESS 9 WALTER DAVIDSON

Walter was the son of Joseph Davidson, a collier whose family lived on Brimington Common. Walter's father was apparently a well-known Derbyshire cricketer as stated by the Sheffield newspaper. Walter had just turned 13 years of

162

age. Not long before he would be starting in work. His 14 years old elder brother was already an iron moulder. For now though Walter was playing with others in the recreation ground opposite the Miners' Arms on that fateful Saturday, a mere 6 days ago! He thought it was about 12 o'clock when he saw Gough outside the pub. This time does not tally with Mrs Neale's account as she claims she originally saw Gough about 12.15pm. From Cotterill Lane to the Miners' Arms is roughly a 14 minute walk so one of these witnesses is mistaken with the time. If Mrs Neale is correct Walter could not have seen Gough until around 12.30. In fact by Monday when the Magistrates assemble again it is Mrs Neale's evidence as to the timings that will change but this isn't helped by the local and Sheffield papers reporting different times in her account as well! Perhaps in the investigation Superintendent Carline is not so worried about precise timings. It was more important to get the sequence of events right.

Walter Davidson's evidence was:- *"A man came up wheeling a hand-cart, with paper toys in it, from the direction of Brimington. I had often seen the man before, but did not know his name. I went up to him, and asked him for two windmills. I have bought windmills before from him. Sometimes he has been "snappy", and sometimes he hasn't. He was "very snappy" that morning."* This candid remark caused the spectators to laugh and even Gough "could not restrain a smile". *"He sold me the windmills. He said he would have no children behind the cart, but he would have us all in front. A little girl went behind, and he told her that if she did*

163

not go in front he would give her a "good clout". (A good hit.) *I looked inside the cart, and saw that it contained a bag which seemed full. (This bag was like an onion bag - like the one produced.) The bag was lying across the middle of the cart.*

The man did not stop above twice in the village (Brimington Common), *and only blew his horn once.*

He went as far as Steele's house, (passed the Miners' Arms pub and even further away from Brimington. 267 yards according to the official measurement. Mr Steele was a retired farmer in his late 20's who lived on the Common. His retirement may have been due to ill health for before the year was up he was a dead man) *and then turned round, and wheeled his barrow back towards Brimington. He walked very fast---- almost as fast as I could run. I have pushed the man's barrow along for him twice. I asked him to let me do so last Saturday, but he refused. He would not let any of the children choose their toys, although he generally did so. He offered me a broken one but I would not have it."* "If I can't have a good one," said the lad, "I must have my rags back." The prisoner's attempt to foist a broken plaything upon him seemed a great enormity in the boy's eyes, and his earnestness made Gough smile again."

Mr Middleton, on behalf of the Windle family asked young Walter a few questions:

"Did you see what was in the bag?"

"No."

"Did you notice the opening?"

"It was tied with some band."
"Was it a big bag?"
"Yes."

Before the next witness the jury was given time to examine the cart said to have been in Gough's possession. Carline had entrusted his men to bring the exhibits into court although the Sheffield newspaper claims the cart was "too large for the police to bring into the Coroner's court". Perhaps it was outside in the corridor. So far a bag had been produced and now the cart.

WITNESS 10 SARAH ANN THORLEY

Mrs Thorley had already given her evidence on Monday to the Magistrate, Mr Barnes MP. She was now to repeat it before the Coroner, Mr Busby.

"I was at home on Saturday last. The lodge is situated at the end of the private road leading from the Chesterfield turnpike road towards the Staveley Works, and Barrow Hill. It is between quarter and half a mile from Brimington. I saw a man come along with a hand-barrow between 1 and 2 o'clock on Saturday. I first saw him just as he was turning through the gateway to the private road. I had seen him pass several times before that day, and knew him by sight. The prisoner Gough is the man. I noticed that he had many toys in his cart. He came through the gateway and went towards Barrow Hill. Our house is about 120 yards from Hoole's Plantation, which he would have to pass in order to get to Barrow Hill. (In fact the

measurement from bottom lodge to the railings by Hoole's Plantation where there was evidence of cart wheels was 333 yards.) Mrs Thorley's evidence only indicates Gough's whereabouts and approximations of time that Saturday afternoon. Gough never denied that he was there on his way to Barrow Hill but Superintendent Carline wanted to be thorough in plotting Gough's route. Therefore every little piece of evidence was to be supplied.

WITNESS 11 MISS ELIZABETH HARDWICK

Miss Hardwick was a 28 years old dressmaker living with her parents and extended family on Hollingwood Common, North East of Brimington on the left of the private road that led down to the Iron Works. That Saturday afternoon she was walking with her next-door neighbour's daughter, 17 years old Annie (Hannah) Ward (in her original deposition the friend is recorded as Fanny) on their way to Chesterfield via Brimington. About 20 minutes to 2 (or quarter to 2) they were walking along the private road.

"When we got opposite to Hoole's Plantation, we saw a man wheeling a handcart with paper toys in it about 50 (30) yards away. We passed him on the Ringwood side of Hoole's plantation. I noticed that the cart was heavy by the manner he pushed it, and it appeared to be full. I had not seen him before. I have since identified the prisoner Gough as the man I saw.
I saw the cart as I returned at night".

This testimony does not actually put Gough at Hoole's plantation. Only that he was going in that direction. If only Miss Hardwick or her friend had turned around! No doubt Superintendent Carline would have been happier with such an account but he was having difficulty finding any witnesses to tie Gough to Hoole's plantation and Miss Hardwick and the next witness were the best that he and his men could come up with.

WITNESS 12 JAMES CROPPER

James Cropper was a young married man living in Cropper's Buildings, a development of nine dwellings situated near to the Brimington tollbar, the other end of the village to where Mr Windle lived. He was 26 years old and had already spent ten years working as a blacksmith. He had now added the trade of grocer to his repertoire. That Saturday afternoon of the 20th he was coming back from New Whittington, a village north of Brimington and beyond the iron works, to Staveley Old Works by train arriving at 20 minutes to 2.

"I came along Hollingwood Common, and up the private road (from Barrow Hill to Ringwood (-the Hall)*) leading to Brimington. When I got opposite Hoole's Plantation, I saw a hand-cart standing on the road-side, and no one in charge of it. (Hoole's Plantation is about a mile away from Staveley Old Works.) The barrow contained paper umbrellas and toys.*

I saw the same cart about 6 o'clock on Saturday night, in Brimington village near the toll-bar. Gough was standing against the door of the toll-house (where Charles Abney Hastings Brown lived) *(having something to drink).*
(When I saw the cart near the plantation fence I thought the owner of it had got over it for his own convenience.)
The cart is the same as the one taken possession of by the police, and belonging to Gough. When I saw it against Hoole's Plantation it was near a gap in the hedge, where there are some railings, about 4 (or 5) feet high (and anyone could easily get over it).

WITNESS 13 WILLIAM SORRELL

Young master Sorrell was a lad of 17 years of age. He was working as a telegraph clerk for the Midland Railway. Earlier in the year he had been lodging with a Mr Hall, a miner and his large family in Staveley. William Sorrell was originally from Birmingham but Mr Hall's son was also a telegraph clerk and possibly befriended him and helped him to get settled. Now William states that he is residing in Barrow Hill which is very convenient for where he is presently working.
"On Saturday afternoon I was in the signal box against the bridge over the

road leading from Brimington to Barrow Hill, about 3 o'clock.
I saw a man coming along from the direction of Brimington, wheeling a handcart, containing rags and paper toys. I recognise Gough as the man.
I don't know how far he went, but I saw him coming back about quarter to 5, and go in the direction of Brimington."

WITNESS 14 WILLIAM WINDLE

Eleanor's father, William looking "very haggard and much distressed" was re-called to give further evidence. When William had gone to The Red Lion on Monday afternoon where the Inquest had opened he had not had an opportunity to identify Gough as the man he had spoken to on the Saturday night. This had now been rectified, turning towards Gough he said:

"I identified him at the county lock-up; the man in the corner, (the prisoner) is the man.
After I saw him on Saturday at the toll-bar,(about quarter to 6 in the evening and after he had stopped PC Wright and confronted Gough once again outside The Three Horseshoes Inn) *I went towards Whittington in search of my girl* (Today Whittington is called Old Whittington in order to avoid confusion with New Whittington. The latter being a considerably newer settlement than the old Whittington. Now the two villages almost blend into one but in the 19th century they were two

distinct entities.), *and when I returned home I heard that my girl had been heard of in the direction of Johnson's lane. I went down there in company with the Brimington constable* (PC Wright). *I walked down the lanes and carefully examined the hedge bottoms. When I had got perhaps 10 or a dozen yards up on the left hand side I found some foxgloves (nettles) and other plants which had been very recently crushed down quite flat, for a space of about 4 feet (and a width of 2 feet). Sitting upon it or lying upon it would have produced the same appearance. We proceeded up the lane and noticed 2 gaps in the hedge on the right hand side, one about half-way up the lane and the other a few yards higher up. The first one was at the bottom of the hedge and he could have crept through it and the next one a person could easily have stepped through. We walked up to Miss Johnson's house door. The constable knocked and she came out.* ("The constable asked her ------"

The Coroner had interrupted William at this point: "This is not evidence. What the policeman said to Miss Johnson or what she said to him I cannot take as evidence."

"Well, sir-------"

Again Mr Busby interrupted:" I cannot take any of the conversation."

"Not what passed between Miss Johnson and myself."

"No, certainly not."

After a "long pause" William surprised declared: "If that cannot be done I cannot bring to light what I wanted to bring to light." "She conveyed information to me, sir, "he continued "Can- not I give it?"

"No."

"We cannot take it as evidence at all."

Mr Windle had no other alternative than to leave the witness box with his secret untold, if it was a secret he had to tell."

What could William want to reveal? He was very anxious to state what transpired between himself and Miss Johnson. Perhaps he should have told more to The Sheffield Telegraph reporter. Intriguing! Perhaps he will be allowed to enlighten us at the magistrates' hearing?

WITNESS 15 PC ARTHUR WRIGHT

Twenty four year old Arthur Wright was originally from Nottinghamshire but he was working for the Derbyshire Constabulary. Earlier in the year he had been living in Holymoorside (Brampton) with his local born wife and two young sons. He was now stationed in Brimington over 6 miles away from Holymoorside and one hopes he was living closer to his beat though it cannot be assumed. All patrolling was done on foot and a policeman could walk upwards of 20 miles a day on his beat! Luckily after 1873 the police were given a boot allowance.

"I was coming to Chesterfield on Saturday morning last, about a quarter past 10 in the morning, and when I was about 80 or 100 yards on the Chesterfield side of Lockoford Lane, I met the prisoner, Gough, pushing a hand-cart towards Brimington. I noticed that the cart contained a hamper filled with parasols. I next saw the man just before 6 o'clock, between the church and Brimington toll-bar. Mr Windle told me that his child had been lost, and that the prisoner had seen it. I said to Gough "What about the child?" and he replied "It followed me from below the Cemetery up to the stone row." (Almond Place, where Eleanor lived) I then asked him if he noticed it particularly. He replied "It left me against its own home." I had some conversation with him about his trade, and, just as he was going away he said "I hope it will soon be found. It's a bad job." He then went off in the direction of Chesterfield. (Mr Windle went off in the direction of Whittington but with no success.)
Between 8 and half past I examined Johnson's lane in company with Mr Windle. About 25 yards from the bottom I found a place on the right hand side

going up as if someone had been sat or laid down.

I(t) would be 6 or 8 feet long, and from 2 to 3 feet wide, and at the back was a hole in the hedge bottom large enough to admit a man through. About 10 yards higher up was a large gap—large enough for a man to walk through. Further up still near Miss Johnson's house, was another gap. I noticed 2 places on the left hand side of the lane where the nettles and grass had been crushed down, but they were not so large as the other. I found no paper or rags or anything of that sort."

WITNESS 16 CHARLES ABNEY HASTINGS BROWN

Mr Brown had already given his evidence to the Magistrate on the Monday morning and to Mr Busby, the Coroner on Monday afternoon. Now on the Friday afternoon Mr Busby re-called Mr Brown and re-read his evidence before the court. The only evidence Brown wanted to add was *"that he pointed out the body of the deceased whilst in the plantation, and in the same state that he had left it to Police-constable Twigg. He identified the prisoner, he had no doubt whatever about his identity."*

Brown's original deposition describes Eleanor as being "not much discoloured".

According to the Sheffield newspaper the description of the position of Eleanor's body in Hoole's plantation caused a "great sensation in court" as also did the next witness' evidence.

WITNESS 17 DR WILLIAM ABRAHAM WALKER

Dr Walker like Brown had already given his findings to the Inquest jury on the Monday in The Red Lion. Now Mr Busby re-called the doctor and read aloud his deposition but not before clearing the court of all females and children. Obviously the doctor's evidence was of such an intimate nature that Mr Busby felt it was wholly unsuitable for female sensibilities. Afterwards the Coroner asked if there was anything further the doctor wished to add.

"I examined the cotton handkerchief(s) (and rags) which I received from Supt. Carline (on the Monday). *I found on them dark coloured stains that looked like blood, and on further examination under the microscope I found that it was blood. It was the blood of a mammal, and most probably human blood (judging from the size of the corpuscles).* However it was not until the early 20th century that scientists were able to identify blood traces with certainty let alone distinguish between animal and human blood!

"I examined the prisoner Gough at the police station on Sunday afternoon. I

examined his hands and found them those that one would expect to find in a man of his occupation—strong fingers and unkempt nails.
I examined his outer clothing, but found no blood upon it (or anything to attract my attention). I found no excoriation (the abrasion of the skin) *or injury upon him in his private parts.* (His "belly was free from scratches or bruises.") *His shirt was not soiled, nor were the insides of his trousers."*

Surely this latter piece of evidence could have caused an inkling of doubt in the jury?!

The females and children were obviously re-admitted to the hall whilst the next witness was called.

WITNESS 18 THOMAS HOLMES ALIAS "MANSFIELD TOM"

If the jury had any misgivings with regard to the medical evidence then Thomas Holmes was going to dispel all doubt with his sensational evidence!

The Sheffield and Rotherham Independent colourfully described Holmes as "a gentleman experienced in roving and known well to the people of Chesterfield for his Bohemian tastes"!

Thomas Holmes, a man in his mid-50's, was better known as "Mansfield Tom". He was born there and had lived most of his life in the Mansfield area, south east of Chesterfield by some 14 miles. He had been married over 30 years but was now a widower. His address was given as Spowage's lodging-place in the centre of Chesterfield—The Beehive Lodging

House on Knifesmithgate "near the Chesterfield church". Tom gives the address as Church Lane but this is probably because lodgers could go out of the back of the building into the lane by the side of the graveyard. He was at this lodging place the night of the census in April of 1881which gives the impression that Tom was a lonely individual. However, he had fathered at least 13 children and the boys followed him into the trade of framework knitters and appear to have stayed in the Mansfield area. Tom, himself gives up framework knitting at this time to become a cattle drover for Mr Lingard, one of the farmers that took him on to do casual farmwork (but as an aside by 1891 he is back as a framework knitter in Mansfield and head of his own household that consists of one of his married sons and his family and two of his daughters!)

*"I am a stockinger by trade, but as I can't work at that I act as a drover. Last Saturday evening, about 6 o'clock, I was going along the turnpike road to the house of Mr Lingard near Brimington Church. When between Almond Place and Tinkersick (*or the cemetery*) I met the prisoner Gough wheeling his hand-cart. (I have often met him before, although I did not know his name.) I was walking slowly, and he was going middling fast. As he passed he said, "Mansfield, where are you going?" and I said I was going to Brimington.*
Gough then said, "We have passed one another many time along this road, but

this is the last time we shall do so. I have done wrong, and shall never be happy anymore."

I said, "What have you done wrong?" and he replied,

"I'll tell you some other time, when we meet again." (And away he went hurriedly as if in great fear.)

That was all that passed between us, and Gough went on in the direction of Chesterfield."

Mr Middleton, on behalf of the Windle family asked if Holmes saw Gough again after this meeting to which he replied: *"I did not see Gough again that night."*

Imagine the whisperings going on in the hall at this so-called revelation of guilt or was it? It certainly stopped Gough's continuous yawnings in their tracks. He looked earnestly at Tom with an occasional smile of disbelief. What was this man talking about? Gough would have something to say about this evidence but the Inquest was not the arena for him to ask questions of the witnesses. Here he was only to listen.

WITNESS 19 THOMAS NEWBERRY

Mr Newberry was 52 years old; he was a native of Staffordshire but had spent time in Yorkshire, where his daughter was born, before moving to Brampton on the edge of Chesterfield. It is probable Mr Newberry was on his second wife for she was only 24 whereas his daughter was 16! The census describes him as a glass and china dealer but in court he states he is a marine store dealer. He had known Gough for a year but purely in a business sense.

"He has sold me his rags and bones at different times. I saw him last Saturday at our warehouse at Brampton about 7 o'clock in the evening, as near as I can tell. He had his hand-cart with him. I bought 5 stones of rags and bones (that is 70 pounds or 31 kg 751g. in weight) *from him and paid him 3s* (shillings) *for them. He went after he had disposed of the things, but left his hand-cart behind, asking permission to put it into my warehouse.*

The cart remained there ("in a safe place") *till about 2 o'clock on Sunday, when Police-sergeant Eyre came and fetched it away. It was in exactly the same condition as when it was left.*

On Monday I sorted the rags and bones, which Gough had left with me, ("its contents had not been disturbed in the slightest degree up to that time,") *and, finding the pieces of handkerchief and rags produced* (as exhibits) *amongst them, I handed them over to Supt. Carline."*

WITNESS 20 ANN ELIZABETH CLARK (E)

Ann was working for Mr and Mrs Spowage in their lodging house as a deputy. She was unmarried but how old she was or whether she was a local is not known. It is possible she had not worked at the lodging house long for she does not appear in the April census and cannot be tracked anywhere else as yet.

"I saw Gough last Sunday morning in our kitchen between half past 12 and 1 o'clock.

He said "Morning," and I replied "Morning" to him.

He then said—"Have you had any flags left here?" and I said—"Yes we have. Are you an old pensioner?"

He replied "Yes." I then said, "There have been five policemen looking for you this morning."

He said, "Haven't they got the man yet for the child."

I said, "I don't know what they wanted."

He went across to the Buck Inn. I followed him, and stood near the railings, against the church. Gough came out of the Buck, and returned to our kitchen. He stood with his back to the fire a few seconds, and then went across to the Buck again. I afterwards saw him in the custody of the police."

WITNESS 21 PC TWIGG

PC Twigg was stationed at Barrow Hill, the purpose built village for the workers of the Staveley Iron Works. From Barrow Hill the constable would pass the iron works and then follow the private road that leads up to Ringwood Hall and on to Brimington. This route would also take him past Hoole's Plantation.

"I went to Hoole's Plantation last Sunday (21st) about 12.30 in the afternoon and the witness Brown pointed out to me the body of the deceased lying in the plantation, under a tree amongst some long grass. It was lying on its back with its head a little inclined to the left, its hands across its chest, (The Derbyshire Times and the Sheffield newspaper uses the word "breast". Is this to give it more sexual connotations?) *one leg slightly drawn up and the knees inclining outwards a little. The dress was not disarranged. The piece of sacking produced was tied round its neck twice, so tightly that it was partly embedded in the flesh. I also found the bag produced a few yards (some 2 or 3 yards) away from her. I assisted to place her in the trap, and afterwards took her home to her father's house at Brimington.*

WITNESS 22 POLICE - SERGEANT THOMAS EYRE

32 years old Thomas Eyre was stationed in Staveley. He lived with his family on the Chesterfield Road, a continuation of the turnpike road that actually led away from Chesterfield and out of Brimington beyond Ringwood Hall. Next door to the Eyres' lived the Calow family who were friends of the Windles. It was Mr Calow who had helped take Eleanor's coffin out of her home the day of the funeral.

Sergeant Eyre now entered the witness box to reveal some good detecting that would be damning evidence for Gough.

"I went down to Newberry's, at Brampton, about (20 minutes to) 2 o'clock last Sunday afternoon, and I received Gough's hand-cart from the witness Newberry. It contained children's toys, flags, parasols, etc. It was the same cart as the one produced today (the one viewed by the jury). At the bottom of the cart I found the two coloured pieces of wallpaper (produced). (It also contained ....a knife and scissors) (and a hamper according to the original deposition.)

On the following day (Monday) *I compared them with the piece found by the witness Brown, in Hoole's plantation, and found that they exactly corresponded in pattern. On placing them together I found that the three pieces had originally formed one piece, as they exactly fitted together."*

These bits of paper were then placed on the table, at which the jury sat, for their inspection. It was ascertained that they fitted exactly with another piece of paper of the same pattern found in Hoole's plantation near Eleanor's body. Damning evidence if ever there could be.

WITNESS 23 SUPERINTENDENT ELIJAH CARLINE

Elijah now went into the witness box. Only one more witness after himself and then the proceedings would be over. Such a long day and he and his men had still to get Gough back through the town to the lock-up in Marsden Street!

He explained to Mr Busby how he had heard of Eleanor's disappearance on the Sunday morning about 9 o'clock. He had an "imperfect description" of the prisoner but nevertheless went in search of him through the town (Chesterfield). He had no success but "a little before one" news came that Eleanor had been found strangled in Hoole's plantation.

"About a quarter past one I visited the Buck Inn in Chesterfield.....Gough was sitting in the tap room, with a pint can containing beer before him. I looked at him, and said, "I believe you were at Brimington yesterday?" He said, "I was."I said, "Then I want to speak to you."

He at once got up, and went with me to the door. I said, "A child that has been missing since yesterday has just been found dead in a plantation, and I shall

182

arrest you on suspicion of having murdered her." He said, *"I know nothing about the child."*

I then took him to the lock-up at Chesterfield, and wrote the charge down. I said, "I am going to arrest you now on a charge of wilfully murdering Eleanor Windle, at Brimington, yesterday. You need not say anything, but whatever you do say will be taken down and may be given in evidence against you."

He said, "I know nothing about the child except that I saw her against her own house yesterday."

I then went to Brimington and received the piece of paper produced, from the witness Brown, and on the following day (Monday) *the rags produced from the witness, Newberry. The rags I handed to Dr Walker, and received them back from him."*

That was all the evidence Elijah was to give but Mr Newberry was re-called. The Coroner wanted to know how he had received the rags from Gough to which he replied that he had bought them loose not in a bundle.

WITNESS 24   MR GEORGE ROPER

The final witness was a mere formality. Mr George Roper ("the younger"), a 30 years old architect and surveyor working from Glumangate, in town, was asked to provide various measurements of the murder scene and the environs of Brimington. This he duly provided. It was left to Elijah to state that this was all the evidence. The Sheffield and Rotherham Independent felt Superintendent Carline had "admirably worked up the case".

It was now up to the Coroner, Mr Busby, to ask if there was anyone present who wanted to give any evidence. Silence! All eyes wide, looking around and at him but no person forthcoming.

Therefore he proceeded to address the members of the jury:

"Upon careful consideration of the evidence that has been put before you will depend the verdict which it will soon be your duty to give. And in arriving at that verdict I ask you to put aside the private thoughts, all reports from newspapers, or anything you might have heard, and consider your verdict simply on the evidence which has been laid before you at the first inquest at Brimington and at the adjourned inquest" (here at the Municipal Hall). (This was a necessary reminder for the press reported far more than they should yet nothing seemed to be done about it.)

"Perhaps it might assist you somewhat in arriving at your verdict if you consider two points,
Firstly as to how the child came to her death,

and secondly if you are of opinion that she came to her death by violent means; then who was the person who inflicted the injuries which caused her death.

As to the first of these two points I do not think you will have much difficulty in arriving at a conclusion. The medical evidence was most conclusive on that point, for you have Dr Walker's direct evidence that in his opinion the child died from the effects of a cord or ligature which had been tightly tied round her neck and which caused asphyxia from which she must have died very speedily indeed.

Then having arrived at a conclusion on this point there arises the second one, which is by far the most difficult to consider"

In his summing-up Mr. Busby proceeded to detail the principal points in the evidence of all the witnesses and of Gough's behaviour that day. However when he recalled Miss Johnson's evidence "he said the most strange part of the whole affair was the manner in which, according to that witness, both the man and the child disappeared. What happened to the girl he could not tell. If she crept through the hedge Miss Johnson must have seen her. It was possible, of course, that the man might have had the girl in front of him, but then, surely, she must have been visible to Miss Johnson from the end of the lane. Miss Johnson must have been in a great state of excitement at such an unusual occurrence (she said it was a common occurrence in the neighbourhood), for she did not appear to know how either the man or the girl disappeared. After running to the end of the lane, she, instead of going, as he considered she ought to have done, to inform the nearest police constable, whether at Chesterfield or Brimington, returned to her house and did not say a word about what she had seen until in the evening, when the child was missing. It was most extraordinary conduct on her part"!

"*In conclusion,*" he said, "*if you find the case to be one of murder it seems to be one of the most hard-hearted and cruel murders that could possibly be perpetrated. If from the evidence placed before you, you consider there is sufficient evidence to find the prisoner guilty of murder you will be bound to return that verdict against him. If, on the other hand, you think he was not the person who committed the murder, but that it was committed by some person or persons of whom you have no knowledge, you must say so. Consider the question very carefully indeed, very impartially, and return your verdict without any bias whatever against any party!*"

At this point the court was cleared in order for the jury to consider their verdict where they sat. (A common procedure at this period.) Within minutes, four at the most, a decision was reached. Hardly time for the foreman to ask each juror in turn for a "guilty or not" let alone have a discussion! Gough stood up, "still maintaining that coolness of demeanour which he had exhibited throughout the proceedings."

The Coroner then said "Gentlemen are you agreed upon your verdict?"

The Foreman (Mr Lingard): "We consider that Gough is the person guilty of murder."

The Coroner: "You will have to return your verdict in this form, as to how and by what means the child came to her death, and then who committed the deed. By what means, by strangulation or otherwise."

The Foreman: "Yes, by strangulation, we believe that she was strangled."

A Juryman: "We believe as a body of men that she was strangled."

The Coroner: "Then you find that she was wilfully strangled, and your verdict is that of Wilful Murder Against Alfred Gough."

The Foreman: "Yes."

During most of the proceedings Gough had "yawned, looked about him, played with his beard and moustache, and struck one as having no concern in the proceedings" apart from when Mansfield Tom gave his evidence. Now the foreman's words seemed to suddenly strike home to him the importance of the situation. "He turned pale, quivered and tears were in his eyes" but not for long.

The Coroner then proceeded to draw up the formal verdict." This was in written form and known as an "inquisition" signed by the Coroner and also by the jury members. As it was charging Alfred Gough with murder it was equivalent to an indictment that should go to trial by jury in a higher court (the Assizes). In such circumstances it was the duty of Mr Busby to immediately commit Gough into custody and order the witnesses to attend the future trial.

"Alfred Gough, you are committed upon my warrant to Derby Gaol to take your trial at the next Assizes upon the charge of wilfully murdering Eleanor Windle."
The Prisoner (who had paled a little on hearing the verdict, but who on the whole maintained a very calm demeanour): "I didn't hear what you said at first." It could have been because the public within court were making their feelings known and Gough could not hear Mr Busby or maybe he just could not take in what he was hearing. The Sheffield press stated that Gough "looked carelessly about the court, as if he were a spectator rather than one who stands, as it were, within the shadow of the scaffold."

The Coroner repeated himself emphasising the words "WILFULLY MURDERING". To which Gough merely replied: *"Yes, Sir"* bowed his head slightly and resumed his seat.

"Take him away".

Proceedings over, two constables "deftly handcuffed" Gough and "supported him" out of court and back to the cell he had occupied when he first arrived at the Municipal Hall that morning. It was now 6.30 in the evening and the inquest had originally opened at 9.30 in Brimington. It had been a long day for all concerned and for Carline and his men it was to continue for some hours yet. The jury's verdict had been welcomed with great satisfaction to the crowds assembled outside the Hall. They were now hoping to catch a glimpse of this child killer and loitered around the building. Carline was not prepared to move his charge until he felt he and his men could handle the situation and so they played a waiting game.

10.30 pm and there was still a large crowd hovering outside the Hall.

It wasn't until the early hours that the Superintendent saw his bed and Gough was tucked away in his cell in Marsden Street without incident.

CHAPTER EIGHT

SATURDAY 27TH AUGUST 1881

AN INTERLUDE

This day, the 41year old proprietor of The Derbyshire Courier, John Toplis got his first chance at reporting the murder of Eleanor Windle. The events of the previous Saturday, the daily happenings of the week and the verdict at Friday's Inquest were reported in great detail. Toplis could not wait to go to print –this story was sensational! The local inhabitants couldn't get enough of it and already it had been reported as far away as Glasgow, London and Bristol before he could publish anything. Thanks to the increasing use of the telegraph system to disseminate information all over the world let alone in Britain the local reporters were having a field day. The press telegram was cheaper than the normal rate-1/- (a shilling) for 75 words, the night rate was even better value and a duplicate message cost only 2d. (2 pence) The journalists at this time could work for more than one paper and sold their stories wherever they could. And who could blame them? Certainly Toplis wouldn't. How could you sit on such a story for a whole week when there would be others ready to make money out of it? Toplis's rival, the younger Wilfred Edmunds of The Derbyshire Times had already published on the Wednesday and he would be in competition with Toplis now as Edmunds printed on Saturdays too. The Sheffield and Rotherham Independent and The Sheffield Telegraph had been publishing the story daily since Monday. Many rumours were floating around and

Gough's career was "being very eagerly canvassed, - every little event of his life which shows him in an unfavourable light is magnified, and detailed by gossipmongers as evidence of his detestable nature." The Sheffield paper could be purchased from the bookstall at the town's railway station and no doubt was very much in demand until the Chesterfield papers got into print. The Derbyshire Times found a story regarding Gough the details of which give a hint of truth to the account though it is apropos of nothing except that it paints him as a dubious character:-

"A correspondent writing to a contemporary says:- "Three years ago the prisoner Gough was engaged as a bathman in a hydropathic establishment at Harrogate. He had at that time relatives residing in the neighbourhood of Harrogate, but his conduct was such that his relations, who were very respectable people, shunned the acquaintance of Gough, and he eventually lost his situation at the baths owing to misconduct towards the female servants of the establishment. Gough supposed that his dismissal was due to complaints made respecting him by the housekeeper, and it was reported to the manager of the establishment that Gough was loitering about the place apparently with the intention of doing some mischief.

The police were requested to watch his movements, and if needs be to take him into custody. A few nights later a constable, who was on duty near the baths, detected Gough concealed at the rear of the premises, and removed him to the lock-up. Gough was under the influence of liquor at the time, and as the manager did not press against him a charge of being on premises for an unlawful purpose the prisoner, on promising not to trespass again, and to leave the town, was committed for 14 days on the minor charge of drunkenness. After being released from gaol, he was seen in Leeds, where he hawked herrings as the means of gaining his livelihood."

Amazingly there is some truth to the story as an Alfred Gough appeared before the magistrates of the Knaresbro' Petty Sessions on Wednesday 30th October 1878 according to The Harrogate Advertiser.

This story meant nothing to Superintendent Carline but he did want to see how his witnesses had come across in print at the Inquest. Already the Sheffield newspaper had reported that "Miss Johnson saw the girl struggling with Gough"! And then "She went into her house without giving the slightest alarm"! The Derbyshire Times was a little more even-handed though it is doubtful most people would read it as that:- *"A deal of blame is laid on Miss Johnson, the Schoolmistress who saw the* man behaving indecently towards the little girl for not going at once over the fields for assistance and a large number of the inhabitants think that had she gone direct to Almond place (the nearest dwellings, coincidentally, to where Miss Johnson lived) and informed the people there what she had seen, the man could not have got out of the Lane. And without going as far as the Row of Houses she could have raised an alarm, as a man was working in the field next to the Pit field which is only a distance of about 30 yards from the spot where the man was seen by her. Indeed several of the Brimington women appear as if they would not treat Miss Johnson with much cordiality if they could be on the jury, their opinion being that had she come down the lane directly she saw the little girl in front of the brutal fellow, her life would have been saved. But it must be remembered that Miss Johnson did go to her house to obtain a broomstick wherewith to try to prevent any outrage and that on her return the man had decamped, doubtless taking the girl with him. It is very easy for people to state what they would do under certain circumstances but action speaks louder *than words, and we believe Miss Johnson acted to the best of her judgement*"! Was this article really defending Elijah's witness? It did not look too good for Miss Johnson and she must have thought the same!

Although the whole district was preoccupied with the child murder regular policing was still going on. Whilst Superintendent Carline was attending the Inquest with Gough the day before, one of his men – PC Moorcroft had apprehended another supposed murderer. Carline considered to himself that "if a superintendent encourages the men to bring frivolous cases, they will do so, but I have always tried to impress upon the men under my charge not to do so, and if they do, the reports always find their way into the waste paper basket." This matter may ultimately appear frivolous but actually it could have had serious consequences! Now Elijah was back before the magistrates in the Municipal Hall attending a County Petty Sessions. Present were the two friends and fellow magistrates Mr Barnes MP and Mr Markham Esq., the man in charge of the Staveley Iron Works.

Elijah, however, was more relaxed about this matter. It was even a light relief! There had been posters put up in police offices giving a description of a one, Joseph Taylor, the supposed murderer of a woman in Bradford, Yorkshire. Age-56-57 years. Height: - 5 feet 7 inches. Features:-stout build, pale complexion, blue eyes, white bushy beard, dark grey hair and bald on the top of the head. A reward of £100 was offered for his capture!

It is no wonder an enthusiastic police constable, eager to please his superintendent, for Carline was universally well-liked, arrested a man he thought matched the description. Mr Carline agreed the man did bear a remarkable resemblance to the wanted felon "judging from the bills circulated" and handed a copy of one to Mr Markham so that he could see for himself. Indeed Elijah "scarcely had any doubt" that it was Taylor. He subsequently telegraphed to the police in Bradford that he had their man. (When Elijah found time to do all this as well as be at the Inquest is hard to imagine. One presumes he would delegate the task to one of his junior officers.) However the Yorkshire police informed him that unless the arrested man's head showed an "indention" it could not be him. The final distinguishing feature of the murderer on the poster was that he had a "very large dent on the left side of the head." Apparently this mark was unmistakable and impossible to hide! Subconsciously Elijah put his hand to his fore head. He could there feel his own battle scar. A reminder of a "very nasty blow" he had endured in the course of duty when in his mid-20's.

"I now therefore apply that he be discharged, as I am quite sure that he is not the man." "It was a well-known trait....that sooner than convict a man unjustly he would give him the benefit of the doubt however slight and recommend acquittal." Carline continued- *"He states that he has previously been arrested on the same charge at Skipton"* (in North Yorkshire over 84 miles away.)

At this information the assembled court could not help but laugh. Mr Markham wanted to try and assist the poor fellow:

"It's a great hardship on the man this strong resemblance; why not give him a note stating that he is not the man?"

Carline ever practical and the professional that he was, remarked:

"That would hardly do, sir; there is a

196

possibility that he might give it to the real man."

The magistrates could see the sense in what the Superintendent was saying and after further questioning the man's circumstances and past history Mr Barnes discharged the prisoner. The relieved man, Joseph Thompson, left thanking the Bench. He'd spent the night in a cell but it was in the same lock-up as the child murderer of Brimington. No doubt he could spin a tale-"The Inside Story" in exchange for a drink or two!

Carline walked back up from the Municipal Hall into the Market Square. The stalls were laid out for market day and there was always a crush of people going about their shopping on Saturdays. He pushed through and carried on up the hill towards Marsden Street. He had had two supposed murderers under his roof last night both old soldiers who had fallen on hard times. He had had it in his power to release one but Alfred Gough was a different matter!

Waiting on Elijah's desk upstairs in his office was a piece of paper one of his men had picked up in the Market Place that day. He thought the superintendent would want to know about it though the officer did not want to be there when his superior read it! Elijah looked at it with growing disgust. It was about young Eleanor Windle and Gough. The writer had penned "lines of the most wretched doggerel ever printed". Why would someone do this?! He got up out of his chair and went downstairs in search of his sergeant pausing only for a minute to glance towards the heavy iron door that was closed across the corridor that led to the four cells for the male inmates. Did Radford know about this? Carline waved the paper before him. The sergeant had to concede that a lot of people knew about it. Copies were being sold in the Market

Place and so great was the demand the seller had succeeded "in disposing of very nearly 1,000 copies." Carline just left the room speechless and prayed the Windle family did not get wind of this.

CHAPTER NINE

SUNDAY 28ᵀᴴ AUGUST 1881

MAYHEM IN BRIMINGTON

The "Brimington correspondent" for the Sheffield newspaper claimed that on this day there were thousands of people visiting Brimington to see the scene of the murder! The curious from the local area had already begun their sight-seeing earlier in the week. Carline had to move quickly even on the day Eleanor was found. He had the cart brought from Chesterfield to check it against the cart tracks by the side of the Plantation before the evidence was obliterated by the feet of the villagers. This Sunday though, gave the opportunity for others as far away as Sheffield, Nottingham and Derby to see the locality. The numbers may well be exaggerated but even Superintendent Carline claimed there were an "immense number of people" about the village doing a tour of the sites that Gough was supposed to have visited with his victim dead or alive the week before. No doubt Eleanor's grave was also on the itinerary. A large number of people had already begun to visit her resting place the day after the funeral as the weather was fine and so the cemetery authorities decided to leave the gates open for the present. The "tourists" continued throughout the day until darkness fell. Elijah had been kept informed that there were relic hunters on the prowl. In Hoole's Plantation the bark had been completely stripped off the tree "near to which Gough had laid his victim"! The "macabre" Carline could contend with but the mutterings against Miss Johnson were something else. That morning the Superintendent upon a personal request for protection ordered PC Wright to keep guard of the property owned by Miss Johnson's brother. No doubt Miss Johnson felt some ease at seeing a police presence even though it was only one man. The young PC Wright remained on duty all morning watching the curious come and go. It was a private lane but with so many people about it was impossible to keep them completely away, trying to get a peek of the house at the top of the drive. Wright did what he could. He overheard smatterings of conversation as to what had happened in the lane and what conclusion one could come to as to the guilty party and what might have happened if Miss Johnson had taken another course of action. Indeed there had been dark rumblings all week from "certain of the lower orders residing in the district" who considered Miss Johnson "did not act in the manner she should have done on seeing Gough (if it was Gough) behaving indecently to the poor child"! And where was Miss Johnson?! Miss Johnson and her brother remained indoors.

During the afternoon PC Wright took himself off to get refreshment. In the early days when Carline was a constable there was no allowance for meal breaks and one had to be ingenious to find somewhere to grab a bite in private without being detected by a superior or anyone else. It was at this point that Superintendent Carline claimed "several hundred people" not content with being in the lane went right up to Johnson's house and got into the orchard at the back of the property. "The Derbyshire Times" described these people as *"a gang of roughs who behaved in a most excited and disgraceful manner ...not satisfied with using several threats and improper language,* (they) *betook themselves to doing what damage they could and to helping themselves to the fruit on several of the fruit trees in the orchard."*

Imagine the horror on PC Wright's face at such a scene and the imagined reprimand he would receive on having left his post. A fine at least! How frightened must the Johnsons have been, hearing the insults and watching the damage done to their fences and trees. Would the rabble commence attacking the house next and then their person and where were the police when you wanted them?!

PC Wright rushed into the orchard and apprehended one of the miscreants who was in the act of picking up an apple. By the bulges in his pockets it was not the first. Whilst having hold of this youth he could see a number of other youngsters robbing the orchard and causing damage. The constable called upon Thomas Martin, a local stonemason, to come to his assistance and detain the youth (later known as Wragg). Martin put his hand on Wragg's collar to assist PC Wright but this was the signal to Wragg to try and get away. Martin wasn't the law and there were plenty of other people taking the fruit, why should he be arrested?! A struggle ensued and somehow one of Martin's fingers got in between the teeth of Wragg. Wragg bit down on the finger "very severely". The Derbyshire Times stated that Mr Martin was "very severely assaulted" having a piece of his finger bitten off! Obviously now George Wragg was arrested for assault as well as stealing and taken to Chesterfield along with Seth Allen and Joseph Carline (no relation to the Superintendent) who had also been captured stealing or damaging the Johnsons' fruit and their trees. They would be appearing before the magistrates in due course as would Gough.

CHAPTER TEN

MONDAY 29TH AUGUST 1881

PRISONER BEFORE THE MAGISTRATES ADJOURNED FROM LAST MONDAY.

Today Alfred Gough was to return to the Municipal Hall where he had been all day Friday. A week earlier to the day he had been at the County Magistrates' Clerk's office. The clerk was the 52 year old solicitor, Mr John Hallewell whose place of work was the Georgian house on West Bars. The building was only used as "an occasional courthouse" and due to its smallness it was decided to continue proceedings at the Municipal Hall. No doubt to the relief of Mr Hallewell. Last Monday his office had been besieged by people out to get Gough and it had not been without incident in trying to get the prisoner back to the lock-up. This week who knows what the crowds would do? His office may not escape unscathed a second time.

Carline was pleased to be going to the Municipal Hall it was less of a security risk. He had given orders to have Gough up and ready for the cab that would be waiting at the gate. He and Sgt. Radford as on the previous two occasions escorted the prisoner through the town to reach the Municipal Hall by 7.30am. An hour later than Friday but Carline was still able to reach the court building without anyone seeing Gough and thus avoided any public demonstration. As on Friday Police Constable Nicholls received the prisoner and conducted Gough to the same cell he had occupied that day. "**He bore himself as quietly and composedly as on the former occasions.**" Today his cell did not give rise to amusement.

He needed to think. It was his opportunity to question the witnesses for he was undefended. This would be his only defence.

The newspapers were reporting that "the excitement over the event in which the accused is said to have been concerned has to some extent cooled down." However Elijah and his men were not taking any chances.

The court assembled shortly after 11 but a large crowd had formed outside the building long before this. As soon as the doors were opened to the public the space limited for their use was immediately filled and to avoid a crush, although the court was "densely crowded," the doors were closed again "and well-guarded". A large proportion of those attending were surprisingly female and some even had babies with them! The space outside, in front of the Hall, was filled with "hundreds of people", many of whom had come from Brimington but were unable to gain entry. But their intentions were to wait outside throughout the Inquiry despite the rain falling heavily and forecast to continue throughout the day. "As the small army of witnesses in couples or singly" arrived to gain entry to the building "they were keenly criticised by the crowd and freely commented upon". Poor Miss Johnson was particularly singled out. Her reception was "more demonstrative than flattering"!

The public inside had to wait for the main event for there was the ordinary business of the Borough Police Court to be disposed of first. The 70 year old magistrate Mr F. Swanwick, (one time pupil of, and private secretary to George Stephenson) was on the bench.

13. Mr Frederick Swanwick, Officiating Magistrate.

The Mayor, Alderman Brown, was an ex officio justice due to his office and, "during the greater part of the hearing" sat by Mr Swanwick's side along with Mr Lancaster Esquire another of the borough's magistrates.

The young man by the name of George (W) ragg who had been arrested yesterday on Miss Johnson's property in Brimington was brought before Mr Swanwick charged with two offences. The Derbyshire Courier claimed the youth was "respectably–dressed" but that did not alter the fact that he had stolen apples to the value of 6d (6 old pence), which had been produced, and assaulted Thomas Martin. Wragg pleaded guilty to both charges.

Superintendent Carline explained to the magistrate what had happened the day before –the numbers of people in Johnson's lane, how PC Wright had been on protection duty, how he had gone for refreshment and the crowd "took advantage of the fact". (Elijah would always support his men. He would never forgive a falsehood but young Wright had told him everything and had bitterly learnt his lesson. Elijah had come up through the ranks himself and knew what long hours were expected of a policeman.) Carline continued his account of Wragg's arrest by his constable and what had happened to poor Mr Martin.

The Superintendent was applying for Wragg to be held in custody until Saturday. Mr Swanwick asked the young man if he had anything to say why he should not be remanded. The youth, however had no good reason and so was removed into custody.

"Mr Swanwick then said that the fact of the man having admitted the charges showed that a most disgraceful disturbance had taken place, and Mr Carline had taken a very wise course in affording Miss Johnson what assistance he could. The affair was extremely

disgraceful." "It was disgraceful." piped up the indomitable Miss Johnson!

In 1867 when Elijah had been Inspector for just a year he had been in charge of the police dealing with a coal strike in the South of the county. Those were "troublous times amongst the miners" which lasted some while. Yet it was said he came through it with "flying colours." The Derbyshire Times in later years described Elijah's "dogged determination, good-humour, keen appreciation of human nature and his tactful handling of men saved many a disturbance and quelled others much more easily than would have been the case if less care and ability had been shown." The disturbance in Johnson's Lane would have been nothing in comparison to a coal strike but Elijah appreciated Mr Swanwick's words particularly as his superior –Captain Parry- the Chief Constable of Derbyshire was there to overhear them !

Captain Parry late of the Royal Marines, a military man, like so many other chief constables had not come through the police ranks. A career in the forces counted for much more in obtaining his position. He was now in his mid-40's and had already spent a decade as a chief constable. He had been appointed by the Home Secretary and once in the post had the power of a virtual autocrat. He could hire, promote, fine and fire his men. In the towns it was the Watch Committee who performed the same duties as the Chief Constable of the County. Chesterfield's Superintendent of Police; John Else held his position by the good graces of the six gentlemen of the Watch Committee. He had no connection with Captain Parry and vice versa. The Chief Constable was here to see his man-Elijah Carline- in action and of course to look upon Alfred Gough.

14. Captain Parry, Chief Constable of Derbyshire.

At 25 past 11 the prisoner was brought into court. Initially Gough did not attract a great deal of attention. He was accompanied from the cells by PC John Curtis and Sgt. Thomas Eyre, two of Carline's more mature police officers. And *"on his entrance turned coolly round to observe the time from the clock above his head"*! PC Curtis was to remain in charge of Gough throughout the whole proceedings.

"He was dressed precisely as on the last occasion, but there was a slight difference in his conduct. He still played with his necktie, twisted his head, often looked at the clock, and occasionally yawned; but he also listened very attentively to the evidence." Gough gave no impression to those about him that he was concerned with his situation. He surreptitiously touched his vest just to check his hymn book, recently given to him, was still in his pocket but no one saw. What was going on inside his head?

Mr Hallewell, the Magistrates' Clerk read the charge against Gough to which no reply was made. He then sat down and the main event for which all were waiting, commenced:-

Mr Middleton, the young solicitor of the local firm of Jones and Middleton had represented the parents of Eleanor at the Inquest on Friday. He had intimated then that he was in communication with the Public Prosecutor "in the hope that the Treasury (Solicitor) will take the matter up". The position of Director of Public Prosecutions had only been set up by the Home Secretary two years earlier. The first Director was a cautious man. Of the cases referred to him he took up only a third and these he passed on to the Treasury Solicitor. Once the decision had been made to prosecute, the handling of it was taken over by the Treasury Solicitor and presumably that meant the costs would come out of the public purse. Before this time the responsibility of bringing a criminal matter to court rested with the "victim" and his/her family. This could be costly and the preserve of the wealthy. However with the new developing police forces their roles were evolving and gradually over the century they were taking over the responsibility for bringing prosecutions to court. Mr Middleton must have pleaded the Windle family's circumstances well.

Today he opened the case by stating that he was now instructed by the Treasury to prosecute the prisoner for the murder of Eleanor Windle. *"His duty was to lay before the bench such evidence as would warrant them in committing the prisoner to take his trial before such a tribunal as would inflict upon him the punishment that the law provided. Having detailed the evidence that he proposed to lay before the Court commenting specially on the evidence of "Mansfield Tom" and the similarity of the pieces of wallpaper found in Hoole's Plantation and in the prisoner's handcart; continuing he said that if he showed there was a case which would warrant the bench in sending the man for trial he apprehended the bench would send him to take his trial at the next Derby Assizes."* In whatever county the crime occurred it was a common law rule that the accused would be tried by a jury from the same county. Even so this would be a journey of more than 25miles, Derby being in the south of the county and Chesterfield in the north. It is doubtful the witnesses would be looking forward to such a prospect! However the first witness was now called:-

WITNESS 1   MR GEORGE ROPER

Mr Roper was the last witness to appear before the coroner on Friday but thankfully for him and his practice the first to appear today. The architect-surveyor had produced a plan of the locality, from Lockoford Lane as far as Barrow Hill, including Brimington, Brimington Common, and Hoole's Plantation. (Literally the whole of the murder scene with the village at its centre and all points –North, South, East and West radiating out from that middle point.)

Superintendent Carline during the Inquest proceedings on Friday had shown Mr Roper the handcart and asked if he could provide measurements for that exhibit for today which he did:-

"the cart was a two-wheeled one, that it was 4 feet long, 2 feet 6 inches wide, and 1 foot 3 inches deep. The gauge of the wheels was 3 feet 2 inches, and the breadth of the tyres was 1 inch and a half."

WITNESS 2   ELLEN HADFIELD

Ellen, a 9 year old scholar of the Brimington Board School, repeated her account of blackberry picking with Eleanor and some other little girls, their fateful meeting with Alfred Gough along the turnpike road and Eleanor leaving them to go with the man back towards Brimington.

Gough was defending himself and although given the opportunity to question these two witnesses declined. Well, there was nothing controversial with their evidence.

WITNESS 3   JOHN INSLEY

Mr Insley was a 56 year old married man. As well as describing himself as a carrier he was also a greengrocer living in Burnell Street off Brockhill Road in Brimington. His

17 year old son John would have known Mr Windle for he was an iron fettler and William would have been his foreman.

Mr Insley's narrative of driving along the turnpike road to Brimington that Saturday morning differed little from his account at the Inquest on Friday. He saw ahead of him the girls blackberrying, Gough and his cart, and Eleanor leaving the other children to follow and walk with Gough. Insley did add that he went alongside Gough "some yards and noticed it contained paper sunshades of a dark pattern". He continued that after he had passed them he did look back and see Eleanor by the cart and Gough going towards Johnson's lane. It was now Alfred's turn to question the witness. *"Had I any rags in the cart?"*
Witness (Insley): "No. I could not see any rags, I could see the windmills."
Prisoner: "Oh!"
There must have been a lull for Mr Swanwick states: *"Have you any other question to ask him?"*
Prisoner: "No."

WITNESS 4   Dr W. A. WALKER

Before Dr William Walker's evidence the court was cleared of all females and children as it had been at the Inquest on Friday. The doctor repeated his evidence of last week. He described Eleanor's condition after she was brought home on the Sunday afternoon (21st) by Mr Knighton. The post mortem results that were carried out the next day on the Monday (22nd). His opinion was that the "unfortunate child" had been outraged and that her death resulted from asphyxia caused by strangulation.

"The mark round the child's neck might have been produced by the hem of the sack, (produced in court).
Mr Swanwick: Do you wish to ask the witness any questions, Gough?"
Prisoner: "Yes, sir, (to the doctor) did you find any marks about me?"
Dr. Walker: "About you?"
Prisoner: "Yes."
Dr. Walker: "No."

At this line of questioning Mr Middleton (on behalf of the Public Prosecutor) intervened to ask the doctor about certain bloodstained rags that had been handed to him by Superintendent Carline for examination. These had supposedly been in the haul Gough had given to Mr Newberry on the night of the murder. Newberry had handed them over to the police on the Monday (22nd) and these had been passed on to the doctor.

Now Mr Swanwick asked Gough if he had any further questions.

"No more than what I just asked him. I asked him if he found any marks upon me and he said "No."
Mr Swanwick: "Is there any other question?"
"No."

WITNESS 5   JOSEPH TURNER

A young bricklayer's labourer of Brimington had seen Gough, whom he had known for 2 years, that Saturday morning (20th). He had first seen the handcart and then espied Gough up Johnson's lane with a little girl who was wearing a "Zulu" hat. He believed the girl found in Hoole's Plantation the next day was one and the same owing to the "Zulu" hat.

"Mr Swanwick (to prisoner): "Have you any question to ask this witness?"
Prisoner (to witness): "Did you see me doing anything else but cut sticks?"
Witness: "No, but you were cutting sticks."
"Yes."

WITNESS 6   MISS HARRIOT JOHNSON

Miss Johnson was the next witness called. She was the retired spinster schoolmistress residing with her brother at Oak House situated in what was known locally as Johnson's lane.

"She described the circumstances under which she first saw a man and a child in Johnson's Lane on Saturday morning. (Due to the man exposing himself)*She described how on the occasion of her going out of her house with a broom handle, the man ran down the lane and disappeared at the end of it. She did not know what became of the child but believed the man took it with*

him. (Her attention was more particularly directed to the man.) She went down to the end of the lane and looked out, but saw nothing of either the man or the child, nor yet did she see the handcart. (There were some gaps in the hedge, and she looked through them but failed to see anything of the man or the child.) From the general appearance of the man she believed the prisoner to be him.

Mr Swanwick (to prisoner): "Do you wish to ask the witness any question?"

Prisoner (to witness): "Could you swear to the man?"

Witness: "I think I could swear to you."

Prisoner: "On your oath?"

The Sheffield and Rotherham Independent reported that Gough was "somewhat surprised" to hear Miss Johnson could identify him and reminded her that she was on oath.

Witness: "I could not swear to your face but I could swear to your general appearance."

Mr Swanwick: "Any other question?"

Prisoner: "No, Sir."

Somewhat exasperated the Sheffield newspaper wants to know why Gough did not question the lady's evidence regarding "his indecency in the lane", a matter "that forms the most important part of her statement"!

The magistrates' clerk, Mr Hallewell, a solicitor in his own right, must have asked Miss Johnson something to do with her eyesight for it is reported her stating "her eyesight was not very good, but from the man's attitude and general appearance, she believed him to be the same."

WITNESS 7   JOHN COOKE

John Cooke was the old highway labourer who had been sat on the steps at the bottom of Johnson's lane smoking his pipe. His evidence today, before the Magistrate, appeared to be more precise than before the Coroner on Friday. His facts seem assured.

"Between half past 10 and 11 o'clock on the morning of Saturday, August 20th, he sat for a considerable time, smoking his pipe on the steps opposite the end of Johnson's lane. He saw a hand-cart placed against the side of the turnpike, about 8 yards (24 feet or roughly 7 and a third metres) *above the steps. There was no one in charge of the cart but he knew the prisoner was the man who generally went about with it. He examined the cart and found in it a hamper containing paper toys in front and a bundle of sticks at the back. There were one or two empty bags at the side of the cart and with the exception of the space covered by the hamper and sticks the bottom of the cart was bare. He*

afterwards went to look for some mushrooms in a field and on his return in about 15 minutes the cart had gone.
Mr Swanwick: "Have you anything to ask this witness, prisoner?"
Prisoner (to witness): "Were there any rags in the cart?"
Witness: "Not one."
"Was there a single rag?"
"I did not see a single rag of any description."
Prisoner: "That's all I wish to ask."

WITNESS 8   SARAH CANTRELL

Young Mrs Cantrell on her way to Chesterfield stated that about 11.30 that morning she had seen Gough standing by his handcart. The cart was still where old Mr Cooke had claimed it to be.

Her evidence today was more matter-of-fact rather than melodramatic.

"She observed that the cart contained some paper toys and parasols, and in the body of the cart was something bulky over which the prisoner was placing some empty bags. She saw the prisoner start and he appeared to have great difficulty in moving the cart.
Alfred could not wait to ask her some questions: *"I think you said in your last evidence that there were some rags in the cart?"*

Witness: "Yes, I said rags or------------
Alfred jumped in: *"There were no rags in the cart; the bottom of the cart was empty."*
Witness: "I said rags or something dark coloured."
"You said rags last time."
Witness: "Rags or something dark coloured."
"There were no rags in the cart; the bottom of the cart was empty."

WITNESS 9   ERNEST H. WINDLE

Ernest was the 10 year old half-brother of Eleanor. He again described seeing Gough alone walking quickly up the turnpike road towards him from near to the cemetery. Ernest thought it was about noon (although at the Inquest he had said 11.45 a.m.) when this occurred but he hadn't taken any notice of the cart or its contents.

No questions were asked of him by Gough for what was there to ask? He had gone in that direction and he may have been seen by a boy. Nothing unusual in that.

Mr Middleton's memory was jogged by Gough being alone at this point and recalled young Mrs Cantrell. Had there been anybody with Gough when she had seen him?
"No, no-one".

WITNESS 10   MRS ELIZABETH NEALE

The 21 year old mother of two recounted how she had seen Gough twice around the middle of the day.

Once as *"His cart seemed to be half full in the front, of something which was covered over with two onion bags, similar to the one produced in court* (as an exhibit). She had spoken to him regarding the large number of parasols he had and so few rags to which Gough replied: *"No, I haven't come far."*
Her second encounter with him was on his way back from the Common and on his way towards Brimington. He was now in his shirt sleeves having now removed his jacket and placed it on the cart. The Derbyshire Times reports that Mrs Neale said it was between half past 12 and 1 o'clock, The Derbyshire Courier and The Sheffield and Rotherham Independent claim she said from quarter to half past one. The latter time seems more feasible. Her Inquest testimony was 1.20pm.

"Mr Swanwick asked the prisoner if he had any questions to ask the witness"
Prisoner (to witness): Did you see anything but rags in the cart?"
Witness: I only saw rags at the bottom end and towards the top end of the cart. I could not see what was under the bags."

WITNESS 11   WALTER DAVIDSON

Walter was the 13 year old witness who had encountered Gough outside The Miners' Arms whilst playing with other children. It was reported that young Walter kept Gough's "face in a continual glow by answering each time a long series of questions with a monotonous "Yes, Sir". He had seen Gough carry on towards the Common and then return to go back towards Brimington. He had obtained two windmills in exchange for rags. Walter's recounting of this with great seriousness nearly had Gough "ready to break out into a hearty laugh" when he felt that Gough was trying to cheat him by offering him a broken parasol! He recalled that Gough would not allow him to stand near the cart's handles even though he had on previous occasions. To Walter the cart appeared to be full. There was also a bag in the middle of the cart which was tied up and Gough's coat thrown over it.

To return to the timings - Walter believed he had originally seen Gough about 12 o'clock but that was also the time Ernest Windle claimed to see him outside his home at Almond Place. The Miners' Arms is more than a mile away! Therefore young Mrs Neale's timings tie up better with Ernest's perception of the time and Walter is possibly out by about half an hour. However time and the perception of it are difficult at the best of times. In 1881 the children would not have owned timepieces and neither would a working class woman. In our modern world the means of knowing the time is everywhere for young and old, male or female alike. Alfred Gough does not question the timings. It was probably enough that he was seen early in the morning, around noon, early afternoon, etc. Therefore let not the modern day mania for time-keeping worry us here!

WITNESS 12   SARAH ANNE THORLEY

Mrs Thorley was one of the first witnesses to give evidence to the Magistrates last Monday as well as at the Inquest on Friday. She was now back in the witness box recounting for the third time what little she had seen from her vantage point at Ringwood bottom lodge situated at the top end of the private road that led down to Hoole's Plantation, Staveley Works and Barrow Hill. She stated that she had seen Gough turn off the main turnpike road to go down the private road between 1 and 2 o'clock with a cart containing paper-toys. It was reported, as early as last Tuesday (23rd), that Superintendent Carline discounted part of a woman's testimony who resided at the "gamekeeper's house at the commencement of the "private footpath "leading to Ringwood Hall". This sounds as if this could be Mrs Thorley. She was saying then that she had seen Gough enter the plantation twice. Superintendent Carline felt this was incorrect. Why?

WITNESS 13   ELIZABETH HARDWICK

Up to last Tuesday (23rd), the day of the funeral, the only witness to have seen the handcart by the Plantation on the Saturday was James Cropper. The police made efforts "to get further information as to the accused being there in the afternoon." Those efforts only produced Miss Hardwick.

Miss Elizabeth Hardwick, a single woman living with her parents at Hollingwood Common used the private road to walk to Brimington en route for Chesterfield that Saturday afternoon. Today there is no mention of her companion in the newspaper reports. Perhaps it was decided by Superintendent Carline that it was unnecessary to involve somebody else in Miss Hardwick's deposition. After all nothing would be revealed from yet another witness' account of Gough's where-abouts.

Elizabeth claimed she met Gough along the road some 10 yards (9.1m) before he had reached Hoole's Plantation at about a quarter to 2 (The Derbyshire Courier reported 1.30-

2.00.) He was wheeling a hand cart that appeared to her to be full and heavy, going in the direction of Barrow Hill.

WITNESS 14 JAMES CROPPER

The blacksmith, James Cropper saw a hand cart drawn up outside the Plantation against the railings. He had come from Staveley Old Works that Saturday afternoon and was on his way to Brimington by way of this private road. *"He did not think the prisoner was in the wood or he would have tried to fetch him out."* This statement caused some laughter in the courtroom. Possibly a young blacksmith with ten years work experience was a well-developed and muscular individual who thought he could take on Gough. Not that he would have known there was anything amiss on the Saturday. It was just a parked hand cart! Gough was not amused he just "cast a meaning look upon him (Cropper)" The blacksmith knew nothing about him or his life except what was in the newspapers and that was not necessarily accurate. Why, the neighbourhood were prepared only to believe the worst of him! He was supposed to have blown his horn whilst plying his trade and frightened some doctor's horse a few weeks back. The valuable horse ran off and smashed into a dog cart worth about £30 or more! This supposedly occurred in Wirksworth nearly 15 miles away from Chesterfield but no charges were brought against him! Why was that?

The police had been given the usual and exaggerated false rumours concerning Gough since he had been arrested and it was with difficulty that Carline had to separate "the chaff from the wheat". Did a Jephson girl, a neighbour of the Windles in Almond Place who presumably had not gone blackberrying with her sister really get propositioned by Gough to accompany him after he had supposedly murdered "Nellie"? She was saved from his clutches by stating she was going blackberrying! Although Carline might discount the gossip, the newspapers would print anything to do with Gough. This was all good business. It was supposed to be illegal for the press to stir up prejudice against someone awaiting trial. This was contempt. But the press took little heed to the penalty and it even failed to be enforced by the police. (It was usually left to the victim of such press attacks to start court proceedings.) It was not unknown for false reports to be published in an attempt to pre-judge guilt and even inadmissible evidence found its way into print on the grounds of public interest!

Gough's attention went back to the blacksmith. James Cropper finished his evidence by stating he saw the same hand cart near the Brimington toll bar that Saturday evening about 6 o'clock. James lived nearby so this is not a surprise. The prisoner was talking to the toll-bar keeper (Mr Brown) at the time and his cart was just a few yards away.

WITNESS 15 WILLIAM SORRELL

The teenager repeated his evidence of Friday. He was a railway telegraph clerk and that Saturday afternoon whilst on duty in the signal box at the side of the bridge over the road that led from Brimington to Barrow Hill he saw Gough. It was about 3 o'clock when he saw the prisoner and his hand cart coming towards him. Gough went in the direction of Barrow Hill and an hour and three quarters later young Sorrell saw the man returning back towards Brimington.

Five witnesses had come and gone in the witness box and Gough still had nothing to ask. Everything was as it had been that day.

WITNESS 16 CHARLES ABNEY HASTINGS BROWN

Brown, the toll-bar keeper, had given evidence to the Magistrates Court last Monday morning when the entire furore was going on outside on West Bars. He had been at the Inquest on that Monday afternoon back in Brimington and then again at the adjourned Inquest on the Friday in town. Now he was repeating his evidence yet again for the Magistrates.

The "aristocratic" name of Charles Abney Hastings Brown "seemed to tickle the prisoner very much". Gough had probably thought of him as Charlie Brown! Brown had seen the prisoner going towards Brimington that Saturday morning between 9.30 and 10.00. He detailed the interview he had had with Gough that evening at 6 o'clock at the toll-house when Gough called for a glass of ginger beer. He related the conversation that subsequently took place between Eleanor's father, Mr Windle and Gough. He also stated at length how he had found Eleanor's body in Hoole's Plantation with the hem of a sack tied round her neck, how he had found a hemp sack and then discovered the piece of coloured wallpaper about 5 yards from the post and rail fence which he had handed to Superintendent Carline. Gough asked nothing regarding the wallpaper. How had it found its way into the Plantation? And amazingly matched with two pieces of wallpaper found in the bottom of his cart! That is some coincidence! Surely Gough would not be so reckless as to leave incriminating evidence lying around particularly as he allegedly was being so careful to hide the body. If he was so reckless he could have left the body where he had supposedly strangled Eleanor rather than take the body with him! The Sheffield newspaper reports that Gough only asked questions of some witnesses and in everything he was "very brief". "It did not appear that he had any direct purpose in his questions, as he passed the greater portion of the important part of the evidence unnoticed."

WITNESS 17 WILLIAM WINDLE

Eleanor's father re-told his version of the conversation he had had with Gough at the toll-house. He asked him "What sort of a girl was that that came up the road with you this morning?" Gough described the girl to Mr Windle and said that he left her at the top of the hill. Gough's final words to him at Brown's were *"I'm very sorry, it's a bad job."* Later that evening Gough was spoken to by PC Wright. Mr Windle added that it was PC Twigg who brought home his dead daughter on the Sunday afternoon.

No mention is made of William's conversation with Miss Johnson that he was so desperate to tell at the Inquest on Friday. Was he given advice by Mr Middleton or Superintendent Carline that it would not further the case? Did the solicitor and policeman think they had a solid enough case without this evidence even though it was all circumstantial? They seem to have persuaded William. Would they persuade Mr Swanwick, the magistrate?

WITNESS 18 PC WRIGHT

Young PC Wright now needed to be every inch a policeman in the witness box. Superintendent Carline had not blamed

Wright for what had happened at Miss Johnson's house the day before. Carline had thankfully supported him but the events had all come out in court earlier in the morning .That would not have been so bad if the proceedings had not been heard in front of his boss, THE BOSS, the one who hired and fired! Word was that Superintendent Carline, who had been head of the Repton and Gresley Division, based at an ungodly place called Wooden Box over 13 miles south of Derby, had moved to the Chesterfield Division in 1874 but that the following year, Carline had heard there had been a missive to his old division from Chief Constable Parry. The order was that a particular police constable should resign because he was "too small and of a youthful appearance"! If that was a sacking matter how did he rate incompetence?! The 24 year old stood to attention and again related the conversation he had had with the prisoner in the vicinity of the church and Brimington toll-bar. The girl's father was present also. PC Wright stated that when Gough left them he said: "I hope it will soon be found. It is a bad job." That was his evidence and on leaving the witness box Wright felt he saw a faint smile of approval pass over the lips of his Superintendent.

WITNESS 19 THOMAS HOLMES, ALIAS "MANSFIELD TOM"

"The features of the prisoner entirely altered when Mansfield Tom entered the witness box. He looked Tom straight in the face, and seemed to regard him with the bitterest scorn. Whilst the witness was detailing his evidence the prisoner never moved his eyes from him. He often shook his head and seemed to clench his teeth."

Gough had heard Tom's evidence on Friday at the Inquest but that arena did not give him the opportunity to question witnesses. He had been thinking about it all through the weekend. Did he know Thomas Holmes, had he met him somewhere else, had he done something to him? Why would "Mansfield" say these things? Gough listened closely to what was said.

Tom was a drover in his mid-50's. He claimed to have known Gough for 4 or 5 months but did not know his name until the day of the Inquest on the Friday. He maintained that he had met Gough the evening of Eleanor's murder on Saturday 20th August between Almond Place and the Cemetery.

"The prisoner was wheeling his cart and as he passed---said, "Mansfield, we've met many times on this road, but we'll never meet no more. I have done something wrong and shall never be happy no more."
Witness said to him "What have you done wrong," and prisoner replied, "I'll tell you if we meet again," That was all that passed between them."

Mr Swanwick then asked Gough if he wished to ask the witness anything. Did he!

"With an air which seemed to express the satisfaction he felt at having a chance of pouring his wrath upon his enemy," "I have, sir," and he proceeded forthwith to question Holmes in the most pointed and emphatic manner."

"Where did I speak to you before that Saturday night? Did I ever speak to you?"

Witness: "*You never spoke to me before we met on the road?*" Tom asked incredulously!
Prisoner (excitedly); "*No you lying old villain.*"
Mr Swanwick: "*You must not talk like that. Ask him any questions you may desire.*"
Gough's "anger was thoroughly aroused, and he gave his opinion of Holmes in the most expressive and violent language he could command."

"*You are a lying old villain and want transporting, Gentlemen;* (addressing the bench) *I never spoke to that man in my life if I was to go to heaven or hell this minute.*" This statement caused a sensation in Court! "*I never spoke to him, I never knew him before the other day, I never spoke to him.*"
Witness: "*You never passed me on the road without having something to say.*"
The Magistrates Clerk, Mr Hallewell then spoke to Gough: "*Have you anything to ask him?*"
At this point in the proceedings "Mansfield Tom" took it upon himself to step close to the prisoners' dock. Why would he do this? He had already aggravated Gough, what was Tom's motive in making matters worse? Tom's closeness was in order to explain "that he was as near to him as that (indicating the space between the two of them with his hands) when the conversation took place." This must have been within arm's length because Gough was described as becoming "excited" and "white with passion," he lifted up his clenched fist to strike the witness, but was prevented by the police officers. PC Curtis made a grab and pinned Gough's arm who was endeavouring to lay a blow on Tom and would have "floored him" but was stopped by other police

reinforcements probably in the guise of PC Wright or Sgt Eyre. Superintendent Carline was to hand but his men were bringing the situation under control without him.

Prisoner: "Don't you come near me you d---d old scamp, you lying old villain, you liar you.
"Witness: "Didn't I---"
Mr Swanwick: "You must not ask the prisoner any question, but you must answer him."

Do you mean to say I spoke to you on Saturday night? Gough continued.
"Yes, about 6 o'clock."
Prisoner: "You are a liar, you are a liar. I never spoke to the man in my life."
Mr Swanwick: "Have you anything else to ask him?"
Prisoner: "No, sir, I never spoke to him in my life, (looking at Tom he hissed) *I wish I could have satisfaction out of you. You lying old rascal."*
The depositions of the evidence were then read over to Mansfield Tom *and he stated them to be correct whereupon* Gough with "great passion" called out as Mansfield Tom left the witness box)*: "Every word of that is perjury."*

What was to be made of Gough's outburst? Throughout the proceedings he had sat attentively, asked brief questions and was even amused by some of the witnesses' answers. He gave no indication as to what his conduct would be when Mansfield Tom entered the witness box. Is this why he had slept restlessly over the weekend in the lock-up? Up to this point everything was circumstantial. Tom was putting the noose round his neck by this trumped up confession. Why?!

WITNESS 20 THOMAS NEWBERRY

Whilst Gough "gradually cooled down" Mr Newberry was called. He was the man that Gough had taken his rags and bones to on the Saturday night and on whose premises Gough had left his cart. In sorting the rags Newberry found that "they were covered with blood marks"! That is according to the Sheffield newspaper, the Chesterfield newspapers are less sensational. "Certain of these rags" were handed to Superintendent Carline.

Prisoner asked witness: "Was there an old bag, a dark coloured bag in the cart?"
Witness: "No I didn't see one, there was a bag that I lent you before."
Prisoner: "You did not see a black bag with the cart?"
Witness: "No I did not."

By the time Newberry finished his evidence Gough had "assumed his usual calm appearance."

WITNESS 21 ANNE ELIZABETH CLARK

This person was a deputy at Spowage's lodging house where Gough had spent the Saturday night (20th). Her evidence was in regard to the conversation she had with Gough and his conduct in the kitchen of the lodging house on the Sunday morning (21st).

"Mr Swanwick: "Do you wish to ask her anything, prisoner?"
Prisoner (to witness): "Was you talking about the child before I came down into the kitchen?"

Witness: "No, the child was never mentioned until you named it to me."
Prisoner: "Were the men in the kitchen talking about it before I came down?"
Witness: "No, the child was never mentioned, I knew nothing about it before you mentioned it to me."

WITNESS 22   PC TWIGG

William Twigg was a 36 year old married man living in Barrow Hill. He repeated his testimony of the Inquest stating the body was pointed out to him by Brown in the Plantation and that he arranged for the child to be carried home in a trap.

WITNESS 23 SERGEANT EYRE

The 32 year old sergeant now took the stand. Here was a competent officer destined for future promotion, a good detective in the making. Eyre stated that he had taken possession of Gough's cart from Mr Newberry and within it found two pieces of wallpaper that corresponded exactly with the piece of wallpaper found by Brown in Hoole's Plantation. The three pieces all matched in colour and design and "also fitted exactly" "showing that they were of one and the same piece."

Did anybody ever wonder what an amazing coincidence it was that Brown alone found Eleanor's body on the Sunday even though volunteers were out looking for her all night? Brown found the wallpaper. Gough was in the toll house the night before where Brown had sold him a drink. Could Brown have slipped outside and pulled out a piece of wallpaper from the cart and the next day planted it in the Plantation? But you would only do that if you knew something already about Eleanor's disappearance or death. Brown did have the opportunity. However it was obviously not a question that Gough considered exploring with Brown. The police and general public were convinced they had got their man so why should they look for another suspect elsewhere?

WITNESS 24 SUPERINTENDENT CARLINE

Nearly all the witnesses had been called and it was up to Elijah now to *"prove* (d) *the apprehension of the prisoner at the Buck Inn at 1.15pm on Sunday August 21ˢᵗ"*. He also stated that when Gough was taken to the police station and charged Gough remarked: *"I know nothing about the child, except that I saw her at her own house yesterday."*

Towards the end of the day the very first witness Mr Roper was re-called. It is to be hoped that he managed to deal with some of his everyday work before being called back late afternoon! He had presented his plan of the area at the start of the day. Now he was to present the distances between one site and another.

"From Lockoford Lane to Tinkersick, 396 *yards;*
From there (Tinkersick) *to Johnson's lane, 484 yards;*
(The embankment from the turnpike (road) *to the end of Johnson's lane was from 5 to 6 feet high.)*
Johnson's lane, 133 yards in length;

From the bottom of Johnson's lane to Almond Place, 333 yards;
From Almond Place to the Miners' Arms, Brimington Common, 2000 yards;
From the Miners' Arms to Steele's houses, 267 yards;
(And in returning)
From Steele's houses to Brimington Churchyard corner, 1,600 yards;
From there to the toll-bar, 200 yards;
From the toll-bar to Ringwood bottom lodge, 700 yards;
From the lodge to the rails in Hoole's plantation, 333 yards;
From there to the signal box near Staveley (Works) *station, 1,530 yards."*

With the final witness departing from the witness box Mr Middleton stood up to declare that that was the case for the prosecution.

Mr Swanwick: "That is the case?"
Mr Middleton: "Yes, sir."

The Magistrates' Clerk then formally charged Gough and said: *"After that caution do you wish to make any statement?"*
Prisoner: "No, sir."
The Magistrates' Clerk wrote down: *"Nothing."* Could that really be the case, he wondered, that Gough on such a serious charge wanted to say nothing? Or had Mr Hallewell at his age heard it all before in former proceedings and was surprised by nothing these days. It was just a matter of fact. Mr Hallewell continued: *"Have you any witnesses to call?"*

Prisoner: "*No, sir.*"

Was there no-one who could vouch for his character in a good light? Mr Newberry had stated in The Sheffield Daily Telegraph that he had always found Gough to be a "very straightforward man." "It happened now and then when a wet day prevented Gough following his occupation he would come and borrow a shilling, and as much as eighteen pence, but these small loans were always repaid when the next lot of rags and bones were settled for. As far as he could see, Mr Newberry considered Gough a decent man, but of course he noticed that he had the misfortune of being too fond of beer, like many more in the same calling." That was the negative! What of the widow Mrs Elizabeth Rhodes who ran the "Castle Inn" lodging house near Walton to the south west of the town? Gough stayed with her and her family supposedly for several months towards the end of 1880 and possibly for some time in 1881. She had spoken well of him to the Sheffield Independent which printed a piece about his time there on the 24th August but she appeared to be the lone voice. He was grateful for that as he had left her lodgings, a couple of months back, under a bit of a cloud. He had struck a man whilst under the influence in a "fresh state" and Mrs Rhodes had spoken sharply to him believing him to be in the wrong and because of that he just upped and left! What could she say of him now? *"She only saw him drunk once, and that was the only occasion on which he was particularly disagreeable."* He was not known to her as being normally quarrelsome. Most of the lodging – house-keepers took a different view and thought of Gough as an unwelcome guest who was very disagreeable when drunk! Mrs Bateman who ran a "cheap" lodging house in Lordsmill Street turned him out after a few days because of the very late hours he kept! Mrs Rhodes claimed that whilst he lodged with her he spent most of his time either mending his handcart or making toys such as flags from old pattern books that he had purchased from wallpaper hangers."**Three figured pieces he fastened up on the kitchen wall, placing a border round each of them, so that they looked like pictures.**"He usually worked on the kitchen table or the long table in his bedroom and afterwards piled his creations carefully in a corner of the room, contrary to what another lodging- house- keeper had said of Gough. Whilst at work he was always humming and he loved singing. Mrs Rhodes stated that he used to amuse his fellow-lodgers with sentimental and comic songs, two of his favourites being the 70 year old song from an opera, "The Death of Nelson" and the more up-to- date (1864) "The Gypsy's Warning". The latter song Gough copied out the words from a book for the female attendant using a pencil and the wallpaper he had to make his toys. On occasion Gough would even entertain all with a tale of his Indian exploits. Alfred claimed "to be a linguist of no mean capacity" and at times would sing in Hindustani though Mrs Rhodes had to admit that no one knew if he was singing in an Indian language or whether it was just "gibberish"! Would she dare to come to court to give him a character reference? And what of young Walter Scott? He had known the 28year old for at least 2 years. Gough had lodged at his premises in Sheffield and it was Walter who helped Gough to get back on his feet (for a time at least) when Alfred had sunk so low that his fellow lodgers advised him to go out begging in order to eat.

15. Sketch from Illustrated Police News 3rd September 1881

Walter had quite a large establishment of some 44 lodgers and yet had gone with Alfred and his army testimonials as to his good conduct to the Sheffield police and obtained a hawkers' licence in order for him to make a living. He also owned a light handcart which Alfred thought would be suitable for hawking and so Walter sold it to Gough for 8 shillings (though that was not the handcart that was in court today). Alfred had been fairly successful in this trade for about 18 months and even managed to rent a pleasant small room from Walter and put some money aside. Gough had been in Sheffield in April and the early part of August staying overnight in Walter's lodging place at 34-36, Water Lane where Alfred collected children's toys for his trade. It was even his intention to return to Sheffield over the winter period. Alfred knew he was not easy to get along with (the papers claimed he was "very intemperate" during his stay in Sheffield, occasionally sober for a week or two" working hard, after which he would have another drinking bout, continuing until all his money had gone and his credit run out) but he still thought he could count young Walter as a friend. Walter had already been linked with Gough as early as two days after the murder by the Sheffield newspapers but maybe this was one "ask too much" for Scott. Perhaps he wanted no more to do with Gough or maybe no one contacted him as to appearing at the Chesterfield Magistrates and he did not know the procedures or maybe it was just too far away for him to spare the time from his business. As it was it felt like Alfred could only count on himself. There would be no friends or acquaintances or even family to support him. Superintendent Carline had informed him earlier in the week that he was allowed to write to any friends he may have but he had not taken him up on the offer and as far as he knew or wanted to tell he had no living relations of whom he was aware except two cousins who he had lost track of.

The magistrate was returning back into Alfred's consciousness: *"Alfred Gough, you are committed for trial for the WILFUL MURDER of Eleanor Windle, at the next Assizes for the County of Derby."* With that Mr Swanwick made a move to leave the court. It was after 5 pm and the court had sat for 6 hours but young Mr Middleton had just one more thing he felt he had to say: *"Before I leave the court I think it right, on the part of the prosecution, to acknowledge the very complete manner in which Mr. Carline has got up this case. I came into it at the last moment, and then I found it in the complete manner in which it has been presented to you to-day."* Carline could not help but smile at the young man for his kind words particularly as Chief Constable Parry was still listening to the proceedings. It was the role of the police to apprehend presumed felons not question them. It was up to the courts

237

to do the questioning and decide someone's guilt or innocence. However Carline and his county policemen had to find the witnesses and put the facts, such as they were, in some kind of sequential order so that they could present a reasonable case to the magistrates. It was still essentially circumstantial evidence but Carline got the result he was hoping for.

The Sheffield and Rotherham Independent reported that day that- "There, probably, never was a case where the action of the police gave greater satisfaction to the general public. The promptitude and acuteness which Superintendent Carline showed not only in capturing the prisoner, but also in gathering up the evidence against him, is acknowledged on all sides, and the people of Brimington especially are very loud in their praises of what the gentleman has done."

When Mr Toplis' Derbyshire Courier finally got to print on the Saturday (3rdSeptember) Mrs Carline must have been beaming at the praise her husband was receiving. Within the newspaper was a comments column entitled "Notes from the Crooked Steeple (Chesterfield's famous landmark, the church with the Crooked Spire)" "by an old crow" Again it mentioned Mr Middleton's compliment to Superintendent Carline and went further by stating it was "fully merited".

"The promptness and assiduity (close and careful diligence) *with which he and his men have acted throughout the whole of the unfortunate affair has been universally praised. The fact that when a solicitor entered the case he did not find it necessary to call one witness more, or one witness less, than appeared at the Inquest, is ample proof of the carefulness with*

which the case was completed." Gough's line of questioning of the witnesses, on the other hand, went into "trivial detail." Did they see rags in his cart; was he holding sticks and so on? Not the "principal points" of their evidence those which "told most against himself".

At the end of Monday's proceedings in the Municipal Hall *"the various witnesses were ---- formally bound over to prosecute* (carry through to the end) *the prisoner at the next Derby Assizes"*. What a daunting thought for young and old alike to travel to the other end of the county. How would they get there? When would they have to go? Where would they have to go? Where would they stay if the trial lasted for more than a day?! This was to be decided at a later date. For now witnesses and public alike, once Gough was removed from court by Superintendent Carline, Sergeant Eyre and PC Wright dispersed from the court and its precincts but that is not to say that everyone went about their business. Far from it!

Poor Miss Johnson was the first to suffer from the crowd outside when she left court. She was "hooted and hissed" after and notwithstanding that, a "great number" followed her walking up South Street from the Municipal Hall to the Market Place shouting and yelling at her all the way. **"It was only through seeking refuge in a cab that she managed to escape from the noisy mob."** What a 48 hours Miss Johnson had had and she still had to go back to living in Brimington amongst very hostile villagers some of whom were waiting for her even as she alighted from the cab!

Gough had been taken back to the court cells there to await his return to Marsden Street Police Station. But that would not be any time soon judging from what had happened on the Friday evening after the Inquest. Therefore "refreshments" were provided for Gough whilst he waited. Throughout this trying time Gough was never a man who lost his appetite even Carline noticed he enjoyed his food. "The Derbyshire Times" felt that Gough was *"much more affected by his position than he cares to show"* and for someone who had spent years alone and rootless this was a possibility.

There was still a crowd waiting outside hoping to see "the last of Gough" but Divine Providence stepped in to provide a heavy, "smart shower" that lasted for some time. This helped to dissipate the crowd enough that by half past nine Carline felt they could make their move. A cab drew up outside and without attracting too much attention Gough was bundled inside and with Carline by his side were off to Marsden Street. However, not attracting too much attention did not mean "no attention" for the cab was still followed by "a number of youths, who hooted and yelled most of the way"!

Once back in the police cell he had occupied all week Gough "behaved with the same reticence that he has shown throughout his incarceration". However it was reported that he was not quite so reserved as on Sunday and Monday, he had even been heard laughing, though he still retained his "indifferent demeanour". "He has made no reference to his crime, and talks only of generalities". He was a man of few words. He had his thoughts to keep him company.

CHAPTER ELEVEN

TUESDAY 30TH AUGUST 1881

REMOVAL TO DERBY GAOL

Much to the disappointment of those curious to see Gough being put on the "mail" train to Derby the night before, Carline arranged for Gough's departure early Tuesday morning. It had been reported that Gough was to leave on the Monday night and no doubt Carline may have had a hand in either spreading the rumour or certainly not stopping it.

Under the cover of darkness and yet more heavy soaking rain Carline, Sergeant Radford and Gough, clutching the book recently given to him, made their way to Chesterfield's Midland Railway station to catch the 4.40 am train to Derby. It would have taken less than 15minutes to arrive at the station to the east of the town. The three figures seemed to hover like phantoms on the empty platform, well; one nearly was if the legal system was to have its way! In the blackness their feet had disappeared under the swirling smoke puthering from the stationary engine. They climbed aboard and settled into a 3rd class carriage. If Gough could have seen out of the window in the gloom he would have realised that for a short distance the railway would have been following his route to Brimington just 10 days earlier. Now he was on the train with the two policemen who had kept him company and protected him throughout his comings and goings to the Inquest and the magistrates' court sessions. Carline and Sgt Radford could for a time relax with their charge. The extra money escorting a prisoner would help supplement the able sergeant's wage which was always a help with his growing family. Elijah watched the prisoner opposite him and contemplated all that he had read about Gough in the papers and then considered his own life. What would the journalists have made of his career IF he was ever to have told them?! He was not one to recount his past exploits at the drop of a hat but sat on the train he let his mind wander. He lived and breathed the police force. The newspapers would struggle to find anything in his past life that was not police orientated. That is, all except one slight aberration in his youth. Something that could never be guessed would happen to a young man Derbyshire born and bred!

ELIJAH CARLINE

Elijah came into the world on 1st January 1839 in Horsley Woodhouse, just outside Smalley in Derbyshire, to one, Edward, a 39 year old agricultural labourer and Mary, a 44 year old framework knitter. His mother had been married before and widowed for, at the time of his birth there were three other children living in the same establishment – Elizabeth, 9 years, Jane, 7 years and 5 year old Matthew. However their surname was Turton and he was a Carline. The family lived in Smalley 7 miles NNE of Derby. In fact in 1881 his parents were still alive and living in the same village though not at his boyhood address. His job allowed him little family contact but he felt they understood and would be very proud of all he had achieved.

He followed his father into labouring but once he had turned 19 he looked to join the police. He was an ideal candidate – a literate, bright agricultural labourer, strong, robust and well-built. Those taking on new recruits felt labourers had both the physical strength and the right mental qualities of "stoicism and deference to become a loyal servant upholding the law and maintaining social order". (The New Police in the Nineteenth Century –David Taylor) He was single at the time; another plus, as many forces stated married men need not apply although once in the job marriage was considered a stabilising influence. He was the appropriate height -5' 11''even though the minimum height was some 4'' shorter. He was a little young; for most recruits were taken on in their 20's but few forces specified a lower age limit. The upper age limit was a different matter. Few men were taken on once they had reached the age of 35. The recruits had to be certified of a strong constitution and free from any bodily complaint. He passed all the requirements and after being recommended by the local Justice of the Peace, Mr J. Radford who found Elijah to be of "irreproachable character and connections" he was signed up.

On 1st March 1858 Elijah - 106 according to the number on his raised collar, was duly appointed to the rank of 4th class constable to the Derbyshire Constabulary that had itself only been in existence since the January of the year before. His green uniform which later became dark blue was issued for a deposit and had to be worn at all times. An allowance was given for his boots. A blue and white striped armband was to be worn on the left sleeve when on duty. The tools for his trade were: - a rattle to attract attention (It was not a whistle until after 1883!) but not to be used lightly otherwise it became a disciplinary offence, a bull's eye lantern to wear on his belt which at night as well as light could give off a small amount of welcome warmth, a very hard wood truncheon kept in a special sleeve sewn within the leg of the trousers and finally, in order to restrain a criminal, a set of handcuffs.

Being discreet in their use was urged even then, as a prisoner later acquitted could bring an action against a policeman for damages. Duly equipped, though not necessarily adequately trained Elijah was stationed in his own home district of Belper. He would have gone out with a more experienced officer initially who would pass on his knowledge to the new recruit. Promotion for the young man came relatively swift and with it each time a slight increase in pay. By the 1st May he was promoted to 3rd class on roughly 18/- a week, by 1st April 1859 he made it to 2nd class and by July of 1860 at the age of 21 he was a 1st Class Constable. This was the highest grade for a constable with the highest pay.

The census night of 7-8th April 1861 found 1st Class Constable Carline now stationed in Glossop in the north of the county. It was an area devoted to the cotton industry but with open moorland to the east. Geographically it was between Sheffield (24 miles away) and Manchester (14 miles away). He was boarding with a Sarah Ann Woffenden and her young son along with Sarah's married daughter, her husband and their son. Only Elijah knew what was running through his mind (The Derbyshire Times later gave the reason as being a winter spent at "Belper"! though it probably meant Glossop) but 19 days later on the 26th April he just resigned from the police force! The uniform was handed back but no return of the deposit. If no deposit had initially been paid then 5/- was deducted from the wages in order to cover the costs of altering the uniform for the next recruit!

"The spirit of adventure led him to accept a job under a contractor for waterworks to be constructed in Russia"! Where or how he found this job is not known but The Police Register noted alongside his resignation that he had obtained an appointment in St. Petersburg, Russia with free passage out and payment of 6/- a day! This would have been double the pay he was receiving as a constable so although it was a bold move it is not surprising Elijah took the job. He made friends easily, was young and single and nothing was holding him back. Between 1857 and 1880 the median wage rates for 1st Class Constables ranged from 20/- to 27/-depending on where you worked. It was equivalent to the pay of sailors, gamekeepers or quarrymen, slightly more than an agricultural worker or someone unskilled but less than many other workers such as miners.

Yet, six months later Elijah was back in England in his native Derbyshire. The Russian contract "did not satisfy him for long" and he applied once again to join the police force. His superiors must have thought well of him for Elijah was re-admitted on the 15th October 1861.However the Register for November states that it is with a reduction in rank and therefore less money than when he had left the force. Elijah Carline, 2nd Class Constable started making his way back up the career ladder so that within 4 months he was back to being a 1st Class Constable. He acted as clerk to Superintendent Thomas Williams back in Glossop where he had been stationed before resigning to go to Russia. This may have been as a punishment for the police were very much a para-military organisation and discipline was "intolerably" strict. It is doubtful second chances were given to young officers who had the audacity to resign but there must have been something about Elijah that made his superiors want to give him that chance. Nevertheless, back to Glossop he went. It was regarded by fellow officers "as the Siberia of the county"! After all Snake Pass was close by and that is notorious for being bleak and impassable in winter "If a constable was unsatisfactory in any other town or village, if he had been up to any mischief elsewhere, he was sent to Glossop, the punishment district, where he soon received his "marching orders" if the slightest difficulty arose."

However, Elijah stuck it out, kept his nose clean and by the following year (1863) just after his 24th birthday he made "Acting Sergeant" being "awarded a chevron" to sew onto his sleeve. 11 months later, having taken a written examination in reading, writing, maths and law, the "highly successful" young officer's temporary appointment was made permanent. Becoming a sergeant meant that Elijah was also considered able to drill his constables at morning parade before they commenced their shifts and that he himself could ride a horse though it was only the rank of superintendent who actually got to mount the beast if there was one! As sergeant, Elijah was only paid around 4 shillings more than a constable and would still spend much of his time on the beat supervising the comings and goings of his own group of officers. He could take charge of the police station, read out the daily instructions to his men on the morning parade and generally ensure that his men were well presented, clean and tidy with their police equipment in good order. At this time one of the tasks assigned to the police was to arrest all County Court defaulters for which they received 1 shilling per head which helped to supplement, in the eyes of most officers, the poor pay. A few pence could be earned a week by constables who could act as "knockers-up", literally going round on their beat in the early mornings waking workers up by knocking at their doors or windows.(The equivalent to a modern day wake-up call.) The more experienced officers could supplement their pay by escorting prisoners, attending trials at the Quarter Sessions or Assizes or even acting as a javelin man at the ceremony to welcome the High Court

Judges. Further small perks of the job such as, in some areas, free tram travel, subsidised housing, help with the utilities or local rates, the provision of coal, free produce and the keeping of one's own livestock and chickens helped the married man with a family to get by, even if that sometimes was near the breadline!

"Many exciting incidents fell to his (Elijah's) lot during one of the hardest periods of his career. Duty was tremendously heavy." The job was 7 days a week, out in all weathers. If an officer started his shift when it was raining then he stayed uncomfortably wet throughout the shift and no arguments. It was not unknown whilst at Glossop for young Elijah to frequently work 2 days without sleep and once he remembered starting his shift on a Friday morning and not seeing his bed again until Monday night! In later years Elijah never forgot this and did all he could to change the system of such long hours for his men. An "extremely rough class of customers passed through his hands (in Glossop) but strength combined with tact brought him through alright." Assaults to police were high but Elijah only suffered one serious attack in his career and that was when he went to arrest some poachers in their own house. Things turned nasty and a scuffle started in the kitchen. The upshot was a table was smashed and in the fight the poachers took to using the broken table legs as weapons against Elijah. He was struck a "very nasty blow" to the head and to this day carries a noticeable scar on his forehead. The "violent lawlessness" had caused the Chief Constable, W.G.Fox to issue to the Superintendents of the Divisions cutlasses for the protection of their men especially those on night duty.

Elijah remained at Glossop for nearly 5 long years but whilst there he was possibly mentored by Thomas Williams who also acted as the weights and measures inspector in Glossop from 1858-1864. Williams had been a sergeant with the Metropolitan police in London in the 1840's to the early 50's, then by about 1853 he had left the capital and travelled north with his family for a new job as one of eleven "Superintendent, constables" for the county, being based in the Bakewell district and being paid £140p.a. This was an appointment prior to the setting up of the County Police. The county folk were initially opposed to a county police force so the superintendent constable was a compromise measure. He would oversee and assist the old Parish Constables and usually took up residence in the lock-up. The Superintendent Constables were provided with "official buttons" but they had to supply their own uniform, coat and hat and have them vetted by the magistrates! However a new system was coming. By March of 1857 Williams had been appointed to "the office of one of the superintendents of the (newly formed) county constabulary" by the dashingly, young, dark and handsome Irish born Chief Constable. Williams' new post was to be in Glossop. It is stated that the new Chief Constable, Willoughby G. Fox Esq. had considerable difficulty in establishing the new force with the first recruits being prone to drunkenness. A common failing it appears in most of the new forces!

Around 1865 Williams again returned to Bakewell when he became Head of that Division and was possibly instrumental in Elijah's transfer there. When Carline was finally released from his "sentence" it was a reward to be sent south-east nearly 26 miles away to the heart of the Peak District to a "beautiful place" where he was "met with much kindness". In February of 1866 he was promoted to inspector with a change in uniform and a pill box cap to wear. (Little did he know that 2 months later in this same year Alfred Gough was being enrolled as a constable into the Leeds Police Force.) This is an amazing rise for Inspector Carline up the career ladder. The 27 year old had taken only two and a quarter years to go from sergeant to inspector. Even in 1878 a Home Office memo recorded that it took 4-5 years to be promoted to a sergeant and a further 8-10 years to be promoted to inspector! Inspectors were in charge of a sub-division containing several sergeants and their respective constables. They would spend a lot of their time dealing with court business but it was a very varied job- supervising common lodging-houses, reporting on the state of highways and bridges, not to mention the outbreak of cattle diseases. Inspectors were commonly in charge of weights and measures and could even take on the role of assistant relieving officer in dealing with the problems of vagrancy. Useful information could be gleaned from frequenting lodging-houses and dealing with vagrants. One found out who the suspicious characters were!

Whilst at Bakewell Elijah finally met someone, a dressmaker from a nearby hamlet close to Rowsley. Elizabeth Toft was four years his junior. After a courtship of not much more than a year and certainly vetted and approved by his superiors, Elizabeth on 15th June 1867 became Mrs Carline witnessed by her older married sister, Anne and her elder brother by 8 years, Harvey (Henry?). 1867 was an eventful but troubled year with coalminers striking in the south of the county. Elijah was charged with keeping the peace which he did with "flying colours". He was gaining a reputation as a "level-headed reliable officer", one of the shrewdest and cleverest in Derbyshire after "bringing to justice the guilty parties in a most mysterious case of arson, which excited considerable comment and discussion at the time." This zealous and able police inspector was destined for further promotion but it meant another move and always at his own expense. This time to the south of the county, south of Derby.

Elijah and Elizabeth's first child-George Edward was born in late December of 1869 in Wooden Box, later to be known as Woodville, where Elijah was based as the new Superintendent of the Repton and Gresley Division on the death of Superintendent Barton. As superintendent he had to be able to do accounts as well as being more than just literate, he also had to have a good general knowledge of the county and know the means of communication by railway and telegraph alongside a superintendent's duties with regard to paperwork and the law as it applied to the police. From 1870 he also held the post of Inspector of Weights and Measures an appointment reserved for the police until 1875. On Elijah's pay (£75-£150pa) they could, from now on, employ a servant. In 1874 the Carlines moved again, north by some 40 miles to Chesterfield, a division destined to be the largest in the county with, in 1891, some 36 officers. Elijah, at 34 years of age must have thought he had made it as superintendent and "keeper of the house of correction" for Chesterfield! He had reached the top of the ladder in a job that he loved (or had he?)

He looked again at Gough now at the bottom of his ladder and thought there but for the grace of God.....

The journey to Derby was nearing its end. Past memories were to be filed away. The train was slowing into the station and the three men made ready to alight. Superintendent Carline adjusted his heavily braided jacket as he stood up. For Gough this was not the first time he had been to Derby. He had lived here 30 years previously when he was a little boy. He did not remember his father, Thomas Goff, but the newspapers claimed he was an illiterate gardener who went "abroad" and died. This did not necessarily mean "abroad" as in going to a foreign country. Thomas was originally from Cheshire and leaving that county for one nearly 58 miles south east felt just as much like going to a foreign land! Alfred could only remember the family being his mother and older sister, Ann. His mother, Catharine was called a widow and they lived in lodgings with the Bull family. Mr Bull was a publican and there were two other couples, a little girl and a man lodging there too. Life was hard as Alfred's mother worked as a washerwoman to make ends meet. She had her own parents and family not too far away, 9 miles North West of Derby. The relatives lived in the same rural village where Alfred's mother had been born and brought up – Turnditch- but her parents Robert and Catherine Wilmot (Alfred's grandparents) were already in their late 60's at this time and probably could not help their daughter and her two children. As it was they were already looking after two of his cousins. Uncle Robert and his wife had no children that he could remember but Aunt Maria lived next door to his grandparents. At the time she had a little boy and a girl similar in age to Alfred. Two other girls lived with his aunt and although they were related he was not sure how. Aunt Maria had married a Samuel Smedley, more than 10 years her senior but she had known him since her days working as a farmer's servant and he was a good, hardworking man. Aunt Maria and Uncle Samuel had done well for themselves. They now ran a grocery shop. What had he done for himself?! The train shuddered to a full stop and reality set in again.

A few workmen about the place surmised that this was Gough getting out of the carriage and "hooted". Therefore Superintendent Carline kept his charge at the railway station until a cab arrived. "The hour was too early for many people to be stirring in the streets and consequently his conveyance from the station to the gaol caused very little notice." Compared to Chesterfield the journey was uneventful and Carline and his sergeant had no trouble in safely landing their man in the County Gaol.

As they turned off the main road and drove past the elegant Regency villas, and the porticoed entrances of the other houses down Vernon Street it seemed incongruous to Elijah that at the end of this short road was the imposing entrance of what appeared to be some austere temple of Ancient Egypt. This was Derby prison built a mere 54 years back.

16. Only Remaining Section of Derby Gaol

Nearing their destination, the dressed stone frontage of the gaol towered 47' above them. Either side of the main entrance, on a double- stepped platform, sat a thick, solid pillar tapering upwards to a decoration of four simple concentric rings. The weight of the upper storey appeared to flatten out the top of each column giving the impression of the upturned foot of a glass beaker. Here the columns stood like sentinels on guard. The cab passed the huge, iron cased gates opened for their arrival and clattered through the short tunnel created by the lodge, offices and waiting room to either side. Into the cobbled courtyard three men alighted but only Alfred Gough was staying. It was here he would await his trial, kept separate from the convicted prisoners as all prisoners on remand were.

Could Gough remember a time when as a police constable of the Leeds Police Force he had escorted prisoners to the castellated borough gaol at Armley? It seemed so long ago, thirteen years, and so much had happened in his life that sometimes it was hard to believe the fact from the fiction.

The Chesterfield and Sheffield newspapers reported that Alfred only stayed in the police force a few months due to him not settling down to the duties of police life but the police records tell a different story and for Alfred to have lasted more than two and a half years was a magnificent feat. In those days statistics show that in the boroughs, for every 100 men recruited 45 would leave in the first year and of that same 100 men only 22 would stay as long as 5 years. It was long known the main human weakness of the police generally was a fondness for liquor and in the late 60's an increase in crime in Leeds was linked to the beer houses. The Chief Constable had no hesitation in stating these drinking establishments were the resorts of "ruffianism, dog-fighters and racers, prize-fighters and others in demoralising games." Stolen property was directly traced to these places. A great many of the beer houses had a "tendency to foster and facilitate crimes unless a police constable is stationed at their very doors"! A police constable whose character had to be beyond reproach!

For more than one and a half years Alfred worked diligently at his job. He daily paraded with the whole of the Leeds' constables in front of the Town Hall, a folly which meant on shift changeover some unsavoury areas of the town were unpoliced. His night beat covered every back street, court and alley and on average a shift could be 20miles of walking with no refreshment break or hot meal. (Alfred smiled at the thought of Mrs Rhodes, telling the Sheffield newspaper of "some remarkable journeys" that he had taken with his cart whilst he was lodging with her in Brampton. "One day he walked as far as Sheffield and back, and proceeded afterwards to Clay Cross". A distance of some 36 miles but as he had marched over 800 miles in his time in the army in India 36 miles seemed nothing!) In Leeds the day beat covered the "principal streets and most frequented thoroughfares". During all this time, according to The Derbyshire Courier; Alfred had borne the character of a steady and industrious man who took great care of his earnings. Alfred then was a "tall fine looking fellow" when he joined the city police on 20th April 1866 at the age of 21. In the Police Register Alfred Gough was described as 5' 9" tall with dark eyes, dark hair and a fresh complexion. In 1866 the Leeds Police Force consisted of a Chief Constable, 6 detectives, 43 officers and 210 constables. By 1868 this had increased to 263. Police constable Gough was number 72. Leeds then was one of the largest towns in Yorkshire with an estimated population of 220,000! That's a lot of people to police! In fact the ratio was 1 policeman to 787 people.

Alfred's cousin, William Wilmot on his mother's side of the family, though older than Alfred by about 6 years, was also a constable but with the West Riding Constabulary in South Yorkshire. However, by 1881 William was a police sergeant in that force. What did he think when he read of this cousin Alfred and the things he had allegedly done? The shame of such a crime was more than embarrassment to the Wilmots! Thank goodness they did not have the same surname as Alfred! It would be good if one could choose one's relatives but even Alfred knew he and William had another cousin, Henry, languishing since 1875 in the prison on the Isle of Wight so he was not the only black sheep of the family!

As Alfred looked around him now he could see the formidable walls and towers but had no idea of the whole scale of the place. Derby gaol covered an area of some 6 acres and was entirely surrounded by a massive 27' high brick wall that was 2' thick and interspersed by eight dressed-stone circular Martello towers. Two of these towers Alfred saw as he had neared the entrance to the gaol positioned along the front. On top of each tower apparently, were firearms for the warders and officers to protect the prison's safety. This seems somewhat over precautionary but it was due to the riots that occurred in Derby half a century earlier!

If Alfred had been a bird flying overhead he would have seen the prison's design looked something like the spokes of a wheel radiating from a central point. However, at ground level all he could see was to his left, the two-storey 'A' wing and hospital for the females. Ahead on the right a fumigating room and beyond that a male 'F' wing behind which, he found out later, were numerous workshops, the "mill" and other small buildings. Directly ahead was the main two-storey building where the governor and his living quarters could be found along with the three male wings, 'C', 'D' and 'E' emanating from the main building behind. To Alfred's right by the perimeter wall was a sight that must have made him shudder – the graveyard! But he had little time for reflection as Superintendent Carline and Sergeant Radford were handing him over to the prison authorities for due process and taking their leave. Gough shook both their hands. They had treated him decently from the outset. Indeed Carline had a reputation for not at all being harsh or vindictive in his treatment of prisoners. Alfred was a man of few words but his glance of thanks told all. Later, Elijah revealed that Alfred had written "many letters" to him whilst at Derby reiterating "in almost every one that he was the only friend he had in the world"!

An aside from the Derbyshire Times states: *"We have now probably heard the last of the prisoner until the Assizes, unless he should think well to make an admission of his guilt, which, judging from his character is hardly probable."*!

CHAPTER TWELVE

SEPTEMBER and OCTOBER 1881

ON REMAND IN DERBY GAOL

Here was a lull in the reporting of Alfred Gough and Chesterfield and its neighbourhood could try and settle back down to everyday life. For Alfred it was a time of settling down to the prison routine of those on remand. He was allowed to continue wearing his own clothes but if they were insufficient or unfit for purpose the authorities would provide prison garb though not the same colour as the convicted prisoners. Alfred had the option of employment but was not "compelled to perform any hard labour". Here at Derby that would have meant time spent on the treadmill housed in its own building. Nothing is mentioned of any work done by Gough.

According to the Sheffield and Rotherham Independent after Alfred had reached Derby the strain of the previous ten days was lifted and **"his spirits seemed to undergo quite a reaction, and he laughed and joked with the officials in a manner that altogether impressed them with his extreme levity."** This mood however was not to last as time on remand went on. **"When he was taken into custody 4d was found upon him, and that having been returned to him he sent and bought apples with it, and appeared to enjoy the eating of them amazingly."**

From the start, prison routine was that Gough was woken each day by the sound of the prison bell at 6 am. He was to make up his bed, and then clean what seemed to be the always gloomy cell with the water he had used to wash with.

Breakfast "such as it is" was taken at 8 o'clock within the cell. His quarters were something akin to a "whitewashed cube 7 feet by 13, with a barred window of ground glass at one end" and a painted door with a spy hole at the other. 9am was one of two 30 minute exercise sessions when Alfred was let out of his cell and into the adjoining "airing yard". He marched in silence keeping a specified distance from anyone else until his time was up and then back to his cell. During his constitution he occasionally looked up at the two-storey wings, so much brickwork to either side of him, so oppressive they seemed to shut out the daylight. Everywhere seemed dismal. No wonder the Medical Officer, Mr John Wright Baker kept a constant watch over his charges though it was usually only once a week. He was such a busy man, he had to be at the prison at least twice a week and carry on his practise out in the real world. He was expected to see every prisoner weekly and that was over 300 inmates, sick or well for he needed to check on the prisoners' mental well- being as well as their physical states. For a man of 53years he did the best that he could in the time allowed.

   11.30 was an opportunity for Alfred to leave his cell again. Stepping out into the hall corridor to left and right of him, above and below, were cells. Over 90 on each floor and each of the three wings off the main building were identical. The staircase to each floor was made of stone but the stairways on each floor were made of iron with railings for protection. To reach the Chapel for that was their destination, the prisoners had to cross a bridge that spanned the main building to "B" wing above which the chapel was situated. The compulsory daily service only lasted 15 minutes but to actually get the prisoners there was a military exercise in itself. The wardens had to ensure silence and separation at all times to, from and during the service. So to actually get from and return to the cell could sometimes take longer than the service but Alfred did not mind he was not going anywhere else and in his mind there was no rush to get to dinner!

Dinner was at mid-day for an hour but locked up again until the next exercise session at 3.30. For one being used to walking miles in the open air Alfred found just one hour's exercise a day pitifully lacking. He was back to the cell by 4 o'clock.

Tea at 6pm though the Authorities called this "Supper"! Then bed at 8pm. "Lights out" was an hour later and in this time those who could read were allowed books. Remand prisoners could have books anyway and also writing materials. Alfred used this time to write some of his letters. Sleep, if one could, and then the same routine again when the 6 o'clock bell would ring to start a new day. Sunday was the only day with a slightly different routine. An extra hour in bed, no work for the convicted prisoners, still the exercise sessions but two trips to Chapel!

Unbeknown to Alfred whilst he was awaiting his trial at Derby a certain Mr Tollington received, in the middle of September "a communication from a friend asking him if the Alfred Gough charged with the murder of Eleanor Windle was their relative"? Thomas Tollington lived with his family at a " very comfortably furnished home", 66, East Lamartine Street, Nottingham."The inquiry took them altogether by surprise; and their first inclination was to deny the insinuation with much indignity. They turned back to the papers they had in the house containing reports of the inquest and proceedings before the magistrates and the further they read, and the more they inquired, the deeper became their conviction that their relative was in trouble."

Thomas, a frame work knitter, was Alfred Gough's 47 year old brother-in-law. Alfred's elder sister Ann was now 40 and a lacemaker. She had only married Thomas, a widower, the year before but they had a son together, Alfred, who in December, was to be five. In the 1881 census Ann is described as a widow (though there is no record of her previously marrying and she is still using her maiden name!) This may well be for convenience as she has little Alfred, her son, to explain away. She is also described as head of the household and very clean and orderly it was too. Poor Thomas Tollington is classed only as a boarder although they are now married. However, to the newspapers they gave the appearance of being a hardworking and respectable family! The condition of the house "bears ample evidence of the cleanly, orderly habits of his (Thomas') wife." Ann made ends meet by taking in a lodger and two other boarders, 11 year old Eliza and 9 year old Joseph Tollington. It is doubtful that they are both Thomas' children for Eliza's parents on the 1871 census are William and Catherine Tollington framework knitters like Thomas and also born in Hathern, Leicestershire. They are obviously related in some way but the census does not record it.

Alfred Gough would have met his little namesake and possibly the other two children back in the autumn of 1879 when after leaving the army he was trying to get back on his feet. He had already tried employment as a night watchman in Harrogate the previous autumn but he had been sacked "in consequence of misconduct". He was then found loitering about the premises, drunk and got arrested. He then had to spend 14 days in prison as he could not pay the 10/-fine or even pay the costs!

He left Harrogate and possibly moved on to Leeds but finding nothing for him there went to Nottingham where he had lived with his sister for some 3 months but it was not to last. "As a soldier he had saved a little money, but not sufficient to maintain him for any length of time; and when finding he could not secure employment, and his little store being almost exhausted, he decided to leave Nottingham. ... and from that time his relatives heard nothing of him — where he was, or what he was doing. They assumed that he had fallen into work somewhere, and hoped sooner or later to hear a good account of him. The notion of his being in trouble seems never once to have crossed their mind. His character they thought they knew, as when he left them he was sober, industrious, and saving." "If he got a halfpenny," his brother (in law) remarked, "he would endeavour to obtain another, and then he would put both away. That was the sort of man he was." However "the public now know more about how Gough spent the two years since he left East Lamartine street than his relatives do."

In order to put their minds at rest Ann and Thomas took it upon themselves to write to the Governor of Her Majesty's Prison at Derby to ask if the prisoner, by the name of Alfred Gough, had certain distinguishing marks on his person. The Governor, Captain Charles E. Farquharson, late of the 21st Hussars, and veteran of India at the same time as the man before him, handed the letter over to Gough so that he could read for himself what his sister had written. As a remand prisoner Gough could receive any letters that were addressed to him and in turn could send out letters twice a week. Friends and family could also visit remand prisoners twice a week without any order provided it was at a reasonable hour. Alfred had now to make a decision "the probabilities are that, had they not first communicated with him, he would have concealed, as far as possible, his identity, and would have passed out of the world without ever letting them know of the trouble he had brought upon them." His sister, however, would be expecting some sort of reply to her question. Was it yes or no? Alfred possibly hoped that the Governor would reply and he probably did judging by the first letter printed in the newspapers dated 8th October. It is obvious that the letter Gough refers to from Ann would not have been the initial enquiry letter. A letter to the Governor, one presumes, would have been more formal in nature.

Saturday   Oct.8th, 1881.
"Dear Sister
"i now take my pen in hand to rite thease fue lines to you to say that I got your loving Letter to-day at dinner time. And very pleased to heare from you hoping at the same time that thease fue lines will find you all quite well as this leaves me in good health thank god for it.
"dear Sister and Brother i ham glad to hear that you have heard from my dear ------------rite at once and tell her that i can find myself   and you can come anny Day Except Sunday.
Every Day in the week.

"good night and god Bless you all   with my Best Love to you all.

"i remain your Affectionate Loving Brother,

Alfred Gough,

Derby."

Ann must have mentioned in her letter, (which was probably written by her husband, Thomas, as Ann was illiterate and explains why Thomas is mentioned in Alfred's letters,) something about visiting Alfred though this would have been a 30 mile round trip at least. How would she explain the situation to her employers if she was still working? It is doubtful she would tell the truth. However another version is given by The Sheffield Daily Telegraph which claimed Mrs Tollington, "in an interview with our representative" given after the trial, visited Alfred on Tuesday 27th September after he had initially made contact with her but only remained for a short time. "He then appeared calm and collected, but conversed with her very little, and carefully avoided any direct reference to the crime". This newspaper does not actually print the letters but gives a brief summary of their content. The interesting and obviously censored part of the letter for publication dated 8th October is that Ann has got in touch with someone; a female-friend or relative at this point is hard to surmise. This person was shocked at the reported events and what has happened to Alfred. She has written back to Ann hoping that Alfred can "find himself" not remain the person he seems to have become according to the newspapers.

Did the next few days find Alfred reading and rereading his sister's "loving letter"? Did it put into his mind, not necessarily better days but days when he was together with his sister and mother? As a family the three Goughs left Derby for Leeds where Mrs Gough was thought to have been a member of the Dissenters and brought up her children "under good influences" and "in a scrupulous manner". Sometime before 1861 the three had again decamped south. This time to Nottinghamshire... to Sne(i)nton, South East of Nottingham. Alfred's mother Catharine was now 42, still a widow but head of her own household. She took in a married female lodger, a seamer to help with money matters but still had to work herself as a charwoman. Big sister Ann was 20 and like her 15 year old brother Alfred both were employed as servants. (Alfred had been in work since the age of 11. The Derbyshire Courier stated "His sister soon followed his example" but his sister was definitely the older of the two and probably started employment first.). There was also an addition to the family at this time-a baby girl by the name of Louisa Gough. Ann, unmarried, was the mother of this child born in the Union Workhouse at Radford (North West of Nottingham), less than 3 miles away from Sneinton. Ann was admitted to the workhouse for the birth of her baby in early March but by the following month she was back living with her mother. Unfortunately little Louisa was dead not long after her third birthday in 1864. An occurrence not uncommon at this time.

The local newspapers thought that during the early 1860's the teenaged Alfred worked as a general servant to an ironmonger in Ashbourne in South Derbyshire. He then left that employment to work closer to home as an ostler for the surgeon and G.P., Dr Anthony Unthank. The doctor, a man in his 40's when Alfred was a teenager, had originally been born in London but had now made his home in Nottingham. He had a Derbyshire born wife and by 1862 four daughters to show for his time there. Some period after the birth of his youngest daughter, and a house move, the two house servants were exchanged for a governess and groom and it is this position that young Alfred possibly held prior to the end of 1865.

1865 was the year the Gough family separated for good. By the November Alfred was in a new job back in Leeds. His mother had returned with him leaving behind her daughter who probably stayed in the Nottingham area being now settled there. His new position was that of railway porter for the Midland Railway Company at a salary of around 17/- a week. The job involved carrying passengers' luggage and the loading and unloading of goods but porters' duties could also include washing railway carriages, sorting parcels and attending to the oil lamps. Alfred only stayed in this job for some 6 months but it is doubtful he left under a cloud for, as a fine young fellow, he was recommended to the Leeds Police Force by none other than Mr James Allport (later to be knighted), the General Manager of the Midland Railway Company.

A police recruiting advert of 1836 for Leeds stated that the police applicant must be well recommended for "Command of temper, Sobriety, Honesty, Activity and Intelligence by his last and present employers." It is to be presumed that this rule still held good in the 1860's. Alfred's mother thought he looked so smart in his dark uniform particularly the new one issued in 1868 where Alfred now wore a much shorter single breasted tunic. It still had the high Prussian collar on which was displayed his identifying number-72 but it sported white piping along the bottom edge of the collar and on the lower part of each sleeve. His top hat was replaced with a cap something akin to the headgear of a French gendarme. It was decorated with a black braided band, a black worsted knob on the top and a badge depicting a shield bearing the corporation's coat of arms. However, though he may not have realised it in himself, Alfred at this point in time was on a slippery slope, the consequences of which had him now sitting in a dreary cell contemplating the life he had led.

There was no reply to Saturday's letter and so Alfred wrote again the following Wednesday:-

Wednesday   Oct. 12th, 1881.
"My Dear Sister and Brother
"i now take my pen in hand to rite thease fue lines to you hoping at the same time this will find you all quite well, but as for myself i ham verry low and weak with such low living
i should so like you to try and get as Much to geather as you possable (possibly) could for (from) you and my dear ------------
it will not be long now before i ham tried
 if she (h) as not sent to you yet rite to her as sune (soon) as you can and tell her to help me all she can for to Strengthen me and I trust God will reward her for her kindness towards me   it may be the last time and tell her to send by the return of Post
i remain your Affectionate Loving Brother   Good Night and God Bless you all
                    "ALFRED GOUGH"

No money is forthcoming from his sister or the mystery female. Maybe Ann thought it was an imposition to be asking for money from this female. It is not known if Alfred had been in touch with this person recently. He certainly had not made contact with his own sister for two years!

Saturday finds him writing again to his sister –the opening niceties over Alfred gets down to what is on his mind.

Saturday   Oct. 15th 1881.
"....hoping ....you are all quite well as this leaves me at Present thank God for it but   only verry weak for want of food as it is such a small lot for a man like me in here   i feel quite hungary after it   i feel as if i could eat the tin pot i get my gruel in   they give us such a small quantity wile awaiting trial.
"dear sister i though (t) you whould of ('ve) come before now to me as you (w) rote and sent me word that my--------------wanted to know if i could find myself and i sent you word yes Back by the returne of post on the 8th of the month this day week since due (do) now try and get me as much as you can i dou(b)t you have not got the letter that i sent to you But i hope you get this safe dear Sister and Brother the assizes begins on the last Day of this month so be su(a)re and (w)rite to my ------------- and tell her to be so kind and send me down as much as she can spare for her unfortunate ----------it May be the last time i may trouble anny of you.   I hope you get this letter on Sunday and send (it) to My Dear ------so as she can send back By the returne of post to you and then you could come and make arrangement for me to get a fine days meales so as to get my strength for the trial now be su (a) re and come it will be dear to get my meales from a nother place brought to me.

But you can try your best for this once for me. You can go to the cook shop in the town, and ask them wat they will find me in plean food for a week Breakfast dinner and tea 3 meales a day at 8—12—5 o'clock daily   come as Early as you can in the day so as to arrange   send this letter to my ----------if you like and i have no doubt that she will try her best for me what she can due(do)   i may never ask you again while i live."

As a remand prisoner Gough was allowed to procure for himself or receive "at proper hours" which would have been 8, 12 and 5 o'clock, "food and malt liquor, clothing, bedding, or other necessaries" if he so wanted under certain restrictions. Otherwise he could have the prison's allowance of food. He obviously had some money with him when he first entered prison as he was able to buy some apples but after more than six weeks in prison Gough had no money to buy food and like others before him was complaining over the quantity and quality allowed to him. As a "class 3" prisoner he was allowed for breakfast and supper - 8oz. bread and 1 pint of gruel. Alfred complained to his sister that there was not enough gruel given and felt he could eat the pot that it came in as well! Dinner again was always 8oz. bread accompanied for 4 days of the week by 1lb. potatoes or 2oz cheese (If the potatoes failed in quality). For 2 days the remand prisoner could have 3oz. cooked meat off the bone and for the remaining day a pint of soup was on the menu. This was a man whose rations when in the army in India were 1 lb of meat a day, bread baked with wheat flour and risen with yeast, a pint of beer and a dram of rum! It is no wonder that Gough, in his letters, had food or the procuring of it on his mind!

"My Dear Sister i wish from all my heart that i was out of this fearful trial dewing(doing) some think else for it is a miserable place to be in   hear(here) i must conclude this time my Dear Sister and Brother With my Best Love to you all and the Children kiss them for me.
"i remain your affectionate Brother
"ALFRED GOUGH"
"Dear sister you can come any day   i shall with Gods Blessing be looking out for you Every day and if you like to make me a fatty cake and bring it with you, you can Give it them you make arrangements with. Come that day as sune as you get word."

Food again!

In response to this letter Ann once again made the trip to visit her brother on Monday 17th October. The "visiting boxes" were off the entrance hall in the main building adjacent to a waiting room and diagonally opposite the Governor's office. A prisoner writing of his experiences elsewhere in the 1870's wrote that the visitor spoke to the supposed offender through a wire grating. In this case two wire gratings separated by 3 or 4 feet of space where the warder sat or stood between them. But Alfred would not have been alone. There would have been a row of other prisoners standing by him trying to make themselves heard to their visitors over the din! Ann "noticed that he was much thinner than when she saw him before, and looked very miserable." He spoke little but that was not unusual and although the visit lasted over 20 minutes "very little passed between them, and she experienced great difficulty in eliciting anything from him." He asked after the health of Ann and her children and their aunt but when asked about the up and coming trial he stated he did not know how it would go but would write to her afterwards. His ultimate fate seemed of little concern to him. "As on the previous visit, he seemed to avoid any conversation respecting the murder, and Mrs Tollington did not force it upon his notice." She had done as Alfred asked in his letter and had brought some food for him but when she approached the authorities requesting she be allowed to leave it for him "they replied that the prison rules did not permit of that being done"! Poor Alfred he so wanted that fatty cake! Consequently Ann had to take it back home with her.

Though Alfred said very little he was just pleased to have his sister near and thanked her repeatedly for having come to visit him.

The following Thursday Gough took it upon himself to write directly to the female relative alluded to in the previous letters.

Thursday   Oct. 20th, 1881.

The letter again starts with the usual niceties.(It is to be wondered if he used the same lines when writing to Superintendent Carline?)

"i ham in good health thank God for it to help me
through this Great trial that is before me
this is a very poor place to be in for to rite a letter to
you   i never Thought i should be so unfortunate as
to rite to you from a Prison and charged with such a
crime against me but i trust in providence to pull me

through it   i wish i had but of ('ve) stopped in Sheffield and kept my little Furnished room (Apparently Alfred had a separate sitting-room in order not to mix with the rough customers who oft times frequented it!) i was paying 3s. 6d. per week and going on very wel and putting a fue shillings in the Post Office Bank every Week, and i was very comfortable but it was not to last (This is young Walter Scott's lodging house in Water Lane, Sheffield. Walter had been instrumental in getting Alfred back on his feet.)   i have a handcart Of my owne and if i had but of('ve) settled down and kept on saving as i was i could of ('ve) (h)ad a Donkey or a poney by this time going on my rounds with salt pipe clay rubbing stone blacking and other small things for the household use and Toys for children i use to exchange for rags and bones i had a reglar round to go (to)and regular costumers in Sheffield and round about its nobourhood, but it seams it was not to be.   I Got unsettled and went to Chesterfield   now if i had but stopped at Sheffield and Joined the Pledge i should of been a very happy and different man to what i ham shut up hear like a bird in a cage and starved with hunger on a small bit of sour Bread and gruel   only Just keeps you alive
i feel that hungary after   i have (h)ad it (in mind) that i could eat the soup that i wash myself with (This is Alfred emphasising his hunger in such graphic terms that he could drink up his dirty washing water! He then describes his day.) "So you may think what a time i have of it. The time is drawing on now towards the trial (Alfred had been informed by 15th October that the Assizes were to be held at the end of the month and 5 days later when he is writing this letter he has been informed of the venue and possible trial date.)   i Shall be tried at

Leicester i beleave they commence on the first of next month November i dir (dare) say that they will try us some time next week. (Here Alfred is a little confused with his dates.) it is a Great Pittey that i ever left Sheffield and then i should never of been in (a) Scrape locked up on Suspicion of Wilful Murder. I hope the God above will help me through with it i was seen about w(h)ere the girl was last seen so the Witnesses seams to say and my handcart against The Plantation the day aefore (before) the bod(a)y was found but that is not to say that i committed the crime, how often (h)as it been the case Of Persons Seen on the day that crimes (h)as been committed near the place and have been innocent and seen last as people thought with the Murdered Just before their death and then as had nothing to due (do) with it. But thare is a great deal of false swearing in this case by witnesses, and one man very much so a man i never spak (spoke) to in my life till he gave his evidence in Court against me as true as there is a God in heaven above us I carnt think how he could mak (e) up a statement a nuff (enough) to swear a man (') s life away and every word *of it false.* (This appears to be the only time in print that Alfred actually mentioned the case and what his thoughts were in connection with it. He obviously finds Mansfield Tom's testimony baffling particularly when a man's life is at stake. Alfred is not admitting to the murder but why raise the subject to this relative and then lie to her if he really did it?)

You have been as kind to me as if i had been thy owne Son and a deal kinder to me then (than) some Mothers as (have) been to thare (their) children i hope God above will reward you and give you (h) is Blessing.

I am right down sad at heart to think i (h) am drawn into this mess to give your kind heart such pain. I wish i was in my own room in Sheffield (w) riting this instead of being hear (here). I was for riting to you before when i was at Sheffield but thought i whould wait till i was better of (f) and i have got worse but i will put trust in Providence   i must conclude this time so no more at Present   from yours affectionately

"ALFRED GOUGH"

"rite to me. I hope you are all quite well and kiss the children for me. i (')ll rite to you after God Bless you all

"ALFRED GOUGH"

"i rote this letter last Night i was quite well   i am not this morning   i feal quite Porley (ill) this morning i have not felt so before   i had to sit down several times   so very faint i hope it goes of(f) since Rite to me a fue lines to Let me (k) no(w)   how you are going on."

It is quite difficult to track Alfred's family relationships. Even his birth appears to be somewhat of a mystery. Newspaper reports, the census returns and his army record claim Alfred was born in Swindon, Wiltshire about the year, 1845-1847. The Wiltshire Record Office is unable to track him in the parish registers for the churches in Swindon or Swinton. There is a Swinton in Yorkshire and another north west of Manchester. It could be that people heard the word "Swindon" when Alfred could have been saying "Swinton" and then naturally it was assumed-Swindon, the county of Wiltshire, rather than anywhere else. The Sheffield Daily

Telegraph claimed Gough was a Yorkshireman, native to Leeds whose parents were operatives and he himself spent his early years in a woollen factory but this was not reported in any of the other newspapers and research does not really give credence to this story. No connection has been found so far why Gough would be born in Wiltshire either, apart from the story that Alfred's father went "abroad", whatever that may mean, and subsequently died!

Alfred's mother, Catharine definitely had at least 3 younger sisters but then in the grandparents' household in 1841 there were 4 other children with ages ranging from 2-5 which is to be assumed are grandchildren –Sarah, William, George and Henry. Ten years later George and Henry, (Alfred's cousins,) are still with the grandparents and recorded as grandchildren, presumably brothers but who their parents were is not known? Sarah appears in Aunt Maria's household 10 years later with her younger sister but whether Maria is their mother or aunt is not known either.

In Alfred's letter to the mystery female relative he refers to her as being like a mother to him which implies someone older rather than someone of his own age. At this stage in his life (1881) it is unlikely for his grandmothers to still be alive, which probably suggests an aunt or maybe a female older cousin. Alfred may have had relatives elsewhere in the country for his parents, Thomas Gough (Goff) and Catharine Wilmot were married 2nd March 1840 in the parish of Manchester and at the time, residing in Chorlton cum Hardy. (About 3 miles south of Manchester) Thomas was a farmer but later described as a gardener like his father, James. In the 1841 census the couple were living in Ashton upon Mersey just 3 and a half miles from Chorlton cum Hardy. Alfred's sister, Ann was born at the end of 1840 in nearby Sale in

Cheshire. The newspapers thought Gough was a native of Leeds but it was never found out for certain though they knew he had spent his earlier years in the town. For some unknown reason Alfred and his family spent his teenage years in the Nottingham area and then by 1865 he and just his mother returned to Leeds again. Are there unknown relatives residing there that have not materialised? Alfred when writing to his sister exhorts her to tell the female relative to "send me down as much as she can spare". This implies that the relative is in the North. Northerners today still refer to going down South. Therefore this suggests the relative was North of Derby. The favourite candidate for the mystery relative should be Aunt Maria Smedley. She was younger sister to his mother and as a grocer she would probably have funds to spare. She probably had known him as a child and teenager and knew how proud his mother was of him as a young man. The slight drawback for this candidate is that Turnditch, although being North of Derby is not so north as to warrant describing it as sending money "down" to him and secondly, Alfred asks the relative to "kiss the children for him". This sounds like young children as opposed to adults. However by this time Maria's children are all grown up! Speculation as to the mystery woman is the only option for now!

It is not known what the relative's actions were if any as these are the only letters published that were written before the trial. Indeed The Sheffield Telegraph states this letter was actually sent to Ann for forwarding on to their aunt but Ann did not send it. "She thought it would only increase the intense grief which that lady feels at the awful position in which Gough has placed himself and the disgrace he has brought upon the family." However the Derbyshire Courier claimed *"The poor fare he* (Gough) *had while awaiting his trial troubled him much, and he was greatly disappointed that his friends did not supply him with extra meals."* The Sheffield and Rotherham Independent claimed that Ann Tollington went to visit her brother twice before the trial and that she and her husband, Thomas received three letters from Alfred. These appear to be what was published in early November by the newspapers.

THE MONTH OF OCTOBER 1881 IN CHESTERFIELD

Back in Chesterfield William Windle had also written a letter in October that found its way, (though deliberately in this case) into print by early November. William's letter was addressed to the editor of the Derbyshire Times:-

DEAR SIR -Will you oblige us "The parents of Eleanor Windle, of Brimington," by inserting in your paper, our heartfelt thanks to all both far and near, for the kind sympathy which has been shown towards us as a painfully bereaved family, and to the kind friends who took such unwearying interest in searching for our lost child, and also to Mr Carline, Superintendent of Police, for the vigilant and able manner he has displayed in the case throughout.

I am, yours respectfully,

WILLIAM WINDLE.

Almond Place, Brimington, October, 1881.

This letter may well be as a result of one other publication that appeared in Brimington in the October-"The Brimington Quarterly Messenger" a non-conformist pamphlet that was published by the Brimington Tract Society and bought by annual subscription. A pamphlet that William and his family were bound to have sight of. October was the first opportunity for the murder of Eleanor Windle to be reported and commented upon by the non-conformists though comment was made "at all the places of worship" the week after the murder was discovered. Reference was made that "Mr W. Windle (was) one of the class leaders in the Wesleyan Society" and it was his daughter that was murdered. Then the vitriolic diatribe commences —"We have since heard that the prisoner has said "Never mind it will soon be over; if it comes to the worst, it's only an 8 foot drop." None of the newspapers report this! "If such is the case, it is quite time another law was put into force —hanging is too good for such like villains. No punishment in the Army is dreaded so much as the "Cat", (-o'-nine- tails, a whip with nine thongs or knotted chords used on prisoners) and we are inclined to think that if 25 lashes of the "Cat" was administered in such like cases every 3 months, together with hard labour for life, it would prove more effectual than hanging." How many times in particularly horrific modern day murders is this sort of language heard even now? The Christian ideal seems to have gone out of the window and for Gough the punishment of hanging was just not enough! Some suffering was called for!

The murder of a child was difficult to live down for the Windle family. Those nagging doubts and the guilt of their actions, could they have done more to protect Eleanor? What did their fellow chapel goers think of the family? It was not just a murder; six year old Eleanor had had something unspeakable done to her before she died. Her innocence had been violated. How did one explain to other children what had happened? The answer was probably give no explanation. Wasn't it enough that she was dead?

The Victorian viewpoint was that it probably was a blessing that Eleanor died. Rape against a child was considered a heinous crime yet if the child survived the ordeal she was then considered tainted and corrupted. She had "fallen" from innocence and was a "polluting presence" and a moral danger to the other children she came into contact with. She herself, though physically a child could not be considered one in mental and moral terms. She was "unnatural", a premature adult who had not received a "healthy normal" development. These girls needed to be retrained and reformed in specialist institutions! How would a morally upright family have coped with such a child? Would their friends have shunned them and the child been ostracised? Would their community have wondered about Eleanor's upbringing? Would the family have ever lived down the shame? For the wider Windle family it is possible the answer was "No". The future generations of Windles seem to have completely eliminated the Brimington branch of the family from their collective memory. Only half of the Newbold side of the family have orally remembered Eleanor's story and told it to the girls of the family as a warning to be wary of "rag and bone men"! However Eleanor's name, when and where have been lost in the mists of time, she has become a young woman rather than a child and she has become an ancestor belonging to a wife of a Windle rather than directly to a Windle. What is most telling is that this hapless young woman, so the story goes, was killed then chopped up and her remains wheeled about on the cart for days before discovery. The Windle family could not bring themselves to talk or even think about Eleanor's rape so what could be just as horrific? Previous generations imagined that being chopped up seemed to equate with that horror. Modern day generations may not appreciate that death would have been preferable to rape but even as late as the 1960's the word "rape" was not a word that was mentioned in polite company and certainly would not have been explained even if the curious had asked.

WEDNESDAY 26th OCTOBER 1881

It was reported in The Derby Mercury that

"NOTICE is hereby GIVEN, that the undermentioned Prisoners, now in the custody of the Gaoler for the County of Derby, will be removed therefrom for trial at the Assizes for the Winter Assize County No. 5, to be held at LEICESTER on MONDAY, the 31st day of October instant:-

No.	Name of Prisoner	Offence Charged
2	Alfred Gough	Murder at Brimington, on 20th August, 1881.

(There were 9 prisoners listed in all.)

And NOTICE is hereby FURTHER GIVEN, that all persons bound by recognizance to appear and prosecute, or give evidence, for or against the prisoners so to be removed, are to appear and prosecute, or give evidence, at the CASTLE OF

LEICESTER, on TUESDAY, the 1st day of November next, at Half-past Ten o'clock in the Forenoon precisely.

Prosecutors and Witnesses failing to attend on the day and at the hour appointed will forfeit their recognizances and will not be allowed any expenses whatever."

This notice was placed in the paper at the instigation of the High Sheriff of Leicester from information given to him, some few days earlier, about the prisoners and their offences by the "Gaoler of Derby", Captain Farquharson. He, the High Sheriff, "shall cause to be inserted in one or more newspapers in the Winter Assize County (that was Derbyshire, Rutlandshire and Leicestershire for administrative purposes) the said list and statement and a notice that the persons bound to appear, shall do so in Leicester."

One presumes that this information would have been personally given to the 24 witnesses involved in the Gough trial rather than them have to read about it, if they could read about it as this was a newspaper that was published in the south of the county and six of the witnesses were illiterate. Superintendent Carline would have had notice of the trial which could easily be passed on to 3 witnesses as they were his officers. That left 19 people to contact- Mr Windle would be able to inform his son himself. Six women, 3 children, 2 teenagers and 9 men were to attend the court in Leicester more than 50 miles away! The trial was expected to be held in the county where the crime had occurred and that would have meant a trial in Derby some 24 miles away, but Leicester! Why hold the trial there? How daunting must that have been for some of the witnesses who may never have ventured far in their lives before? However, that is not to say that the majority were born and bred in the Chesterfield area. In fact it was roughly half that were natives of Chesterfield and half were born out of the county. Witnesses' travelling expenses would be paid for and possibly Superintendent Carline organised for everyone that wanted to, to do the journey as a group for, once in Leicester, it is doubtful that anyone would know the route to the "Castle". And how disappointed the children were going to be!

MONDAY 31st OCTOBER 1881

PREPARATIONS FOR THE ASSIZES

That morning James Charles Mathew said goodbye to his family in Cornwall Gardens, Kensington and headed for the railway station to catch the train that was to take him up to Leicester. 1881 so far had been a very propitious year for the 50 year old unlike Alfred Gough. In March, Mathew, as a junior counsel had been appointed a judge in the Queen's Bench Division, part of the High Court of Justice, and the following month he had been knighted. Sir James was now one of fifteen high court judges who were each commissioned to travel a particular circuit of the country in order to hold an Assize court where particularly serious cases were heard. The Midland circuit, in his case, was visited in a set order with so many days allocated to each Assize town. Sir James' last Assize was held in Bedford; today it was the turn of Leicester, the following Monday he would be in Nottingham and then the week after that- Warwick. Now, His Lordship Mr Justice Mathew, Knight, was alighting the

2.46pm from London and being welcomed by a gathered assembly of notables:-the annually appointed High Sheriff-Mr. Thomas Swift Taylor Esq. whose principal duty was to wine, dine and keep safe the High Court judge, the Under-Sheriff-Mr. Samuel Francis Stone, Gentleman, the Acting Under-Sheriff-Mr. R. Berridge and Deputy Chief Constable Moore with a "posse" of policemen. The arrival of the Assize judge into a county before the railway era had been an impressive occasion. The Under-Sheriff would meet the judge at the county boundary and as they neared the county town the High Sheriff and county gentry would ride out to greet him. On entering the town the church bells would ring, trumpeters heralded the occasion and he would be escorted to his destination by javelin men (something like a guard of honour). As a new judge Mr Justice Mathew had never been treated to that ceremonial. It was enough to have the dignitaries meet him off the train and then drive in the Sheriff's carriage to the Municipal buildings. Once there, His Lordship was escorted to chambers where he could take off his everyday attire and put on the scarlet robes and long wig of his office. At the Municipal buildings, Sir James "opened the commission for the borough". From this building the judge then proceeded, no doubt with a retinue, to the Castle where "the commission for the county was opened". The "commission" was the judge's authority given to him by the High Court of Justice to hear county cases at Leicester. This was the commission of the Winter Assize. Originally there had only been two Assizes a year-Lent and Summer but by 1870 it had become the practice to hold a Winter Assize in ALL counties which at the end of October had 6 or more prisoners awaiting trial. This procedure was put in place to try and reduce the time prisoners were held on remand.

Between 1876-77 a fourth Autumn Assize was initiated by the then Home Secretary in a bid to reduce remand time to 3 months stating that the Autumn and Winter Assizes be held ONLY at certain of the selected towns and in these towns would be heard the cases of prisoners from a group of counties not just prisoners from the county of the allocated town. Therefore at this Winter Assize Sir James was not only to try the prisoners from Leicestershire but also any prisoners from the adjoining counties of Rutlandshire and Derbyshire too. Hence the reason why Alfred Gough was not going to be tried in Derby. There were critics to this system from all quarters. This could cause considerable hardship for the witnesses who were "bound" to attend trials and prisoners so far away from their home county had difficulty in finding representation and even greater difficulty in producing their own witnesses. If the prisoner was acquitted he would not be provided with the means of getting home but would be just turned out. Judges complained about their own travelling and that it took them away from London at a busy time for civil cases. Even the jurors of the Grand Jury were not happy. But for now, this was the system and Sir James would make the best of it.

A short ceremony at each venue was followed by a reverential walk to the cathedral (St. Martin's Church) for a service and sermon given by the Reverend J. Bennie. Formalities concluded and the judge settled into his lodgings it would be left to the High Sheriff to entertain Sir James that night and probably every night for the time he was in Leicester.

17. Photograph of The Trial Judge, His Lordship Sir James Charles Mathew. © National Portrait Gallery, London

CHAPTER THIRTEEN

TUESDAY 1st NOVEMBER 1881

THE TRIAL PRELIMINARIES AT LEICESTER CASTLE

18. Photograph of Leicester Castle Today

On this day it is to be imagined Superintendent Carline, his men and the witnesses made an early start in order to arrive at the courthouse in Leicester in good time. They would have travelled by train as there was a direct line from Chesterfield to Leicester. Alfred Gough had a much shorter journey to make though he need not worry about the time, the prison authorities would see to that. It had been ordered that the Governor of Derby Gaol should transfer the prisoners attending the Winter Assizes to Leicester Prison three days before the opening of the commission and that they should remain there until the outcome of their hearings. Whilst at this prison gossip had somehow spread that one of the Leicester prisoners on remand had killed himself the day before. So much blood it was rumoured! Was this place more terrible than Derby?

19. Contemporary Sketch of Leicester Castle. Courtesy of the Record Office for Leicestershire, Leicester and Rutland.

The cobbled road that led up to the "Castle" passed the vestiges of some ancient monument. However, what was once the Great Hall of the fortification looked to all intents and purposes like some simple single storey red brick municipal building with an addition to the left of it. Going to a castle had sounded so exciting to some of the younger witnesses but where were the crenellated thick stone walls, the slit windows for the archers to shoot out of and the large iron portcullis? Not here! Alfred Gough had come from that type of "castle" except its name was Leicester Prison and it was not ancient! All that could be seen of the castle before them was a low symmetrical building built upon a stone plinth, a pedimented dormer window cut into the tiled roof line at each end and below were three long narrow windows either side of a central pedimented section that jutted out slightly from the main structure. A pretty curved Venetian window with "Gothic" glazing bars was positioned above the fanlighted main double doors through which Superintendent

Carline and his officers led the witnesses. Immediately to left and right of them in the foyer was an arched door, for the general public, that led into one of the two courts. Which court should they go into? None for the moment. Just go straight ahead to the foot of the staircase into the entrance hall.

Alfred Gough was to come in through a different entrance entirely. An entrance that went down a dimly lit staircase that led to the cells underneath the court house. Ahead of him was a brick lined corridor but he was escorted off to the left into a corridor that housed the cells and interview rooms for counsel to come and speak to their "clients". Alfred was not the only prisoner down there and it would seem that the prisoners shared cells at this time for the rooms were reasonably spacious. All the windows were heavily barred and the glass the type that one could not see out of. Merely a faint hint of daylight. Conditions for prisoners in court cells at this time were regarded as "quite deplorable". A Home Office Committee in 1887 heard that some court cells were nothing more than "cupboard-like boxes, with bases measuring about 2' square" others " a single dark room, with no seats, no heating and inadequate sanitary facilities" where prisoners were kept unsegregated. (REPORT OF HOME OFFICE COMMITTEE on the Accommodation in courthouses and other places for prisoners awaiting trial at Assizes and Quarter Sessions PP1887 (Cmnd 4791) XLI, 905)

Ten thirty, all eyes were on the judge's door to the right of His Lordship's seat on the bench. Waiting its opening. "Court rise!" and into a packed court stepped Sir James Charles Mathew, a Justice of the High Court of Justice in full wig and regalia. Taking his seat the clerk proceeded to read the "proclamation against vice and immorality" to one and all. A tradition that is still carried out today when High Court judges visit the provincial courts.

The first task of the day was to swear in a Grand Jury-two Knights, the remainder –gentlemen and all justices of the peace.

1) Sir Henry St.John Halford, 52 years old, the Deputy Chairman of the Quarter Sessions, a freemason and Lieutenant Colonel of the Leicestershire Rifle Volunteers (No.31) was foreman.

2) Sir Frederick T. Fowke, 64 years old, Chairman of the Quarter Sessions, Constable of the Castle, Treasurer of the county and Lieutenant Colonel of the Leicester Militia (No.26).

3) George Thomas Mowbray, 56 years old, Joint Deputy Chairman of the Quarter Sessions and Deputy Lieutenant.

4) Philip Peter Perring Goodchild, 42 years old, Captain in the Leicester Militia (No. 26).

5) Gregory Knight, Captain in the Leicester Militia (No.26)

6) Richard Worsley Worswick, 45 years old, Major in the Leicester Militia (No.26).

7) William Pearson, Major in the Leicester Militia (No. 26).

8) Edward Henshaw Cheney, 66 years old

9) Henry Cleaver Woodcock, 62 years old and owner of 300 acres of land

10) Henry Etherington Smith, 69 years old

11) Frederick Palmer, 55 years old, a Deputy Lieutenant

12) Corbet Smith, 36 years old, late captain in the Royal Dragoons

13) Richard Lewis de Capell Brooke, 49 years old, trained as a barrister but not practising.

14) Hussey Packe, 39 years old, living in London

15) Ralph George Pochin, 51 years old, retired naval commander RNHP

16) George William Pochin, 36 years old, annuitant (One who receives an annual income for his lifetime.)

17) Thomas Arthur, 70 years old, retired Lieutenant Colonel in the Army

18) Charles Packe, 54 years old

19) George Shaw M.D., 79 years old.

20) Thomas Charles Douglas Whitmore, 41 years old.

21) The Derbyshire Courier also lists 55 year old Isaac Harrison as a juror but he is not in the actual Crown Minute Book of The Midland Circuit 1873-1882.

Looking at the first seven names and what their interests are it can be seen that the makeup and social class of this jury is nothing like the "farmers and shopkeepers'" jury of the Brimington Inquest! Members of a Grand Jury were the "best figures in the county"- merchants, "middle ranking professionals" and all initially approved by the High Sheriff. At least eight of these gentlemen had an address which was described as a "Hall" and if one considers Mr Whitmore, at random, to be a typical juror:- He was a 41 year old married gentleman with three young children, two spinster sisters and a cousin who was his land agent, all living at the Hall. This family had a retinue of a butler, two footmen, a Swiss governess, a French cook, housekeeper, three ladies' maids, three house maids, a kitchen maid and one other type of maid. All living-in and all unmarried. Then there were five other servants classed as "lodgers"- three laundry maids and two helpers in the stable. Beyond the Hall were other households such as the stud groom and his family who depended on Mr Whitmore for their employment. It can be imagined that this was how the county set lived.

Twenty jurors sounds like a lot but the size of a Grand Jury varied from 12 to 23 jurors and these were not the men who would eventually hear Alfred Gough's trial. Their function was merely to hear the evidence from the witnesses of the various cases that were to come before His Lordship and then decide if there really was a case to answer in each matter. It was not unheard of that malicious actions could be brought against innocents so the Grand Jury was "to weed out any weak and baseless cases" thereby saving court time and not wasting that of the judge who was really only there to hear the most serious of cases. The 20 gentlemen did not have to reach a unanimous decision; a majority vote would suffice where at least 12 had to concur.

His Lordship, once the Grand Jury had been sworn in, was to give them instructions (charge them) regarding the various cases. However as in all legal matters there was some "housekeeping" to be done. The "Calendar of Prisoners" was a document detailing the date, venue and who it was that would be officiating at the upcoming Winter Assizes. It also contained a list of prisoners, their age, profession and level of literacy. (Gough was classed as "Imp."-he could read and write imperfectly. Certainly his letters have no punctuation to speak of and it appears that any important words to him were emphasised by a capital letter.) The names and addresses of the magistrates who committed the defendants were noted in the Calendar and, as in Gough's case, also the coroner, Mr Busby Esq. His warrant was dated 3 days earlier than the warrant of the magistrate, Mr Swanwick Esq. The offence as charged in Gough's case, was detailed both from the magistrate and the coroner and lastly the date was recorded when the prisoners were received into custody at the county gaols. This Calendar was now being referred to by His Lordship stating the number of prisoners from Leicestershire (2 or 5 depending on which newspaper one read), 11 from Derbyshire and none "he was happy to say" from Rutlandshire. The cases though few in number were "very serious and grave" in their character.

Sir James went on to point out that since the Calendar had been printed John Jarman from Leicester had committed suicide (The Calendar states that he had been found dead in his cell on the morning of the 31st October (the arrival date for the High Court Judge to hear his case). He was a 60 year old confectioner with two of his children in the family business. He had been in prison awaiting trial since 20th July charged with attempting to murder his wife. Despair and fear of the outcome drove John to drastic measures-he cut his throat with a piece of glass bottle. The Derby Mercury stated that the carotid artery was cut completely through and the doctor stated that death was instantaneous. His Lordship then commented on this matter of suicides and remand prisoners. A speech that would not seem out of place even in modern times:-

"I believe it is impossible to over-estimate the great suffering that some accused persons have to undergo while awaiting trial. We are *so informed by those who have charge of*

prisoners, and it is *shown in several ways. Of the number of persons who made attempts upon their lives, strange to say, those who were untried were those who, for the most part, made such attempts, and, more singular still, the attempt was most frequently made by prisoners who might anticipate acquittal, or conviction of an offence less grave than the one charged against him. Considerations of humanity would weigh with everybody who had to consider whether it was wise or not to hold four assizes in a year, but at the same time it was obviously extremely undesirable that assizes should be held where there was little to do."* This was the dilemma- costs and inconvenience against people's lives! *"It was most inconvenient that the elaborate and costly machinery provided for the administration of the criminal law should be set in motion where there were no serious offences to be tried."* His Lordship directly looking at the magistrates of the Grand Jury continued:- *"As you have noticed, in some parts of the country the judges have been brought and the grand jury summoned where the amount of crime did not justify such a proceeding but as* you go *on* you will *be better able to ascertain how to provide precisely in that respect, though it* is *extremely difficult to predict, (beforehand) particularly at the length of time the arrangements must be made before the Assizes* are *held, how long it would be needful that the judges should be in the particular towns selected for the trials.*" The London Gazette had printed as early as 2nd September the announcement issued by the Privy Council on 26th August that the three counties of Derbyshire, Rutlandshire and Leicestershire were to be "joined" for the purposes of creating a Winter Assize County number 5 and that the court would sit in Leicester. Administrative matters were also to be put in motion. (At the time the Privy Council was sitting Alfred Gough was still at the Inquest stage of his hearings.)

Behind every High Court Judge was his own Clerk of the Assizes and staff who would follow the judge on his circuit. Sir James' clerk was Arthur Duke Coleridge. It was his job to oversee the smooth running of the Assizes. This involved clerking in court- both the civil and criminal courts, drawing up the indictments (the document that accuses a person of a particular offence), writing up the judges' orders and dealing with the costs incurred by prosecutors and their witnesses. The clerk needed to know beforehand what cases were going to be put before the judge and publish the lists accordingly. Administration was not the domain of the judge.

"Housekeeping" over with, the judge now proceeded to tell the Grand Jury about certain of the cases he "thought it necessary to call their attention" to. Not surprisingly the first mention was that of Alfred Gough. "It seemed that an abominable outrage had been perpetrated on the child, and she was then cruelly murdered." *"The evidence was largely circumstantial, but that was what might be expected in a case of that character."* His Lordship now gives the direction to the jury- "you will *doubtless have abundant reasons for sending the case down for investigation by the petty jury*". Meaning the judge expects this Grand Jury to send this case for trial before an ordinary jury of 12 men (a Petty Jury as it was known) and *"leave the prisoner there to dispose of the suggestions of the prosecution."* How was Alfred Gough going to answer the allegations brought before him? No one knew as yet. "Whether the prisoner would be able to account for his time differently" would be for the Petty Jury to say.

The second matter His Lordship wished to mention was another Derbyshire case. A charge of rape, the prisoner being a 24 year old married man and the victim, a girl of 14. (At this time the age of consent was merely 13 years.) His Lordship was questioning the degree of resistance that was offered, "which might be expected to be offered" in the case of rape by the girl. At this time there was a general tendency to downplay rape charges for a lesser charge and even more so if the alleged assailant was of the middle or upper classes. A gentleman would never do such a thing! As to all the other cases in the calendar Sir James did not think it necessary to make any further remarks.

The Derbyshire Times records that after mention of the Derby rape *"His Lordship said there was a case on the calendar of an abominable description which he could not help referring to, for the reason that it appeared, from what took place before the magistrates, that two persons, a man and a woman looked on and saw the offence perpetrated. And yet it never apparently occurred to anyone of them to take steps to prevent the unfortunate fellow from yielding to the diabolical temptation of which he appeared to be possessed. He could not conceive that it was possible that such a thing could be done, but there again it was for the petty jury to say whether the evidence was sufficient to convict the prisoner."* Whether the judge is referring again to Gough's case or another matter entirely is not clear. The Derbyshire Courier makes no mention of this although the two papers otherwise more or less marry up in their reporting. Is the judge referring to Miss Johnson looking on as Eleanor was stood by a man exposing himself in the lane? But who was the man that the judge referred to? Was it old Mr Cooke sat at the bottom of the lane or someone entirely different? Could he have been referring to Miss Johnson's mysterious brother? Could he have left his house to see why Harriott was rushing in and out? Was he not curious as to what was happening? It will never be known or even if this was the actual case His Lordship was in fact discussing.

For now, His Lordship made ready to rise but not without giving "a dig" to the court arrangements at Leicester! "I have *a somewhat inconvenient course to take."* The judge had to leave the building and return to the "borough court" at the Town Hall to deal with the business there. This took him about ten minutes to walk the distance to Horsefair Street and "as he had said to the Borough Grand Jury" implies he actually started the day there at the borough court arriving at the criminal court for the 10.30 session. *"He hoped that arrangements would be made by which the two courts would be brought together, so that the judges and officials might be saved the inconvenience of having to pass from one to the other"*! The judge left the court sending the Grand Jury to their own room to make a start on hearing the witnesses in all the cases not just Gough's. The court itself was adjourned until the afternoon. Apparently the procedure was that all the witnesses would be taken into open court and sworn in batches and then sent along to outside the Grand Jury room where they would wait to be examined by these venerable gentlemen. The examinations were conducted in private. There would be no members of the public, no press and no accused. The Grand Jury would be assisted by a clerk who would have the witness depositions, explain the case if necessary and assist in the witness examinations. Once the Grand Jury had considered the indictments, heard all the evidence from the prosecutors and their witnesses they would have to come to a decision. Was there enough evidence on the face of it to send a case to trial? If "yes" they would sign the bill "True Bill" (of indictment). If the Grand Jury felt there was not enough evidence against the defendant the bill would be signed "No True Bill". In that case at the end of the session the accused would be discharged but that was not the same as an acquittal. It was possible for the case to be brought back again at a new session! Apparently though, the Grand Jury could be dispensed with altogether if a coroner's jury had brought in a guilty verdict. That would automatically have sent a defendant to trial. That had been the case with Alfred Gough. However he had also appeared before the magistrates which supposedly gave the Grand Jury the right to investigate the matter further. Alfred Gough, as was expected by Superintendent Carline, had a case to answer but what if the Grand Jury had come to a different conclusion from the coroner's jury? Whose opinion would have had the greater authority?!

LEICESTER CASTLE 2pm

Two o'clock and the court was re-assembled, the judge having taken his seat. The 20 members of the Grand Jury were armed with their "True Bills". One, a mere strip of parchment having the names of the witnesses written on the back, was for Alfred Gough. The indictment which had to be absolutely precise read "that he feloniously, wilfully, and of his malice aforethought, did kill and murder one Eleanor Windle, at Brimington, on the 20th August, 1881." Earlier in the century indictments were not allowed to be amended so that if there was a mistake on the document then the accused could be acquitted.

There were eleven prisoners from the Derbyshire area and they were brought up from the cells in turn to plead "Guilty" or "Not Guilty". One of these was Gough.

"The Clerk of Assizes (Mr A. D. Coleridge), asked if Gough was on the premises, and a reply having been given in the affirmative, the Clerk of Assizes ordered that he should be brought before his Lordship. In a very few moments Gough accended from the cells beneath into the dock, being dressed in clothes similar to those in which he appeared when before the magistrates and the coroner at Chesterfield". The Derbyshire Times claimed Gough entered the dock with *"a light step" "displaying the same indifference"* that he had shown all along. This reporter knows that Gough's clothes were the same as when he was arrested by Superintendent Carline.

"He appeared to be in good health, though somewhat careworn (and paler), and having

cast a rapid look round the court, took up his position at the right hand corner of the dock."

Alfred was now to be arraigned by the Clerk of the Assizes who slowly rose whilst looking carefully at the indictment that he was about to read:- *"Alfred Gough you stand charged in this indictment with having in the parish of Brimington in the county of Derby on the 20th August feloniously, wilfully, and of malice aforethought killed and murdered one Eleanor Windle. Are you guilty or not guilty?"*

The twitching of Alfred's face and neck muscles betrayed to one reporter that there were signs of nervousness but Alfred firmly and decidedly replied:

"Not guilty".

With this reply Gough now "put himself on his country". It would be for his fellow countrymen to decide whether he was guilty or not. At some stage, possibly before one of the earlier prisoners pleaded "Not guilty" the common or petty jury of 12 men were sworn in. A juror for the Assizes had to be aged between 21 and 60 possessing certain property qualifications-either land worth at least £10 p.a. freehold or £20 p.a. leasehold, or occupy a house with 15 or more windows or occupy a dwelling with an annual rateable value of at least £20. This was the qualification set in 1800. The make-up of the unpaid jury was mainly small farmers and shopkeepers. It was lamented that educated men rarely sat on these juries as it was relatively easy to buy one's way out of jury service and the vast majority did. This petty jury was only going to hear the trials for that day. Yes, however many trials were to be heard on one day it would be the same jury that heard them. There would be another petty jury sworn in the next day.

Continuing the Clerk asked; *"You stand charged on a similar offence of wilful murder on the Coroner's inquisition. Are you guilty or not guilty?"*

"Not guilty".

His Lordship then addressed the prisoner, *"Are you defended by counsel?"*

"No, my Lord."

"Would you wish the Court to assign you counsel for your defence?" His Lordship knew that as this case could carry the death penalty, the prisoner needed legal representation. It was only common-sense and if that gave the impression to others that he was on the defendant's side then so be it. Sir James may not be an experienced criminal judge yet but he knew proceedings would progress smoother if both sides had representation.

Hesitating Gough replied: *"Yes, my Lord, I have no one."*

There was no guaranteeing that the counsel chosen would be proficient. It was pot luck as to who was in the court at the time and not engaged. Obviously there were counsel in the room who were available. Sometimes counsel volunteered themselves, sometimes a prisoner could choose and sometimes the judge chose. This need not have been someone inexperienced it could be the most senior counsel there.

Sir James looked about the crowded courtroom. Who would his gaze alight upon? *"Mr Weightman, will you take the prisoner's defence?"*

Thomas Turner Weightman, a 40 year old barrister from Nottingham replied: *"If your Lordship pleases."*

This meant Mr Weightman would be giving his services for free! Criminal work, as far as barristers were concerned, was generally poorly paid. Etiquette forbade a barrister from appearing in court for less than 1 guinea (21 shillings) but most defendants would find it almost impossible to scrape together that sort of money. A few barristers would work for less in order to get started in their notoriously difficult careers and even take on other jobs to supplement their income.

A slight nod from the judge and speaking again to Gough: *"Then counsel is assigned to you."*

"Thank you."

Before the prisoner was removed from the dock and taken back down to the cells Mr Weightman asked: *"Will your Lordship kindly allow me a copy of the depositions?"* To give him some idea of what the case was about! The request was acceded to, the prisoner was whisked away and the next matter was called on. The Derbyshire Times reported that the hearing of Gough's case was fixed for that day and that it was expected to last "the whole of the day" as there were 24 witnesses. However time was marching on! It would be in Gough's interest if his trial could be heard the next day. This would give Mr Weightman some time to look at the case. However it was not considered unfair or strange at this time for counsel to conduct their brief after a quick chat with the prisoner over the dock rail. As it was Mr Weightman would be involved defending two of the other Derbyshire prisoners as well!

After the Grand Jury had returned all the bills they were dismissed by His Lordship with thanks for their services. (A century earlier the Grand Jury had had an important role to play in the legal system but mutterings had commenced regarding its continuing usefulness and over half a century later its function would be abolished.) For the present time Mr Justice Mathew proceeded with the first of three trials scheduled to be heard that afternoon before the newly empanelled Petty Jury.

The first trial had two defendants – hawkers like Alfred Gough. Together with a third man it was alleged that they tried to obtain money by false pretences. The 44 year old Mr. Horace Smith prosecuted and for his trouble his fee would be about 2 guineas, rarely more, even at the Assizes, but the defendants were unrepresented. This was not unusual, and at the turn of the century it was common for both victim and defendant to be unrepresented. After hearing the evidence presented by Mr. Smith His Lordship stopped the trial "and ruled that there was no evidence to go to the jury". The prisoners were therefore acquitted. Not a very good start for the High Court Judge who was here in Leicester to try the most serious of cases and not a very good reflection on the abilities of the Grand Jury!

Moving on to the second case that afternoon again with Mr Smith prosecuting. This was a matter regarding a man charged with bigamy. Again the prisoner was undefended but he had prepared a "long" statement professing his innocence in thinking his first wife was dead (until she turned up where the new bride lived!).This unsworn statement, though not allowed to all defendants, could be read by the prisoner himself or a court official and in effect was the prisoner's only defence. The bigamist was seeking leniency from the court. It was the closest approximation to giving evidence which at this time was forbidden to defendants. However, being written before the trial, the statement would not necessarily address any witness evidence given that may reveal something of importance during the trial. The legal view was that this procedure was a protection for prisoners who might incriminate themselves in the witness box. Previously, prisoners who had no written defence were generally hopeless in defending themselves- "not knowing what to say they said nothing"! Those defendants who did manage to say anything simply gave a denial but no reasoning behind it, the explanation was something akin to "I was drunk" as if that excused all and failing that just begged for the court's mercy.

The Petty Jury found the bigamist guilty but recommended mercy. His Lordship sentenced him to15 months hard labour as the offence was a serious one!

The third trial was of a man from Brimington. This time 36 year old Mr Gilbert Kennedy prosecuted. The charge was "an abominable crime" The True Bill makes mention of carnal knowledge of a calf! Was this the crime referred to by Sir James earlier when addressing the Grand Jury?! Whatever the evidence it was not enough to convict him and the judge acquitted him.

Meantime whilst these three trials were in progress it was obvious to Superintendent Carline that even if His Lordship sat late, Alfred Gough's trial would never be completed that day. He obviously had to make arrangements as to what to do with all of his witnesses. They surely did not go back to Chesterfield that night? There were expenses available for witnesses, certainly for travel. One assumes there would be some money available for overnight accommodation. With

24 of them this was going to be costly. And, it is known there were 24 witnesses but were the youngsters and women chaperoned by one or more of their parents, guardians or husbands? Was William Windle accompanied by his wife or any of his other relatives or was he just with his son, Ernest? The logistics would be something of a worry but no doubt Elijah Carline would take it all in his stride.

For the witnesses, apart from the morning session with the Grand Jury, it was a lot of waiting around. No doubt after staying at the foot of the staircase in the entrance hall, for a short time, the witnesses started to explore their surroundings. There were other doors here in the encaustic tiled hall leading into the two courtrooms. At the top of the short seven stepped staircase were two large windows overlooking a river at the back of the building. The stairs then split into two, each staircase coming back upon itself into a large and airy room to the front of the building where the public had access to the railinged balconies the full length of one side of each court. This room contained the Venetian window that was seen above the front door when the witnesses first entered the "Castle". The church opposite filled the whole of the window. "That's the church of St Mary de Castro" remarked a passing usher who could see that some of the witnesses were showing an interest in the beautiful building opposite. "Part of it was built about 800 years ago as a chapel. It was once part of the original castle buildings. It's obviously been extended though. The bell tower on the right was built about 1300 and the recessed spire was rebuilt over a hundred years ago." The children told the usher that where they came from the church spire was crooked! "And where would that be?" "Chesterfield!" The surprised usher went off to perform his duties while the witnesses lingered about the windows looking at the views. Near to the Venetian window if they were quiet they could hear the proceedings going on in front of His Lordship. When was it going to be Alfred Gough's trial? It was getting late in the day.

Whilst the witnesses and Superintendent Carline waited upstairs Alfred Gough waited downstairs in the court cells. At some point in the afternoon it can possibly be assumed that his barrister, Mr Weightman may have visited him but then again if it is anything like the procedures that occur in modern day courts it may well have been that the interview did not take place before Wednesday morning just before the start of the trial. For Alfred this could have been an anxious time wondering when he would have the chance to speak to his counsel and whether he was going to be tried that day but no doubt he kept all this to himself.

Obviously both Alfred and the 24 witnesses were told at some point late in the afternoon that the jury had been discharged and the judge had risen for the day. Alfred would be returned to Leicester Prison whilst Superintendent Carline and his officers probably made provision for settling in the witnesses at some accommodation in the town for the night. Meanwhile back in Brimington the families of the witnesses would be wondering where their loved ones were? Would Elijah send a telegram to the telegraph office in Brimington or to Marsden Street Police Station in Chesterfield to have his constables get word to the families and even let his own family know? It is to be hoped he did.

As an aside, a wag of a journalist reported that some Italian necromancer had foretold that on this day- 1st November-the destruction of the world was to commence. For Gough this prediction was possibly to come to fruition but for the journalist, he writes "the sea was to have overflowed the land, and caused a great destruction of human life." "It is the 4th as I write this, and I have received no telegram of such an awful visitation. Surely this Mother Shipton (a prophetess) of fair Italy has made a mistake; or else the prediction is so verified that there is no one left to wire the news"!

CHAPTER FOURTEEN

WEDNESDAY 2nd NOVEMBER 1881

ALFRED GOUGH'S TRIAL BEGINS

Again the 24 witnesses made their way up the cobbled street pushing through the throng now gathered outside the courthouse. This time though they knew they would be called into court, the one on the left as they entered the building. The whole day would be given over to Alfred Gough's trial. Alfred was waiting as before down in the cells. He finally got to see Mr Weightman who had read the depositions from the witnesses. They met in one of the secure interview rooms next to the cells. They must have spoken about the Brimington area and the local colliers and mines which must have been information given to Mr Weightman by Gough. It is not likely Mr Weightman knew that area of Derbyshire and yet it would figure in Gough's defence.

10.30am. The judge's door opened and the packed court rose to their feet. Not only entered Lord Justice Mathew but also the High Sheriff, Mr Taylor Esq. and his chaplain who were there to hear the proceedings. A reporter claimed "the seats on the Bench set apart for magistrates desirous of witnessing the proceedings are so limited in every respect that an extraordinarily small number of the "great unpaid" are to be seen there." Today it was two guests. Once settled the nod was given for the prisoner to be brought up from below. Alfred left his cell accompanied by his minders and turned left down the brick lined corridor that he had seen when first arriving in the building yesterday. This time he would try to take in his surroundings. This short corridor had an arched brick ceiling and at the end of it he could see the bottom of a staircase. At the foot of the staircase he took a deep breath and then slowly ascended- 1,2,3, the staircase then took a dog leg to the right, 8,9, the brick wall had become wood panelling . He was reaching the court, 13,14. Fourteen steps and Alfred was in the very heart of the court. This must have come as a surprise when he entered the "unusually small" dock yesterday to give his plea but he may not have taken it all in. The Sheffield and Rotherham Independent claimed that Alfred caused a "slight sensation" with the spectators. "He walked erect and soldierly, but was somewhat nervous on first entering the dock." It is hard to believe with the boxed pew arrangements in the court and Gough coming up the staircase and immediately turning right towards his seat that the crowd saw any of this unless they were standing and vigilantly watching for movement on the stairs leading down to the cells. Gough "cast a hurried glance" as he stood before his seat but then took a more leisurely look around him to see where he was yet still with his customary indifference. The room itself was "exceedingly small" for a county like Leicester –"a compartment of limited dimensions-" and consequently was "crowded to its utmost capacity." The Derby and Chesterfield Reporter was scathing about every aspect of the room. The journalist could not bring himself to call it a "hall" as it was so "diminutive"! "In fact, I don't think, though my experience of Assize Courts in various parts of the kingdom is extensive, that I have ever sat in so inconvenient a Court as this one at Leicester. Everybody is huddled closely together"! It is a wonder that if this court was so inconvenient the administrators did not choose Derby as the Assize venue? The irate reporter continued: "The construction of the Court is, in fact, somewhat similar to that of the one at the Town Hall, Derby, in which the Borough Sessions are held; but oh! what a difference between them. The Court at Leicester is so cramped…Derby Police Court is far superior to it"!

Apparently, according to the Sheffield and Rotherham Independent "**the audience included a fair sprinkling of the inhabitants of Chesterfield and the neighbourhood**"! The Derby and Chesterfield Reporter claimed "on reliable authority" that the locals had wanted a special train to be run from Chesterfield to Leicester and back in order for people to attend the trial. At cheap fares, of course! This never materialised but if it had the reporter stated that "many would have been disappointed" "for no sooner were the doors thrown open this morning than the Court became crowded, and admittance, as it was, had to be refused to scores, whose number, doubtless, would greatly have been swelled by many of those from Brimington, for people living near Leicester and neighbourhood were early upon the scene, and, taking up positions close to the doors, were among the first to enter."

Above to Gough's right in the gallery (which appeared from below to be "very close to the ceiling") and behind him on raised forms and standing beyond were the general public. Behind these onlookers at the back were three long rectangular windows and above the end one, a dormer window giving light to the room on this November day. Directly ahead he was looking at the clerk and behind him on the higher bench the light, bright eyes of His Lordship who sat between a cleric and some other gentleman. Everywhere there was mahogany wood, panelling, "pews" at differing heights, little doors, single cubicles and steps up and down.

All so difficult to negotiate around with the flowing gowns of the legal profession!

20. Photograph of Prosecuting Counsel Chandos Leigh QC

Sat in front of Alfred were the two rows of counsel and solicitors though they had their backs to him. Mr Weightman took a quick glance at him but prosecuting counsel were considering how they should open the case. The Honourable Edward Chandos Leigh QC was prosecuting on behalf of the

Public Prosecutor. It was here that worthwhile fees could be earned for those fortunate to be working for the Treasury Solicitor. Due to the seriousness of the case it was young Mr Middleton who had arranged for it to be so prosecuted. An action the 26 year old solicitor from Chesterfield had arranged when he had appeared before the magistrates there. The silk gowned Chandos Leigh QC was a 48year old married man, top of his profession living in Marylebone, London but some time in 1881 he was appointed Recorder of Nottingham which meant he also sat in judgement. It was the rule that a QC must appear with a junior barrister and that was Mr John Etherington Smith, aged 40 another married barrister up from Putney in London but he did have connections to Leicestershire as his father was one of the justices on the Grand Jury! It is interesting to note that all the prosecuting counsel mentioned at the Assizes had come up from London or Kent- Mr Horace Smith, Mr Gilbert Kennedy, Mr John Etherington Smith, Mr Chandos Leigh QC yet the defence barrister was from Nottingham!

The two prosecuting counsel received their instructions from young Mr Middleton of the firm of Messrs Jones and Middleton of Chesterfield. It was up to him, as the solicitor to prepare the case and brief the counsel though Superintendent Carline had on this occasion done most of the work for Mr Middleton already.

Sat in two raised pews to Gough's right were the press, scribbling away. The Derby and Chesterfield Reporter disgruntedly claimed there was only room there for four pressmen yet there was at least a dozen journalists attending the Assizes! "Doubtless (these seats) met all requirements some years ago, but now-a-days, as may easily be imagined, they are practically of very little utility"! "Were it not for the courtesy of those of the learned counsel who do not happen to hold briefs, I really do not know what we should do, but, thanks to the gentlemen of the long robe, we are perhaps almost better off than any present, although we find quarters quite close enough. Our friends- for the learned gentlemen certainly deserve that appellation- have earned our gratitude by placing at our disposal the sittings in front of the Clerk of Assize which they might claim, and content themselves with standing near the dock." A good number of pressmen were therefore on the front row of the court where His Lordship could keep an eye on them. A good vantage point to watch at close quarters the witnesses and jury but only those reporters sat in the press pews would be able to see any reaction from Gough. It was they who later reported that he looked "very careworn but maintained a very firm demeanour during the progress of the case" "appear(ing) to be one of the least interested persons in the Court."

However, now the names of the new jurors for the day were announced.

1) Samuel Barber, 42years old and a farmer

2) Joseph Clayton

3) Digby Lyon, 43 years old and a civil engineer's assistant

4) William Hurst

5) Samuel Calladine, 55 years old and a framework knitter

6) Henry Clemenson

7) Jennings Barrington, 54 years old and a master grocer

8) Edward Start? 54 years old and a grazier and carrier

9) Joseph Wright

10) John Slater? 63 years old and a farmer

11) Ernest Cooke

12) Charles Martin

(A lot more research would be needed to pinpoint the remaining jurors' occupations. However, the jurors' names are correct and what occupations are given follows the pattern of the Brimington Inquest jurors.)

Each in turn was shown to their allocated seats, to Gough's left. Then after each was sworn in, the prisoner was "delivered into their charge". The clerk once again read out the indictment to Gough. Yesterday at this point the press claimed Gough was "suffering from great trepidation". Now his face, "by no means repulsive" was "pallid and pinched, his limbs trembled, and the muscles of his face and neck quivered exceedingly." Gough became "the observed of all the observers"!

It was the Honourable Chandos Leigh QC who got to his feet to deliver the opening speech to the jury. It is interesting to note that both The Derbyshire Times and The Derbyshire Courier identically report this speech almost to the letter and yet diverge again on the witness statements. Could there have been a copy of this speech given out to the press or maybe one reporter took down the speech to pass on the details to a fellow reporter in a sister paper?:-

"I appear with my friend Mr Smith on behalf of the prosecution, and it might not be amiss to say at the outset that there could be no possible doubt that the girl Eleanor Windle was murdered by somebody - that an outrage of a

most severe and abominable nature was committed upon her, and that afterwards her life was taken away by strangulation. It will *be* my *duty, however, on the part of the prosecution, by laying the facts before* you, *link by link, and chain by chain"* (This phrase was often used by the press when reporting the murder in Chesterfield) *"to show without a reasonable doubt that Gough, the prisoner at the bar was the person who outraged and murdered the child.*

The prosecution then told the jury in detail who Gough was and what the events were from the time of Eleanor going out blackberrying on the Saturday to the witnesses that would be called to recount what they had seen or heard through to Sunday's events and Gough's arrest. Most of the information will be familiar but as this is a case being heard in Leicester then this local jury have no idea of the Brimington or Chesterfield locality. It is up to the prosecution with the aid, no doubt of Mr Middleton and Superintendent Carline and his men, to set the scene more vividly.

"The prisoner is a man between 30 and 40 years of age, (Interesting that Gough's exact age has not been pinpointed.) *and for the last two or three years he* has *been gaining his livelihood as a rag and bone man, in the neighbourhood of Chesterfield. He had no particular fixed place of abode, lodging first at one house and then at another. He made and sold paper sunshades, parasols, and other children's toys, and it was his habit to give these toys in exchange for the rags brought to him. The*

314

little girl in question, Eleanor Windle, was a child of six years of age, and she was the daughter of a man holding a respectable position as foreman, at the Staveley Iron Works. He lived at a small house close to the Chesterfield and Brimington Road. On Saturday morning, August 20th, about 10 o'clock, Eleanor Windle was out with some companions gathering blackberries on that road, close to a hamlet called Tinkersick. At about half- past nine on that morning the prisoner Gough was seen trundling his handcart, in which he carried his toys, and the rags and bones which he obtained for them, in the direction of Brimington.

21. Sketch from Illustrated Police News 3rd September 1881

He passed the party of children -six in number. Five of them went on their way, but the poor little girl, Eleanor Windle, said she would follow the prisoner. She was seen to do so, and to overtake him, and they were also seen talking together at a place called Johnson's lane."

"We must now pause a moment while I describe to you Johnson's lane, because the theory of the prosecution is that the murder was committed at the side of that lane, and it will be for the jury to consider carefully the whole district about Johnson's lane, and what he was doing at the time he was there.

Some important evidence will be given by a woman named Harriott Johnson who lived at Oak House at the top of the lane. I have told you that the prisoner was seen with the little girl at the bottom of Johnson's lane. Johnson's lane ran down to the high road and there were five or six steps from the high road to the lane, the carriage way (the lane) itself turning and sloping to the road. The lane was 133 yards in length, and at the top was Oak House, where Miss Johnson, a retired schoolmistress, lived with her brother. At one side of the lane was some thick underwood, and on the left hand side, looking from Oak House, there were several gaps. When the prisoner and the little girl were seen together, the latter was wearing a light dress, and what was called a "Zulu" hat. The handcart was also seen near the end of the lane.

The next witness happened to look up the lane, and saw the prisoner about 16 yards up, with the little girl. He had known the prisoner before, and also knew the handcart. What happened next? Miss Johnson to whom I have already referred, came out of her house, and she will describe more particularly the distances when she comes as a witness before you. She saw a man and a child, and as they came somewhat nearer to her, she will tell you that she saw the man's trousers unbuttoned, and that he was exposing himself. She will also describe what was her action at the time. It seemed that she ran back to her house in order, as she will state, to get some sort of a broom handle to drive away the man. This would be about half-past ten in the morning. The man came a little further up the lane, and was still indecently exposing himself. Then something which certainly seemed rather curious occurred. The man saw Miss Johnson coming, and at once turned away and disappeared. I have told you the jury that there were gaps in the hedges, and that there was a quantity of thick underwood, but Miss Johnson will say that although she ran after them, yet for some strange reason, she never saw them again. The man must have got through the gap in the hedge, and there will be evidence put before you the jury to show that near the gap the grass and underwood were crushed flat in two separate places. The theory of the prosecution is that the man having exposed himself, as seen by Miss Johnson, must have attempted to do something to the little girl, and that being near the road, he resorted to the abominable act of strangling her, near one of the gaps in Johnson's lane. You might ask what became of the handcart all the time? The handcart was left standing at the bottom of Johnson's lane, and a witness named John Cook, whose evidence will be most important, saw it there. Cook had known the prisoner and also knew his handcart and, seeing nobody in charge of it, he went and looked in. He saw that it contained a hamper filled with toys, such as paper sunshades and parasols, and noticed that the cart was not full. He watched the cart for some time, but eventually went away to gather mushrooms. On his return in about a quarter of an hour the cart had gone. Now what had become of the cart? The next witness was a woman named Sarah Cantrell, who was passing about half-past eleven, and saw the prisoner Gough moving the cart, apparently with some difficulty, in the direction of Brimington. The cart contained something bulky, and appeared to her to be full. About noon on that day the prisoner was seen by the little girl's brother, Ernest Windle, to come up

Brimington hill. This would become important because, at a later stage, the prisoner was asked where he left the child, and he replied that it was at the top of the hill, whereas Ernest Windle's statement would prove, beyond question, that no living child was with him as he came up the hill. About a quarter past twelve, the prisoner reached a place called Cotterill- (Cottrell) lane, where a woman named Elizabeth Neale got some rags to purchase a toy, and she noticed that the hand-cart was full. A lad named Walter Davidson, who also bought some toys from the prisoner, on Brimington Common, would state that the prisoner refused to allow them to touch the cart, and told them not to go to the front. The prisoner went on (in) to the Miners' Arms, which he reached about half-past twelve. Let us pause a moment, and recapitulate exactly the position of matters at that time. We have got the prisoner at Johnson's Lane, a little after ten o'clock; we have got him going with the child there and being seen by two people; we have got him leaving his handcart at the bottom of Johnson's Lane; we have got him staying in Johnson's Lane a considerable time; we have got it that when the handcart was left it was not full, and that after it was moved away it was full according to two witnesses; and lastly, we have got him at the Miner's Arms about half- past twelve o'clock. What was the next step? If the theory of the prosecution is right that the cart was full owing to the child being placed inside it, in the sack, and being trundled along by the prisoner, it was absolutely necessary that the prisoner- being well known in the neighbourhood-should dispose of his ghastly burden as quickly as he could. He returned from the Miners' Arms to Brimington village, and thence in the direction of Barrow Hill, passing the Ringwood Lodge at the junction of the road from Staveley village, and the private occupation road from Staveley works. Down the private occupation road the prisoner went reaching there about one o' clock. He was seen to pass through the gates and proceed in the direction of Hoole's plantation, which was at the side of the occupation road. This seemed to be the most convenient and accessible place- and one where discovery would not be probable- for the prisoner to get rid of his burden. A witness named Elizabeth Hardwick saw the prisoner near to Hoole's plantation about one o'clock; and she will tell the jury that the cart seemed full and heavy. A short time after that- about twenty minutes to two-a witness, of the name of James Cropper, saw the hand-cart with the paper toys in it close to some railings at Hoole's plantation. I should explain that Hoole's plantation was separated from the road by a thick blackthorn hedge, except at one point, where there was a gap, filled in with posts and rails. That was where the cart was standing. Shortly afterwards, the prisoner was seen by a signalman, passing under the railway bridge at Barrow Hill, and he was seen returning, at about a quarter to five, by the same man. Now we get to the evidence of a very important witness-the man who kept the toll bar at Brimington. That witness, Charles Abney-Hastings Brown, would speak to three separate occasions. First, he saw the prisoner at half-past nine in the morning; then he will speak as to what took place as the prisoner was returning from Barrow Hill, between five and six o'clock in the afternoon. He will state that the prisoner came to him at the toll-bar, and strange to relate, the poor child's father, William Windle, was present. Of course, as the child had been missing since ten o'clock in the morning, inquiries were being made as to what had become of her. The father had a conversation with the prisoner, but as I prefer in cases like this not to open with the conversation, I will leave the witness to tell the story first-hand. The sum and substance of the conversation, however, was that the prisoner did not know what had become of the child, that it was a "bad job", and that he had left the child at the houses near the cemetery. As to the latter statement, Sarah Cantrell will swear that she saw the prisoner passing the cemetery, and that there was no living child with him then. Ernest Windle, the brother of the little girl, will also say that he saw the prisoner passing Watson's houses, and that there was no living child with him, so that the statement of the prisoner, under any circumstances, could not be correct. From the toll-bar the prisoner passed through Brimington in the direction of Chesterfield, and the next person he met was an old friend of his, named Thomas Holmes, on Brimington Hill about six o'clock. He addressed Holmes by his nickname just as they were passing between Johnson's-lane and the Cemetery, and evidently wishing to unburden himself, used some very remarkable words. He said that he had done something wrong, and that he should never be happy again, promising that he would tell him what it was the next time they met. Gough then went on in the direction of Chesterfield. He had been in the habit of leaving his cart with a man named Thomas Newberry, and on this occasion it was left on that person's premises all Saturday night, not being touched until the police took possession of it. That cart contained a most material and important piece of evidence against the prisoner. At his lodgings the prisoner was told that the police were after him, and he at once said, "What, about the child?" I do not lay much stress on that, however, because he had heard about the loss of the child before, and had had some conversation both with the police and the father of the child about it. But why was it that the police were searching after him? (You,) The jury would remember that I told you that the cart was seen at the corner of Hoole's plantation. On Sunday morning the toll-bar keeper, amongst others, went out in search of the child, and when he arrived at Hoole's plantation he saw against the post and rail already mentioned, wheel marks, as if a cart had been moved backwards and forwards in order to get it as close as possible to the rails. He went inside the plantation, and the first thing he found was a bag or sack. On proceeding a little further, he discovered the body of the missing child, with her little Zulu hat, and light dress on, as described by one of the other witnesses. The hem had been torn off the sack which the witness found, and was tied tightly round the neck of the child. In addition to that, the same witness found a piece of wall-paper, similar to what would be used by the prisoner for making his sunshades and parasols. Brown at once gave information to the police, who also saw the child, and the piece of sacking round its neck. There was an extraordinary thing about this wall paper. I have told you that the prisoner's handcart was left with Thomas Newberry, and when it was taken possession of by the police, it was found to contain, amongst other things, two pieces of wall paper corresponding exactly with that found in the plantation. This I think is the substance of the case. When the prisoner was arrested by Supt. Carline, he repeated the statement he had previously made as to leaving the child near its own house and thereby reiterating for the third or fourth time the falsehood. The doctor will be called, and the prosecution will not only be able to prove the facts of the case as I have stated them, but to show that the child came to its death by strangulation. The evidence of the doctor will show that there was no doubt as to that point. The fact that the piece of sacking was tied tightly round her neck left no doubt in the minds of reasonable men but that the child was foully murdered. In addition to that, I will be able to show by the evidence of the doctor that the child had been assaulted in a foul manner - too loathsome for me to describe - and that murder supervened upon that. Having detailed the circumstances of the case as well as I possibly can, I will ask (you,) the jury to carefully consider the evidence I will lay before you. If at the close of the evidence you entertain a reasonable doubt that the prisoner did commit the crime, I will ask you, in God's name, to acquit him; but if you have no doubt, or no reasonable doubt, then it will be your duty, however painful it might be, to say that he was guilty."

The opening speech to the jury over, Mr Chandos Leigh QC took his seat whilst his junior counsel, Mr Etherington

Smith rose to call the first witness and conduct the examination in chief. Whilst the court waited for the witness to enter the room, Alfred Gough was finally allowed to sit down.

WITNESS 1   GEORGE ROPER

Mr George Roper, the 30 year old architect cum surveyor, was the first witness from Chesterfield to enter the crowded courtroom. He was to produce "the plan of the district around Brimington, correctly drawn to scale, and said the tracings produced were exact copies of the plan". Five of his measurements were the same as given at the Magistrates' Court but others differed slightly. Perhaps Mr Roper felt that before the Assizes he should just double check the measurements once more. Hence the different figures. He also explained the geography of the place more fully to the jury which was unnecessary before as, in Chesterfield; most people knew the area he was dealing with.

"The distance from Tinkersick (Lockoford Lane) to Johnson's Lane was 833 yards. Johnson's Lane was on the right hand side of the road leading from Brimington; it was higher than the road, and was approached by some steps up the embankment. The embankment opposite the end of the lane was six feet in height. Standing in the road opposite the end of the lane one could see over the embankment. Johnson's Lane sloped up hill, as shown in the sectional plan produced, and the distance from the high road to Oak House was 130 yards. From the end of

Johnson's Lane to Almond Place, which was the place where the deceased child lived, the distance was 332 (333) yards." The remaining distances were as before. Mr Roper now produced his sectional plan of Johnson's Lane. (See page 37) *"The fence on the left-hand side coming from Oak House commenced in a garden fence, (with an opening for the front door) then came a wall, and next to that there was a gap, marked third gap on the section, which led to a field. An old and very thick irregular hawthorn hedge, about six or seven feet in height, then commenced. There was no ditch on either side of the lane. (The hedge goes to the end of the lane.) There was another gap lower down the lane, and still further down there was another gap communicating with two fields, and an elder tree covered the gap. The hedge from thence continued to the gate posts at the bottom."* Young Mr Roper had also managed to make an enlarged plan of Hoole's plantation (See page 44). It *"had a good hawthorn fence round it, with the exception of one spot where (some posts and rails had been placed so that they could be removed at any time to admit carts). There were trees and shrubs in the plantation, and also two mounds or "spoil banks" from collieries."*

Mr Roper finally gave the handcart's dimensions as requested by Superintendent Carline. Nothing was to be left to chance. The jury needed to be able to picture the locations in their minds' eyes.

Mr Etherington Smith had no more questions to ask so now it was the turn of Mr Weightman to cross examine. The newspapers only report the answers to Mr Weightman's questions and so it has to be imagined what the question could be.

"The carriage road from Johnson's Lane joined the main road at a level."

"There was no embankment at the side of the lane (The gaps in the lane were level with the lane, there was no ditch, but the hedge overhung the lane)."

"The distance between Johnson's Lane end and the Cemetery Lodge was about 130 yards."

"The lodge was inhabited."

"The road into which Johnson's Lane ran was the high road, between Staveley and Chesterfield, and is well frequented especially on Saturday, which is the market day at Chesterfield."

"There were many colliers in the district but I did not know that there were two collieries in work at the back of Kidnapper Lane." (This was a lane running parallel to Johnson's Lane and the houses at Almond Place.)

The Hon. Chandos Leigh took the re-examination in chief of Mr Roper.

"It was possible to see the entrance to Johnson's Lane from the Cemetery house, but not to see up the lane."

His Lordship then wished to ask a question- *"Where the hedge in Johnson's lane turned with the carriage way it was about the same height as the other portions of the hedge."*

WITNESS 2 ELLEN HADFIELD

Now ten years old, Ellen next came into court and entered the "tiny" witness box. It was to be Mr Chandos Leigh who would lead the questioning this time. She recounted how she, Eleanor and four others went blackberry picking that Saturday morning at Tinkersick. This is where they saw the man with the "parasols". There was "sensation" in the court when Ellen declared the prisoner was that man! Eleanor left them to follow the man of her own accord towards her own house and the other girls went on towards Lockoford Lane.

Mr Weightman then asked young Ellen a question to which she replied: *"The prisoner did not speak to any of us as he passed. Eleanor Windle said she wanted to get a parasol."*

WITNESS 3 JOHN INSLEY

Mr Etherington Smith was to take the examination in chief of the carrier Mr Insley. This differed little from his evidence before the magistrates except that his timings are more precise. *"He passed Tinkersick about 10.30"* when he saw the girls blackberrying. He repeated Eleanor's actions, (a little girl whom he knew "perfectly well".) -where Gough and Eleanor were in relation to each other after he had passed them and turned around looking for someone who should have been following him out of Chesterfield.

Mr Weightman then proceeded to cross examine with Mr Insley's replies being:

"The prisoner frequently came to Brimington with his toys."

The judge wrote in his notebook that Insley had "many times" passed Gough on this road "where I have been carrier for the last sixteen years."

"The top of the cart was full of windmills."

"On the same side of the road as Johnson's-lane there were three gates between where he first saw the prisoner (at Tinkersick) *and where he passed him. There were two grass fields, a fallow field, and one, containing an old pit, which was partly sown with oats."* The pit though disused still had "open" shafts.

"(He knew the neighbourhood well.) There were no working collieries near Johnson's-lane. The nearest one to Brimington was the Tapton colliery, about a mile from Johnson's-lane."

"A number of colliers live at Brimington, and they work for the Staveley Company, who employ 4,000 to 5,000 hands (but he had not seen much roughness in these men)."

"From Staveley Works to Brimington they would come past Hoole's plantation."

Mr Chandos Leigh took the re-examination: *"There was nothing in the bottom of the barrow."*

The "top of the barrow was full of windmills" and "the sunshades had wood handles" noted His Honour.

WITNESS 4   JOSEPH TURNER

Mr Chandos Leigh began the questioning of this bricklayer's labourer who claimed to have known Gough for two or three years. He and a friend, Henry Witham, had passed the unmanned hand cart on the way to Chesterfield and at the bottom of Johnson's lane he noticed Gough and a little girl "about 16 yards from the road, standing close together". (Since the Inquest and Magistrates' Court appearances Turner's distance has increased.) *"The man had five or six small sticks under his arm, and he had another in his hand, which he was splitting."* Turner described the child's attire and the viewing of a body with similar clothing on the Sunday.

Mr Weightman's cross examination of the witness brought forward these replies:

"The sticks which the prisoner had in his hand were such as he used for the (handles for the) parasols which he sells."

"He and the child were standing in the middle of the lane, and the prisoner had his face towards the road, so that if he had looked up he could not miss but see them (Turner and his friend)*."*

"If he had met the prisoner on the road, he should have wished him good morning."

"Her hat was laid on her chest" when he saw the child next day in Hoole's plantation noted the judge.

WITNESS 5   HARRIOTT JOHNSON

Apparently when Miss Johnson entered the witness box Gough "ventured a smile". What was he thinking? Did he think it amusing that Miss Johnson, such a respectable woman, must have been highly embarrassed repeating to all and sundry what she had apparently seen him doing in the lane? It was Mr Etherington Smith's turn again to take on this formidable lady in examination in chief! She was the 53 year old spinster who looked after her brother at Oak House at the top of Johnson's Lane. She saw Gough and Eleanor in the lane that Saturday morning and explained her actions on seeing Gough behaving in an indecent manner. She could not explain the disappearance of the two and in particular what happened to the child. No matter how much Miss Johnson had been pressed there was still no proper explanation given. Did her short sightedness have anything to do with this?! Was she really telling all that she had seen?

When Mr Weightman cross examines this witness the two local Derbyshire papers feel it important to actually state Mr Weightman's questions as well as Miss Johnson's answers.

"When she first saw them the man and child were standing on the embankment at the end of the lane." (She could see from the top of the lane to the bottom.)

(She could not say how far she came down the lane but...) "They were somewhere about 100 yards from her and the man was looking towards Bradbury's field which was on the right hand side of the lane going down."

"When she went out the second time the couple were up the lane and even though the child was in advance of the man she could clearly see that he was exposing his person. She ran as hard as she could to the house for the broom handle, and on returning" "the child was standing towards the hedge on the left-hand side. The hedge hangs over. The child was standing nearly under the hedge." A point the judge would want to remember. *"The man ran swiftly down the lane and disappeared round the corner. She went and stood on the embankment but could see no one."*

(He ran towards Brimington, for had he gone towards Chesterfield, she would have seen him go down to the road.)

Mr Weightman: *"Do you know what became of the child?"*
"I don't know what became of the child, I fancy it went with the man."

Mr Weightman: *"You fancy it went with the man?"*
"Yes, sir."

Mr Weightman: *"Did you see a cart?"*
"No, I did not, but that is no reason that a cart should not have been stood there." (There

was a bush there which might have hidden the cart.)

Mr Weightman: "When did you first mention this matter? When did you first mention what you had seen in the lane?"
"On Saturday evening."

Mr Weightman: "To whom?"
"To a policeman."

Mr Weightman: "Did he come to see you?"
"Yes, he came up to see me."

Mr Weightman: "What time did he come to see you?"
"I think about eight o'clock in the evening. I can not say to a quarter of an hour."

Mr Weightman: "He was the first person to whom you mentioned it?"
"No."

Mr Weightman: "I asked you who was the first person to whom you mentioned it?"
"He was the first person to whom I gave any information."

Mr Weightman: "My question was to whom did you first mention anything of this matter?"
"Well, I mentioned it first to my brother. I made no formal statement."

Mr Weightman: "No formal statement?"

"Well, I suppose when you make a statement to a policeman it is a formal statement."

Mr Weightman: "When did you first hear of a little child being missing?"
"On Saturday evening, after tea."

Mr Weightman: "Did you not mention something about it to the mother?"
"Yes; she came up to enquire."

Mr Weightman: "When?"
"It would be sometime before the police officer came." (Just as it was getting dusk.)

Mr Weightman: "Why did you not tell the mother all when she came seeking for information about the child?"
"Well, because she was a mother."

Mr Weightman: "What did you not tell her?"
"I told her that I had seen a man behaving indecently in the lane and that she had better communicate with the police."

His Lordship (to witness): "Will you tell the learned counsel what you did not tell the mother. That is what he asks you to do."
"I perhaps kept back the worst part of it, as anyone would have done. I begged her to communicate with the policeman and send him to me."

Mr Weightman: At the time you were on the embankment, did anyone pass?"

"A man in a trap, drawn by a grey pony."

Mr Weightman: *"How long did you stay on the embankment?"*
"A few minutes."

Mr Weightman: *"I suppose the man in the trap would see you with the broom handle?"*
"Yes, he turned and looked towards me."

Mr Weightman: *"Which way was he going?"*
"Towards Chesterfield." Cross examination over Miss Johnson left the witness box.

WITNESS 6   JOHN COOK

Mr Chandos Leigh now rose to examine old Mr Cook, the highway labourer who also claimed to have known Alfred Gough for about two years. Not quite the impression given at the Inquest or Magistrates'! He repeated his story that between 10.30 and 11.00 of the Saturday morning he was sat on the steps at the bottom of Johnson's lane on the turnpike road for some time. *"He knew Johnson's Lane, he had been by it hundreds of times."* Whilst seated there he noticed the cart parked some yards *("nine or ten")* higher up the road towards Brimington. He claimed to know it was Gough's cart and on three occasions curiosity led him to investigate the unmanned vehicle and its contents in between smoking several pipes of tobacco on the steps. John Cook stated the cart was close to the side. So much so that one wheel was in a rut. (Would not this fact alone make the cart difficult to manoeuvre when Gough got back?) Cook never was reported at the Inquest or Magistrates' stating a wheel was in a rut. This evidence was new.

"He then went about 150 yards down the road into a field (to look for some mushrooms) for ten minutes or a quarter of an hour, and on his return the handcart was gone. Numbers of people "about a score" *went past him as he sat on the steps. It was a field owned by Mr Bradbury, on the right hand side of the turnpike road, and at the bottom side of Johnson's Lane."*

Mr Weightman now stood up to cross examine. John Cook replied to a question regarding where he went mushroom-picking:

"It was a grass field (the next field but one to that sown with oats) and he entered and returned from it through a gate. He could see straight up the turnpike from the gate of the field." (Could he not have seen Gough then pushing his cart up the hill towards Brimington? Obviously not.)

"On leaving the field he went on to Brimington."

"He was on and about the steps for nearly an hour and thought it was strange that Gough did not come to take charge of the cart."

"The bag was in the bottom of the cart (but he could not say whether there were one or two bags) *and the hamper, which stood above the cart was fastened to it."*

Cook was then re-examined by Mr Chandos Leigh: *"**The onion bag was empty.**"* Cook had already explained that the hamper was filled with toys "some in and some out". "Those of the toys that were out had no handles. The split sticks were like the handles" and in the cart itself was nothing but a thin onion bag and the split sticks.

Before the next witness was called Mr Weightman asked His Lordship if he could ask for Miss Johnson to return to the witness box? He had a question to put to her.

Miss Johnson was out in the entrance hall thinking that her ordeal was over. It must have come as a surprise to hear the usher calling her name again. Surely he was wrong! "No, please follow me back into court and remember you are still under oath." Miss Johnson entered the witnesses' door from the hallway and immediately stepped up into the back of the witness box. The usher closed the little door behind her.

Mr Weightman was on his feet explaining that he had one more question to put to her:

"The child when in the lane had something in her hand which witness believed to be a piece of ribbon or (pink) paper." (With Miss Johnson's poor eye sight could this have actually been the hem of a sack that Eleanor may have found in the bottom of the cart and was wafting about only to be snatched from her and used in anger round her neck or was it just a strip of wallpaper?) It is not clear why Mr Weightman wanted this piece of evidence in the public domain. How was this to fit in with his scheme for Gough's defence?

WITNESS 7 SARAH CANTRELL

It was back to Mr Etherington Smith who called the next witness. Young Mrs Cantrell recounted that she was passing the stationary handcart about 11.30 on her way to Chesterfield. She had noticed one of the two wheels was in a rut. She, unlike John Cook stated that as well as the paper toys the cart was quite full. "I was as close to the cart as I am to this desk, (witness box)." She then dealt a blow to the defence. Rather than being melodramatic as on a previous occasion she merely said *"It appeared as if there was something very bulky inside in a lump."* "Lump?!" Where did that emotive word spring from? Mrs Cantrell never used that word before! She continued, elaborating on her original statements, Gough *"was in the front of the cart between the shafts and he was engaged placing what appeared to be like a sack or rags on the cart top."* When the young woman had passed by she did turn round to see Gough trying to move the cart *"with great difficulty"* in the direction of Brimington and alone.

Mr Weightman now had to deal with this "lump" in the cart.

"What he was placing over the cart was not rags such as he would gather, but a piece of old cloth, or bag."

WITNESS 8   ERNEST HENRY WINDLE

Mr Chandos Leigh was to question young Ernest. His father had given him a look of encouragement before he entered the crowded courtroom. So many people! Luckily for the witnesses, the witness box itself was right by the door to the court as they entered and the counsel that was to question them should already be on his feet. There was no time to look around. Look at prosecution, direct your answers to the judge on the right, if you can remember and make sure the jury can hear you. Keep focussed. The ten year old, (half-) brother to Eleanor recounted his seeing Gough on the turnpike road about 11.45 (on the previous two occasions he had said noon) quite close to his own home, Almond Place. He first saw Gough down the hill near the cemetery coming up towards him en route for Brimington. He was alone. When Gough passed Ernest the boy remarked it was "at a quick pace".

Mr Weightman had only one question: *"Prisoner was wheeling the cart up hill."*

WITNESS 9   ELIZABETH NEALE

Back to Mr Etherington Smith to question 21 year old Mrs Neale. She lived with her collier husband, Jacob and two year old daughter at the top of Cottrell Lane which led from Brimington village to the Common.

"She was going to Brimington village. About half-past twelve o'clock." (The Derbyshire Courier reports the time as 12 o' clock but in her original depositions before the Coroner and the Magistrate she had said a quarter past twelve!) She saw Gough coming in the other direction, going towards the Miners' Arms and the Common with his handcart containing paper toys. She was with her little daughter and thought to get her a parasol. Mrs Neale went back into her own house to fetch some rags in order to exchange them for the parasol "with a pink ribbon on it". She had to call Gough to stop. She then was *"close to the cart, which had in it a hamper containing paper toys. In the middle of the cart there was a very small bundle wrapped in black, and at another side of the cart was a small tin which she believed contained spice. The cart also appeared to be three parts full of something*

which she could not distinguish but which was covered over with two onion bags. She could not see the bare bottom of the cart. She remarked to prisoner "You have a many flags and parasols this morning, and you have not many rags."

He replied "No, I have not come far yet you know." Gough then took up his horn as if to blow it (to get the attention of potential customers) but no sound came out. They each then went their separate ways and later met again going in the opposite direction- Mrs Neale back to her house and Gough on his way to Brimington village. Gough, on the return trip, had taken off his coat and it was thrown over the top of the cart. This was around half past one.

Cross examining Mr Weightman was interested in the "black bundle": *"The black bundle in the cart was about the size of a gentleman's hat."*

"She knew the prisoner by sight, he had often come to Brimington before."

"On previous occasions he had blown his horn, but that day it would not sound."

"Prisoner did not call out as he went along the road."

"She talked to him for about five minutes."

"He had many toys, and very nice they looked."

Following on from Mr Weightman's cross examination Mr Chandos Leigh re-examined:

"The black bundle was not covered up (with the onion bags) *but what was under the bags she could not see."*

WITNESS 10   WALTER DAVIDSON

Mr Etherington Smith was also to question 13 year old Walter Davidson. The pattern of the prosecution each taking a witness in turn had just changed. Walter encountered Gough near the Miners' Arms about twelve o'clock coming from the direction of Brimington village. He wanted two windmills. Gough gave him one that was broken but young Walter was not having any of that and eventually got two good ones. *"The cart was standing still and* Walter *went to within two or three inches of it. Prisoner said he would not have him so near the cart. There were some bags in the cart which appeared to be full and there were also a number of rags in it. The cart seemed to be very full inside but what it contained* Walter *could not say. Prisoner had a dark jacket on at the time, but at a later period when prisoner was returning from Steele's Houses, towards Ringwood, he had his jacket off and it was thrown across the cart. When prisoner came up the first time he went into the passage of the Miners' Arms, but did not stay there long."*

Mr Weightman continued the questioning about the Miners' Arms:

"He stayed in the Miners' Arms for perhaps five minutes, leaving his cart standing outside in the road."

"There were about 20 children near the Miners' Arms when prisoner passed, and he was stood still with his cart when he sold witness (Walter) *the windmills."*

His Lordship wanted a little more clarity regarding the location of the handcart whilst Gough was in the public house:

"When prisoner was in the Miners' Arms the cart stood in the road near to and opposite the door leading into the Miners' Arms."

Walter's evidence over, it was now one thirty. His Lordship, obviously hungry, decided to adjourn for half an hour for luncheon. The court rose and the judge and his two companions exited by the door to his left. The jury went out by a door behind the judges' bench-twin to the judge's own door. Whilst Alfred was escorted back, down the staircase immediately behind his seat, to the cells, the counsel lingered in the court. How was the trial going so far? Who was being called to the witness box next? Would all the witnesses be dealt with today? Let's eat before the court reassembles! The majority of those who had seats in the assembled crowd refrained from leaving the room for fear that they would lose their places and so stayed put and hungry.

Two o'clock and the crowded court was ready to continue with the witnesses. Alfred ascended the stairs and took his seat on the plain bench. The judge seated himself on a chair behind which was a narrow wooden "screen" and at the top of it, jutting out from it, was heavy elaborate carving; even the royal coat of arms, found in every court ,was worked in wood above his head. A wooden upturned boat shaped canopy was above that. The whole resembled a medieval throne. Well, the court was part of the ancient Great Hall of the castle. If His Lordship cared to look around him he could still see vestiges of that time. Above the wood panelling on the wall to his right above the heads of the jury were two long arched Norman windows inset into the thick stone wall. Some long dead stonemason had carved a narrow column to either side of each window and half way down the courtroom on this same wall opposite the dock and Alfred Gough was a narrow stone arched doorway again decorated with a carved pillar to either side of the door though slightly more substantial than the window columns. If Mr Justice Mathew leaned forward in his seat he could see the fourteenth century roof trusses and thick cross beams that travelled from somewhere behind his chair towards the front of the building but that would be digressing. The next witnesses were to be called and their evidence probably dealt with quickly

22. Photograph of Interior of courtroom taken from the long gallery. The dock is just out of view at the bottom centre of the photo. Courtesy of the Record Office for Leicestershire, Leicester and Rutland.

WITNESS 11   SARAH ANN THORLEY

Mrs Thorley saw Gough pass the Ringwood Hall lodge on his way down to Barrow Hill.

WITNESS 12   ELIZABETH HARDWICK

Miss Hardwick, questioned by Mr Chandos Leigh QC, stated she passed Gough on the road near to Hoole's plantation (where Eleanor's body was to be found the next day) about a quarter to two and the cart "appeared to be very full".

WITNESS 13   JAMES CROPPER

Mr Etherington Smith questioned the blacksmith, James Cropper who saw a parked handcart containing paper toys against the rails at the side of Hoole's plantation. *"It was about three yards from the hedge"*?

WITNESS 14   WILLIAM SORRELL

The young teenaged William was the telegraph clerk. He saw Alfred Gough pushing his handcart under the railway bridge towards Barrow Hill from his vantage point in the railway box where he was working above the road. Mr Chandos Leigh was the one questioning him. He had seen Gough at three and then at quarter to five when he was returning from Barrow Hill, allegedly.

Mr Weightman decided to cross examine this witness. He was obviously interested in whether there was a different route to get to Barrow Hill from Brimington?

"A person could get to Brimington without going up the private road, but he would have to go round by Troughbrook."

(That was like continuing along the main turnpike road going away from Brimington and heading in the direction of Staveley for about a mile before turning left down the Troughbrook Road that would eventually lead to the works and Barrow Hill beyond. By going down the private works road one effectively cut off the corner of this first route saving the workers' time. It was a short cut.)

"*He*(William) *did not notice what the man had in his cart as he was going, but there were some rags in the cart when he returned.*"

These last four witnesses would have been very quick to deal with. The next witness would take more time.

WITNESS 15 CHARLES ABNEY HASTINGS BROWN

The toll-bar keeper was to be examined by Mr Etherington Smith. Both of the local Derbyshire newspapers retell this witness' account exactly. He told how he had seen Gough that Saturday morning *"a little before ten o'clock"* whilst working on the turnpike road near Lockoford Lane. They had exchanged "Good mornings" and Gough then carried on along the road to Brimington. Brown next saw Gough, having come from the direction of Ringwood, about six o'clock in the evening at the toll house where he lived. It so happened that Eleanor's father also came up to the toll house at this time in search of his daughter and conversed with Gough.

346

23. Sketch of Charles Abney Hastings Brown, mistakenly described as "Henry" in the Illustrated Police News 3rd September 1881

"What (was) the little girl like who had gone up the Brimington road that morning in his company. Prisoner replied that he did not know, so many children followed him, but afterwards he stated that a little girl went up the hill with him from the old machine house to the little cottages on that side of the cemetery (meaning Almond Terrace).

Gough declared that the little girl wanted a parasol and he had told her to fetch some rags and then she should have one.

She left him and once other children gathered around him he saw nothing more of the little girl. Brown said after that conversation Mr Windle went away followed soon after by Gough.

The third part of Brown's testimony was regarding the finding of Eleanor on the Sunday.

"Noticing some wheel marks near the hedge at Hoole's plantation, he got over the rails into the plantation. He went up a path between two spoil banks, and up this path found a bag something like an onion bag. The bag produced (as an exhibit) *was the one, and it was lying on the ground under a tree. He rolled the bag up and put it in his pocket, and then, going down the other side of one of the spoil banks, he saw the child's body lying, it being about 28(25) yards from where he found the bag. The child was lying on its back, with its face inclining to the left hand. A hat lay about half-a-yard from the body. It was a rush or Zulu hat. He noticed something round the neck of the child, which was of a material similar to that of the bag. He put the sack over the body, put the hat over the child's eyes, and having called a man named Tull(e)y to look at the body, he proceeded to inform a policeman.* The "Derby and Chesterfield Reporter" stated Brown covered the body "as the flies were getting at the child's eyes"! *Within five yards of the railing he discovered, on returning, the piece of coloured wall-paper,* (shown as an exhibit) *which he afterwards gave to Supt. Carline. He took P.C.*

Twigg back to the place where he found the body, and showed it him in the same condition as he himself had found it."

It was now the turn of Mr Weightman to cross examine. First regarding the wallpaper found on the scene.

"The piece of wall-paper was similar to what the prisoner would use for the manufacture of his windmills and parasols."

"The largest of the spoil banks would be from 15ft. to 20ft. high, and the other one was under 10ft. high." Eleanor's body was found on the smaller one.

If this was a fictional story, Brown had the opportunity, at his toll-house, to remove from Gough's handcart the "sack" and the wallpaper in order to plant them on the waste ground the following day and thus incriminate Gough. He alone found the body, he alone found the evidence and he had some connection with Gough in that Alfred had served with the 17th Foot Regiment as did Brown's son. Was there a motive there to pin the murder on Gough? Did Brown have the opportunity to abduct Eleanor? He was on the turnpike road at the same time. But what would his motive have been? Could it have just been opportunistic? Mr Weightman's job was not to pin the murder on anybody else. He just had to sow doubt in the minds of the jury regarding his own client. Not even Gough seemed to think that Brown was blackening his name unlike Mansfield Tom!

WITNESS 16   P.C. TWIGG

The Derbyshire constabulary officer was questioned next by Mr Chandos Leigh. It was this policeman that Brown stopped on Sunday afternoon to show his discovery of the body of Eleanor Windle. At this point "the sacking" was produced in court as an exhibit by the prosecution. This sacking was found *"tied twice round the neck of the child very tightly, and appeared to have been drawn tight by a man's hand.* The "Derby and Chesterfield Reporter" described this in more graphic terms "It was twisted twice round the neck with a slip knot, and there was a long piece loose which it seemed had been pulled tight, and thus made the sacking sink deeply into the flesh".(This caused another sensation in court.) *Two or three yards from the body was the sack."* Again produced in court as an exhibit. (If Brown's evidence was correct this sack was actually over the body when PC Twigg arrived.)

"He assisted to put the body in a cart and it was removed to Mr Windle's house. The body of the child could not be seen from the private road but the bag could have been seen from the road." This is the first time that this was mentioned yet PC Twigg could not have seen the sack in situ as Brown had picked it up earlier. It could only be Brown saying that the sack would have been seen from the road. Yet he did not say that he did see it. Brown claims it was the wheel marks by the fence that caught his eye.

WITNESS 17 WILLIAM WINDLE

It was now the turn of Eleanor's father to go into the witness box. Superintendent Carline knew the list order of the witnesses. It was more or less identical to when the case was heard at the Inquest and Magistrates' in Chesterfield. He gave William an encouraging smile. This part of the ordeal would soon be over for the Windles but the torment of Eleanor's death never seemed to leave them for long.

Mr Etherington Smith patiently waited for the witness to be sworn in and then commenced the questioning. As the Derbyshire newspapers had reported in detail the evidence of all the witnesses in August they saw no need to go into the same amount of detail again. William initially stated where he worked and his home address. He said that Eleanor, his daughter, had been six years and three months old and was "a well grown child". "A well formed child" noted the judge! *"They missed the child on August 20th, and his son and others searched for her but without success."* William then retold the conversation he had had with Gough at Mr Brown's toll house. On Gough explaining to William Windle that there had been so many children he could not say whether he saw Eleanor or not or what happened to her William replied *"that the prisoner was alone with the girl, and could not have walked with her 10 or 15 minutes without knowing what she was"*! The judge noted that Mr Windle continued to say "because she would come chatting along with you"! Asking Gough again where he had left Eleanor he replied *"At the top of the hill"* which was where Almond Place was *"If you brought her to the top of the hill, and if she turned back to purchase one of your articles, where is she? The first thing she would have done would have been to have come home either for rags or for money to purchase one."* William then *detailed the conversation that he had with the prisoner in the presence of P.C. Wright* (outside The Three Horseshoes pub) *when prisoner repeated his statement about seeing the child and expressed his sorrow at her loss."*

"On the following day witness (William) *said he was shown the dead body of his child."* This was not quite true. On the Sunday when Eleanor's body was brought home William collapsed in a dead faint perhaps because he did catch a glimpse of her. However he told the coroner, Mr Busby, that he had not seen the body until the day of the post mortem and Inquest which was the Monday.

Mr Weightman asked which of the two conversations with Gough did the prisoner express some concern?

"On the second occasion the prisoner expressed a hope to witness that the child would soon be found."

WITNESS 18 PC WRIGHT

PC Wright was another of Superintendent Carline's officers to be examined by Mr Chandos Leigh QC.
"He likewise gave the substance of the conversation which took place between the prisoner, himself (Wright) and Mr Windle on the evening of August 20th. At the close of the conversation prisoner went away in the direction of Chesterfield. On the same evening witness (P.c. Wright) *together with Mr Windle examined Johnson's lane, and about twenty-five yards from the bottom of the lane on the right hand side going up he found a gap large enough for a man to go through. The hedge was not broken through entirely. The grass on the lane side, close to the gap, was*

much flattened and presented an appearance as if someone had been laid there, there being also a hollow near the hole. Ten yards higher up the lane on the same side he found a second gap and still higher up a third one through which any full grown man could have got with ease. There were also in the lane side two other places where the grass had been flattened."

Mr Weightman then asked the police constable about the gaps in the hedge:- *"The first gap looked as if it had been recently made, the others were apparently of long standing."*

WITNESS 19 THOMAS HOLMES, ALIAS "MANSFIELD TOM"

The calling of Thomas Holmes stirred Alfred. He was to be "deeply interested" in this man's testimony. Mr Etherington Smith was on his feet for the examination of "Mansfield Tom". Tom was a drover at Chesterfield and he now claimed to have known Gough for five or six months. (An increase of a month since the magistrates' hearing.) No doubt Gough was vehemently shaking his head at this. If not in fact then at least internally! The drover claimed that he met Gough on the turnpike road "below Brimington Cemetery" that Saturday evening. He, on his way to Brimington and Gough going towards Chesterfield.

"Prisoner said "Mansfield, we have met many a time on this road, but we shall never meet again." Witness (Mansfield Tom) *asked him what he had done wrong, and he said, "I have done that wrong I shall never be happy again." Witness again asked him what he had done*

wrong, but prisoner said he would tell him when they met again. That was all that took place betwixt them, and it was then about six o'clock."

Mr Weightman had a number of questions to ask this witness of which again it is only the replies that are recorded:

"Prisoner did not stand still speaking to him, but spoke as he was passing."

"He had flags and parasols in his barrow."

"Witness did not know anything about the child being missed until he got back to Chesterfield." (Was this really true? Did he not see any activity of people looking for Eleanor by this time? Or anyone ask him to keep a look out for the girl on his journey? It is just a thought.)

"He mentioned his conversation with the prisoner to several people, and on being taken to the police station related it there." (Was this Mansfield Tom's undoing, bragging about a supposed conversation with an assumed murderer? He possibly thought people would buy him a drink on the strength of it. Little did he know feelings were running high, having been out of the area for some days, and that people would take him so seriously and march him off to the police station with his supposed information. Once it had become official how was he to back out of the story?!)

"The latter occasion would be nearly a week afterwards."

"He gave evidence at the adjourned inquest and also before the magistrates."

WITNESS 20   THOMAS NEWBERRY

For some reason The Derbyshire Times reports Thomas Newberry as witness 24! It is The Derbyshire Courier that claims he is next in the witness box. This witness is the illiterate marine dealer from Brampton where Alfred went to sell his rags and bones. "I put the rags I bought of him, in a bag. I held the bag while he put them in." Thomas had had "several dealings with the prisoner." He sorted Gough's rags on the Monday and some he handed over to Superintendent Carline. However, Sergeant Eyre had removed Gough's cart from Newberry's warehouse on the Sunday. "No one interfered with it."

Mr Weightman's cross examination related to the weight of the rags Gough brought in that night:-

"He (Thomas Newberry) *bought five stones of rags and bones from the prisoner on the Saturday, and gave him 3s* (shillings) *for them."*

WITNESS 21 ANN ELIZABETH CLARKE

Anne Clarke was the "deputy" at Spowages' Beehive Lodging–house in Chesterfield. She saw Gough when he came down to the kitchen on the Sunday between 12.30 and 1 o'clock. He asked her if any flags had been left for him and she replied in the affirmative "if he was an old pensioner". He replied that he was. Clarke then told him five policemen were looking for him. Gough asked after the missing child but Clarke knew nothing about that subject. She said the last she saw of him was going across the road to The Buck Inn. Not quite what was said before in Chesterfield but it has to be remembered the local press may not be reporting absolutely everything as that had been done already over two months ago.

WITNESS 22 POLICE- SERGEANT EYRE

Mr Etherington Smith examined this witness. The sergeant related that he had collected the handcart from Thomas Newberry. The cart "in which he found some pieces of wall paper corresponding with the piece already produced" (in evidence as an exhibit probably during Charles Abney Hastings Brown's testimony.)

WITNESS 23 SUPERINTENDENT ELIJAH CARLINE

Elijah at long last was called to the witness box. It was late in the afternoon and the witnesses were beginning to tire of all the waiting around. Elijah did not like to be hanging around either but courts were like that and there was nothing that could be done except wait. Alfred could have pleaded guilty and then there would not have been a trial but that was too much to hope for! Mr Chandos Leigh was to examine the superintendent.

"He detailed the steps that he took in apprehending the prisoner on a charge of wilfully murdering Eleanor Windle, when the prisoner replied that he knew nothing about the girl, though afterwards he stated that a child had walked up the Brimington-road with him as far as Almond Terrace. The Superintendent also stated that he compared the piece of wall paper which he received from the witness Brown with two pieces of wall paper found in the prisoner's handcart, and found that the pieces of paper were of the

same pattern and had originally formed one piece."

WITNESS 24 DR W A WALKER

Dr Walker the 35 year old general practitioner from Chesterfield who performed the autopsy on Eleanor was the very last witness. No doubt he would have been anxious to be called on if he had been in Leicester since early Tuesday morning and it was now late Wednesday afternoon. He had patients to attend to back in Chesterfield although he knew his assistant, Joshua, would be quite capable of dealing with matters. Still he would like to get back as soon as was possible.

It is not reported in the Derbyshire newspapers here but when the doctor gave his evidence in Chesterfield both at the Inquest and at the Magistrates' Court the women and children were asked to leave the room. His testimony being of a delicate nature. It is to be wondered if His Lordship did the same in Leicester.

Mr Etherington Smith dealt with the medical matters. The doctor described the state of the body after it had been brought home on the Sunday afternoon- *"the deep impression which he found round the neck of the child, and which he believed had been caused by a cord being tied tightly round the child's neck. The wet state of the child's clothing and the injury to the private parts were then detailed,"* His Lordship wrote "considerable injury of private parts", "There was a lacerated wound of vagina. I could see it. The injury began at the opening of the vagina, and continued up the canal."

The National Archives holds the original witness depositions from both the magistates' and the coroner's courts (ASSI 13/12) which means Dr Walker's report can be read in full. The sensitive material the papers dared not publish can now be seen. Nothing is omitted.

"I examined the drawers and found them marked with a recent blood-stain about 2" square at the part that would fit against the private parts. I examined her genital organs, and found the parts which should be naturally opposed and in contact presenting a circular opening into which one could see for the distance of an inch- They did not show any signs of external bruises, nor were there any marks or bruises on the thighs or lower part of the belly- There were two small scratches on the left buttock quite superficial- they were evidently quite recent and must have occurred shortly before death."

"And continuing Dr. Walker alluded to the post mortem examination of the deceased,"
"The uterus was in a natural position and normal- I again examined the genital organs- I found no actual tearing of the skin surface but the internal surface of the vagina was abraided (lacerated) and torn - very severely. The canal admitted my first finger without the least difficulty- There were no signs of the hymen- which ought to have existed- The opening must have been caused by some very violent and unnatural means- In my opinion it has been occasioned by the insertion of the finger of a very strong man, or the point of a walking stick- It has not been occasioned in the first instance by a man's penis, but it may have been partially inserted afterwards. I cannot state positively whether it has or not" but "the injuries to the vagina were inflicted before death." *"the cause of death being in his opinion*

asphyxia, or strangulation due to restriction of the neck. The marks might have been caused by a piece of lining or hemming such as the one produced (as an exhibit).

Mr Weightman's cross examination was referring to Eleanor's weight and height:-

"He believed that the deceased child would weigh somewhere about five stones. He could not tell the length of the child's body."

When Dr Walker's evidence is seen in its entirety it is no wonder that William Windle wanted to get hold of his daughter's alleged killer at the line-up back in August. The poor child was only six! Did she laugh inappropriately? Did she think it was an exciting game being chased by Miss Johnson? Did Eleanor notice someone was not laughing? Did someone lose all control?

WITNESS 16 PC TWIGG

The prosecution obviously felt they needed to close a loophole. Dr. Walker had not seen the ligature around Eleanor's neck but PC Twigg had. The usher came out into the corridor looking for the policeman stood with his colleagues. Twigg was surprised to be recalled "to prove that the ligature ….was removed in his presence by Dr. Bradley" but if it helped to strengthen the case... (Dr. Bradley was the young Irish doctor who lived in Brimington and had been the first medical man to arrive at the Windles' home that Sunday afternoon.)

Throughout the proceedings it was reported that there were several members of the "fairer and gentler sex" who listened to the horrible details of the witnesses with as much interest as their male counterparts and "without scarcely any of those unseemly demonstrations by on-lookers and listeners which sometimes disgrace courts of justice." Only once was there a call to order and a rebuking look from the judge when considerable laughter was caused by a flippant remark from Miss Johnson in replying to one of Mr Weightman's questions." Once or twice sensations of horror ran through the audience" but generally speaking the silence and stillness was almost oppressive. Alfred sat "comparatively calmly and collected" throughout as well. This time paying attention to every word uttered!

The Honourable Chandos Leigh, still on his feet, had reached the end of his prosecution case. *"That will be my case your Lordship."*

His Lordship glancing at the time stated: *"I do not propose to sit much longer."*

Obviously Mr Chandos Leigh was a persuasive man. He suggested that he should now sum up the evidence to the jury of all that had been said by the witnesses. (In effect the modern day closing speech but before the defence has put forward its case!) Sir James agreed to this, misguidedly. Perhaps he thought prosecution would be quick as he had already intimated he did not want to sit late. However, once Mr Chandos Leigh was on his feet there was no stopping him!

"In opening the case (I) *challenged* (myself) *to prove that the prisoner at the bar was the man who had perpetrated not only the outrage on, but the murder of, the poor child, and it would be for* (you) *the jury to say whether, after having heard over twenty*

witnesses whom (I) have called, (you) were not satisfied that the result of the evidence had done that. Although the case was what was called one of a circumstantial kind, (I think I have) link by link established a chain of evidence which in (your) judgement would prove irresistible. It might be said that (my) story was an extraordinary one, and that throughout the proceedings there was conduct on the part of the prisoner which would militate against the idea of his being a guilty man, and that his whole demeanour from the time he met with the children to the time that he passed Hoole's Plantation was not the demeanour, was not the conduct, of a guilty man. (I have) in a long experience at the criminal bar, often heard that argument used, and therefore (I think) it right to call (your) attention to certain reasons which might induce (you) to carefully consider the matter.

Having dwelt for some time upon various points to show that a belief in the prisoner's innocence ought not to be held simply on the grounds of his demeanour during the day. (I ask you) the jurors to approach the case on the evidence, and on the evidence only. The first question which presented itself to (my) mind was how much of the case was uncontested or not. From the cross-examination of (my) learned friend it seemed there were several points the latter did not pretend to contest.

First of all, could it be pretended that the child was not murdered; that it was not brutally outraged before being murdered? Could it be contended for one single moment that the prisoner was not coming along the road from Lockoford towards Brimington on that morning?

Could it be ever pretended that the prisoner was not accompanied by the little girl for something like 80 yards before they got to Johnson's Lane? And ask (yourselves) *if it could be doubted for one single moment that the prisoner was first at the corner of the lane seen by one witness, secondly, he was seen up the lane by two witnesses, and on both those occasions seen in company with the little girl in a Zulu hat and light pinafore?"*

Proceeding, the learned counsel, Mr Chandos Leigh QC, *sketched in an able and concise manner the evidence that he had laid before the jurors, strongly upholding the theory which he had advanced in his opening statement, that the murder was committed during the period that the prisoner's cart remained at the bottom of Johnson's Lane (for three quarters of an hour.)*

Mr Weightman had suggested in cross-examination that the girl followed Gough of her own accord. "The poor child, as the father had said, was of a confiding temperament, of course she had no thought of evil, and of course she followed him of her own accord."

"It might be said that the evidence of Harriott Johnson was of an extremely improbable character. Strange might be the story that she told but (I think) her evidence was given in a manner which carried with it the impress of truth. And when asked by (my) friend (Mr Weightman) how it was that she did not tell the whole of the circumstances of the affair to the mother, Miss Johnson's answer was that of a woman of feeling and of consideration; she replied "I did tell the mother all I could, I kept something back, and made my formal complaint to the police." Was that unnatural? (I) or (you), might have done different, but a person in her position and of her age, naturally had a feeling and a sense of delicacy, and did not wish to wound the mother's feelings, though they must have been cruelly wounded afterwards, not only by the death of the child, but by the disgrace which succeeded it."

Continuing, Chandos Leigh argued that the testimony of Miss Johnson was strongly corroborated by that of Cook. The Derbyshire Courier states it was the doctor's evidence! "It might be asked what personal motive Gough had for strangling the child? Surely Miss Johnson's evidence supplied the motive. When a man, within 30 or 40 yards of a public highway, frequented by a lot of passers-by, and on Chesterfield market day committed the disgraceful villainy of exposing himself to a little child in the name of all that was holy, in the name of all that was just, in the name of all that was right could (you) not think and believe that - on the child uttering those cries which she possibly would do, nay, certainly would do on account of the injuries inflicted upon her by the ruffian - he in a single moment should have used the running noose which it was perfectly clear had been used, and taken away the life of his victim."

Continuing the evidence step by step, and dwelling on the finding of the bag, and the piece of wall paper near the body in Hoole's Plantation, Mr Leigh asked if it could be pretended that another person murdered the child and left it in Hoole's Plantation? If such an idea was consistent with their (the jury's) ideas of common sense for God's sake let them adopt it, but if not, it would be their duty to act on the belief that the prisoner and no other person committed the crime. Going to the evidence of Mansfield Tom, Mr Leigh asked if Mansfield Tom could have invented the statement of prisoner, that he had done something wrong, and would never be happy again? Was that an invention of his brain, or was it really said? It would be for them (the jurors) to consider. But did the case stop there? When challenged as to whether he had seen the child the prisoner said that a great many children followed him up the hill. But could that be? There was all the evidence against it. Prisoner said he left the child at her own home, but did he do so? The witness Cantrell saw the prisoner pass by without the child. The latter's own brother, Ernest Windle, was seated near to his father's home and saw prisoner pass by with the cart, but without the child. How could the prisoner say that?

"(I do) not think (I) need detain (you, the jury) any longer. (I think) that in endeavouring to discharge the duty cast upon (me I am) entitled to say (I have) made out the case for the prosecution. (I have) endeavoured to do so apart from any attempt to rouse (your) sympathies or feelings in anyway against the prisoner and (have) merely discharged the duty devolving upon (me) as representing the Crown. But (I can) not help seeing before (me) a picture of a respectable man like Mr Windle, who (has) undoubtedly brought up his children respectably and well, and an affectionate mother and her children ruined, as it were, and disgraced, and the little one of the flock, in deed and in truth, brutally outraged and brutally murdered. There (is) no contest about that, the question for (you is) whether (I have) satisfied (you) that the prisoner Gough was the perpetrator of that offence, of that outrage, and of that murder.

With that devastating finale ringing in the ears of the jury the Honourable Chandos Leigh QC resumed his seat. The hour seemed late,-4.30- it was certainly getting dark outside. Sir James would have liked to have finished the trial that day but he could see that everyone's powers of concentration had been stretched to the limit. There was nothing for it but to adjourn the trial and continue at ten thirty the next day. It would then be the turn of Mr Weightman for the defence. He had already indicated that there would be no witnesses for Gough but even so it was only fair that a fresh start should be made in the morning. That meant two jury bailiffs were needed to be sworn out in order to keep the jury somewhere safe and together. This was usually a room in a court building but as Leicester Castle was not that large the bailiffs may have decided to take the jury to a hotel for the night. Indeed The Leicester Chronicle states the jury stayed at The Bull's Head Hotel until court reassembled the next day. The Derby and Chesterfield Reporter stated that "every necessary arrangement (was) made, for their comfort, but at the same time (measures were taken) to prevent their being communicated or tampered with."

For Superintendent Carline it meant another evening in lodgings for himself and the witnesses. Alfred meantime was delivered back to Leicester prison for one more night.

CHAPTER FIFTEEN

THURSDAY 3rd NOVEMBER 1881

GOUGH'S TRIAL CONTINUES

The Derbyshire Times reported that *"long before the time fixed for the opening of the courts its precincts were besieged by a multitude of people desirous of obtaining admission."* Foremost amongst them were several ladies *"and no sooner were the doors thrown open"* at ten o'clock *"than every available space was occupied, and the occupants remained steadfastly at their post until the conclusion of the case, until the prisoner left the dock."* Indeed, "owing to the limited dimensions of the room" a large number of persons were unable to secure admission at all though apparently "many of the inhabitants of Brimington and the neighbourhood" were successful. That is, according to the Sheffield and Rotherham Independent!

At 10.20 by the hands of the court clock Gough was being brought up from the cells and Alfred quickly took his seat alongside a jailer. The jury door was opened and the jurors took their seats in the jury box. The capacity of which is such "that the gentlemen in whose decision rests the fate of the unfortunate persons placed upon their trial must, indeed, wish that the architect had treated them more liberally when making provision for them- I was going to say "when making provision for their comfort," but refrain from using that phrase, for the architect surely never thought of such a thing"! So states the unhappy journalist from the Derby and Chesterfield Reporter! The Petty jury seated, the gentlemen answered to their names and now all was ready for His Honour's entrance.

Just before ten thirty the chubby faced Sir James Mathew, under hooded eyelids, was looking at himself in the mirror. Readjusting his gown he had no thought to Gough's fate. That was in the hands of the jury. He was glancing at his curly thinning hair sleekly parted over to the right and his bushy, wispy sideburns that rested on his collar in preparation to him putting on the shoulder length wig of a high court judge. In disguise he became someone else! How many people would recognise him in the street without his trappings of office? Very few he thought. A knock and his door was opened by the clerk. His Lordship was now ready.

As he entered the crowded court all rose to their feet. Once His Lordship was settled all eyes were on Mr Weightman.

There would be no witnesses for Gough it would just be Mr Weightman putting the case for the defence to the jury. Gough watched his counsel closely. The press thought he had a "depressed and unsettled appearance" but what did they know?

"In a case like this it (is) *impossible for* (me) *to disguise from* (you, the jury) *the immense responsibility which* (I feel) *resting upon* (my) *shoulders, responsibility,* (I know) *lightened in this respect, by the careful attention* (you have) *given on the previous day to the evidence which had been called before* (you), *and also by the temperate - the most temperate-language of* (my) *learned friend Mr Chandos Leigh in his opening speech, and in his summing up of the evidence; but still a responsibility which* (I am) *bound to feel, because of the issues that lay*

between the prisoner and the Crown- issues which, if (you find) adverse to the prisoner, could result only in one way, namely, in that sentence which the law (is) bound to pass upon him if he was guilty of the crime laid to his charge. There (is) no pity for him; there (is) not one single atom of palliation in it. It was an absolutely wicked murder- murder of the foulest degree- of the cruelest kind -without a single thing, as (I) said, to be put before (you) in extenuation; but when (you look) at it in that light (does) it not put before (you) the importance of caution, inasmuch as it was a foul crime, inasmuch as the circumstances in the case were so gross-(I) must say almost beyond what the imagination could conceive. Therefore, it behove(s you) to approach the consideration of the case with the greatest caution, to look at the facts if possible most dispassionately and most carefully, and to take care in investigating all the circumstances between the prisoner and the Crown before (you) deliver the verdict which (you) should ultimately deliver. (You) must give (your) verdict according to legal evidence proved before (you); take care that, because of the foulness of the crime (you do) not make the prisoner a victim, a sacrifice to outraged morality. (My) learned friend in his address at the beginning of the case said there were many things which the prisoner would hardly be supposed to dispute. (I am) with (my) friend there; there were many things which the prisoner confessed, and which for him, appearing as his advocate, to dispute would be idle. There was no doubt that the prisoner was on the Brimington road on the morning in question. (It was also true that he met the children, and was overtaken by Eleanor Windle before he came to Johnson's lane. This was proved by a very respectable witness, the carrier, Insley, who saw them before him at the bottom of that lane. Now, Johnson's lane, as far as Oak House, could be plainly seen from the roadway; and the time was eleven o'clock in the morning. It was in the morning-a time when numbers of people were passing and repassing between Staveley and Chesterfield. It was Chesterfield market day, and one of the witnesses said that during the time he sat at the bottom of Johnson's lane scores of people passed. Now, every one of these people could see the whole of Johnson's lane. The theory of the prosecution (is) -as (my) learned friend ha(s) boldly stated - that the murder was committed in Johnson's lane, upon one of those flattened pieces of grass which was referred to by one of the witnesses. The prosecution went further, and alleged that the murder was committed during the three quarters of an hour spent by Cooke at the bottom of the lane. Now, was that theory borne out by the evidence, or was there not some other solution as to what took place? There were four witnesses who spoke to the time the prisoner was at Johnson's lane. First of all (you) had the evidence of Turner, who saw the man standing with the little girl gathering sticks about sixteen yards up the lane. Then (you) had Miss Johnson, who spoke of seeing the prisoner three times in the lane; and she was followed by Cooke, who did not see the prisoner at all, but saw his cart; and lastly came Sarah Cantrill, who passed as the prisoner was starting from the bottom of the lane in the direction of Brimington. Now it was very clear that there was no original intention in the mind of the prisoner to commit the deed, supposing him to have done so. There was no enticing on the part of the prisoner, but the little girl followed him of her own accord. Then the question (is), when did the intention enter his mind? Was it as they were going along? There were four gateways before they got to Johnson's lane, and it should be borne in mind that the lane was a frequented place, there being a house at the top of it. There were shady hedges on each side, but its whole length could be seen from the roadway. As (I have) said, there were four gateways for the prisoner to pass before arriving at the bottom of the lane, and one of these gateways led to a disused colliery shaft. Now if the man's mind had wickedness in it, instead of going up the open lane - open to the view of everyone, to the chance detection of anyone who might happen to go up the lane - he would have taken the little one through the gateway into the field and disposed of the body at the bottom of the disused shaft, where perhaps she would not have been discovered to this day. According to (my) learned friend, the prisoner selected a spot where he was almost safe - so to speak - to be detected The place was close to the highway, and the time was about 11 o'clock one midsummer morning. It seemed highly improbable that the prisoner committed the offence, because, if he was the man, he must, according to (my) friend's theory, have committed the crime in Johnson's lane. It was very clear when the witness Insley came on the scene that the girl was standing by the cart, and the man had moved a few yards up the lane. The next witness was Turner, who saw the prisoner about sixteen yards up the lane. Miss Johnson came next, and she said he was standing on the embankment before coming into the lane when she first saw him, and having returned from her house she saw him a second time a few yards up the lane. Now that was before Turner saw him, and (I) would ask the jury if Miss Johnson's statement were correct - how was it that Turner did not see the man with his clothes disarranged? Turner did not say there was anything indecent in his conduct. Was Miss Johnson to be believed? She had acknowledged to having defective sight. Perhaps, living alone in Oak House, she was a lady whom a little thing disturbed, and, with a great imagination and a defective sight might tell (you, the jury) what she believed she saw. It was a remarkable thing that, although Miss Johnson swore she saw the prisoner when he had just entered the lane with the little girl - and she acknowledged that the little girl was in front of him - yet Turner, who saw them, never saw indecent behaviour on prisoner's part. (My) learned friend ha(s) talked about establishing the case link by link, and step by step, but when evidence came to be sifted, it was astonishing sometimes how the chain broke, and when it did break it was very difficult to mend it again. (My) learned friend ha(s) opened a great deal about gaps in the hedges and ha(s) taken trouble to prove the gaps in the hedges. Miss Johnson ha(s) not said one word about seeing the man go through a gap in the hedge. (Is) Miss Johnson to be believed? (Is) she correct in what she stated? She told (you) she was on the embankment and saw at least one person pass by, and actually did not call his attention. One would have thought that, after seeing what she said she saw, she would have stopped the man and told him something dreadful was being done. It was a remarkable thing that she had not called the attention of any passer-by. She said she did not see what became of the child. It might be that the man went down the lane and turned *the corner, and it might be that the little girl sped through one of the gaps in the hedge into the grass field.) The prisoner must have gone into the road and what was more he must have seen Cook in the road."*

Mr Weightman paused at this point to explain something of how the law operated in the late nineteenth century. Alfred Gough, the prisoner was in the dock and facts were being sworn against him but he could not himself be sworn in the witness box and give evidence. "His mouth was closed"! This complaint to the jury was a common tactic of defence lawyers. Not that Mr Weightman was complaining! "He did not complain because of that, if the criminal law of the country was that no criminal should give evidence in his own defence be it so." It was actually considered as a protection for defendants in case of self-incrimination. If a prisoner was defended then the unsworn statement, if there was one, was inadmissible.

Mr Weightman asked the jury "to take the prisoner more into their care" because he could not defend himself. Gough "stood there unable to tell them on oath, unable to tell them except through his advocate, what were the true facts of the case. Every witness that could be called had been called by the prosecution. But the prisoner at the bar was a poor man unable even to employ legal advice and except through the courtesy and kindness of his Lordship he would have been without an advocate on his behalf. Therefore if he could have called witnesses and had not done so let them not put it down against him, as a charge against him." Gough had been asked at the Magistrates' if he had any witnesses to call. Witnesses as to fact in that they had seen the event or witnesses who could give Gough an alibi and if he had, they could have been bound over to attend the trial. The trial judge had the power to pay these witnesses' expenses out of public funds but only after the trial. That meant that defence witnesses had to get themselves to trial, which may have involved walking for days to some far off venue, and then have the means to feed and provide lodging for themselves whilst awaiting the trial to be called on. This would be a deterrent for most witnesses and not unnaturally so. As Gough had no witnesses to call Mr Weightman had either to get the prisoner's version out in cross-examination (considered only as a "lawyers' tool") or put Gough's version to the jury as a hypothesis.

This hypothesis was – *"Miss Johnson had lost sight of the man round the corner and that the man had gone away from the corner to collect rags and bones from (farmsteads and other) houses in the vicinity,* (looking at a map of the period it is hard to see where these buildings were!) *that then he came back again at the time that Cooke had gone to gather mushrooms, and that he was putting in the rags he had collected when Mrs Cantrell was passing by. It was a most important fact in the case that the prisoner sold 70lbs.* (pounds) *to Newberry that day. It was preposterous to accept the theory of the prosecution that the murder must have been committed whilst Cooke was sitting on the steps, -committed in open daylight, and within the view of everybody from the road.* (Do you) *mean to say that the injuries inflicted on the child, according to the doctor's evidence, could be inflicted without a shriek on the part* of the victim, without a cry? It was almost idle to suggest it, because (you know) that those injuries that were inflicted upon the child were inflicted by the perpetrator of them before the man had strangled his victim. (You know) that, and yet there was not a sound heard by Miss Johnson, Cooke or the scores of persons passing up the road. Not a witness had been called before (you) who heard a shriek or cry. The cries of a little child of six would be piteous; her shrieks would be heard half a mile off, and yet there was no sound heard. Did that fact assist the theory of the prosecution that the crime must have been committed in Johnson's lane whilst Cooke was sitting there? These (are) most important matters, requiring (your) consideration. There was not a shadow or tittle of evidence that the man's demeanour had at any time told against him. He had been calm and collected from beginning to end, as an innocent man would be, and it was another important thing for (you) to take into consideration. On the part of the prosecution it was said he made haste to dispose of his ghastly burden. That was utterly untrue. The man made haste to dispose of his ghastly burden! Why he paraded his cart up and down the village of Brimington. He had plenty of chance of disposing of his ghastly burden if he had so willed. The suggestion that he made haste was almost idle. No man who ever committed a murder, and carried the victim of his violence about with him, made less haste; no man could have appeared less disturbed in his mind. The last seen of the child was by Miss Johnson, and here it was remarkable that the child, having run after the prisoner, and having no money to purchase a toy, he put his hand into his cart and gave her a bit of wallpaper, torn from a large piece. The finding of this piece of paper did not bring the prisoner one whit nearer the scene, because it was proved that the child had it in her hand in Johnson's lane. But, returning to the statement of the prosecution as to how he hastened to rid himself of the body. What did he do? Why, instead of going straight to Hoole's plantation, as it might be imagined he would have done if he meant to dispose of the body there, he turned down Cotterill-lane, and (quietly) had a conversation with Mrs Neale, which was certainly a most astonishing thing if at that time there lay in his cart the ghastly corpse of the child. Was it credible that with this foul piece of dead flesh in his possession he would have acted in that way? (Was it credible that with that knowledge he wheeled the cart over the clattering stones and through the village..?) Besides, he also went down to the Miners' Arms and Steel's houses, and his conduct there surely was not that of a man anxious to get away or conceal a crime. The case did not *stop with the fact that the prisoner had, by offering a child a broken toy, there done the very thing which was likely to bring a crowd of children around him. He actually went into the Miners' Arms, and left his cart outside unattended at the mercy of the whole troop of children, (who, by clambering about his barrow, might have disclosed the thing he wished to conceal.)* Mr Weightman was doing his best to scorn and ridicule the prosecution. *("There was nothing remarkable in the prisoner taking off his coat on a hot summer's day and throwing it across his cart")! Then with regard to passing Ringwood Lodge, there was nothing remarkable in the prisoner doing that, for it was his nearest way to Barrow Hill and Whittington. The prosecution would have* (you) *believe that in that open road, in view of the window of the lodge, just when two young women had turned their backs upon him, the prisoner lifted the body out of the cart and clambered over the fence to deposit it in the plantation, but* (I) *(Mr Weightman) suggest that the prisoner visited the plantation for another purpose, (the purposes of nature) (and his cart might have been drawn up to the hedge not in order that he might remove the body from it, but in order that it might not be in the way of any passing vehicles) and pointed out as a remarkable fact that when the man Cropper saw the handcart standing by the fence it appeared to be full.* (I) *strongly impress upon* (you) the jury the importance of the fact that the prisoner went on from the plantation about his business, and actually returned in the evening through the village of Brimington. (Let me point out) how much more effectually the prisoner, if he was the murderer, could have disposed of the body in the canal and other places in the neighbourhood. It was true that the child was found in the plantation, but there was no evidence to show that the body was put there on Saturday afternoon. The coincidence was certainly unfortunate, but it was not conclusive. As to the statement made about a sack bag, (I am) astonished that during the whole of the case, when the witnesses came up and spoke of it, they were never asked whether the bag was like the one produced and found in the plantation. It had never been shown that the bag produced was like that seen in the possession of Gough and (I) might fairly ask this to be considered to the advantage of the prisoner. (I) contend that the conduct of the prisoner in returning through Brimington, and in conversing with the child's father in the manner he did, was not such as would have been pursued by a guilty man."

"(I do) not think much importance ought to be attached to the prisoner's statement that he left the child near to her own home, because

hundreds of children came to him in a day"
Now this is where Mr Weightman may be stretching the truth just that little bit too much for the jury! *"and it was quite likely that an innocent man -for as such* (I) *put Gough before* (you) *-would not be able to tell where one child or another left him, and therefore his answers were not remarkable. Coming to the evidence of Holmes.....about a week after the occurrence, when people were beginning to talk about the tragedy, when Gough had been apprehended, people were apt to put constructions upon and add to expressions that perhaps originally were innocent enough in themselves. And therefore* (I can) *not help thinking that* (you) *the jury in* (your) *own minds* (will) *warn* (your) *selves from accepting in all their plain, literal meaning, any words that might have passed between the prisoner and Holmes."....*

"The prisoner on his return, went to those places which he usually visited".

Mr Weightman then stated that the prosecution had put before the jury a "most preposterous suggestion" when it was asked if Gough did not commit the murder then who on earth did? How on earth could Gough say who did it if he did not do it?! It was an argument that Mr Weightman thought ought never to be used before juries. He had heard that prosecution tactic too many times in his career. He offered his theory:-

"was it not possible that the little child knowing that she had strayed away, that

perhaps dinner time was past at home, got through the gap in the hedge, and wandered about as little ones would, and did, wander? Was it not possible that she wandered abroad, afraid to go home, in the fields around Brimington, and so in the direction of Staveley Ironworks and Hoole's Plantation." A good theory but flawed. Mr Weightman had done so well in his defence speech but his knowledge of the locality was sadly lacking. Those in the court who knew the district found it "very amusing" to hear his observations as to the neighbourhood of Johnson's lane and Hoole's plantation. It "occasionally produced a smile even on the prisoner's face"! The locals knew that if Eleanor had gone through a gap in the hedge and walked across the fields she would first come to her own home! However Mr Weightman continued:-

"Brimington was not the most innocent place in the world, the calendar of (this) *assize showed that in Brimington was laid the scene of one of the foulest crimes as it was possible for human nature to suggest.* (If Mr Weightman is referring to the trial held on Tuesday afternoon then the judge actually acquitted the man. Not that this jury would have known that.) *It was a place crowded by colliers, 4000 of them worked at the Staveley Ironworks. They were as* (you know) *-though* (I do) *not wish to put upon them a worse character than they bore, a character not the best in the world, and Hoole's Plantation was the spot where a man would dispose of the body of a child that he had murdered."*

(I have) *put before* (you) *the suggestions that came into* (my) *mind on behalf of the prisoner, and if there were any that* (I have) *omitted, and which occurred to* (you) *the jury,* (I trust) *they* (will) *not be visited upon that man's shoulders.* (I have) *done* (my) *duty so far as* (I have) *been able.* (I have) *put before* (you) *on behalf of the prisoner those theories which* (I) *thought the case warranted. If the prosecution* (has) *made out their case as* (my) *friend said link by link - if the chain was complete* (I) *would be the last man in the world, and unworthy of* (my) *position, if* (I) *asked* (you) *to violate* (your) *oaths by returning a verdict other than the circumstances demanded, but if the prosecution* (has) *not made out their case - if there were links wanting in the chain - then, however foul the crime, and however loudly the blood of the child cried to heaven for vengeance, it* (is) *not for* (you) *to visit that vengeance on the prisoner's shoulders.* (You will) *be bound to consider the case upon the evidence.* (I have) *tried to do* (my) *duty, let* (you) *do* (yours), *and* (may) *God direct* (you) *to a right verdict."*

Mr Weightman had spoken to the jury for an hour in defence of Gough's very life. Gough had been surprised that his counsel could say so many things in his favour. This was an experienced advocate "one of the most skilled barristers on the Midland Circuit" and Gough could not have had better. When Mr Weightman took his seat there was "some slight applause" in the courtroom so splendidly did he plead

Gough's cause but a look from the judge and his clerk soon suppressed that enthusiasm.

As there had been no defence witnesses it was now up to the judge to sum up. If there had been defence witnesses then after Mr Weightman's closing speech Mr Chandos Leigh QC would have had the right to reply on behalf of the prosecution. Throughout the nineteenth century the fear of letting prosecution have the final say was a powerful deterrent for not calling such witnesses.

His Lordship explained to the jury that he thought it best not to have tried to conclude the trial the previous evening. He was right. Mr Weightman had just now taken an hour and that should not have been rushed yesterday, it had been dark outside and that made it feel like a long day to everyone and no doubt the concentration of the jurymen would have been flagging. The judge also would have had to sum up. Judges today take at least an hour to sum up and usually it is even longer. In the first half of the nineteenth century the standard of summing up was generally low if not non-existent but by 1850, though not universal, there was an improvement. Therefore His Lordship hoped that the jury "had suffered little inconvenience by being locked up for the night"! Even if they did they would not be complaining to the judge!

Sir James commenced his summing up. He asked the jury to "view the case dispassionately". There had been circumstantial evidence but *"In that respect it was not singular because the same thing was true of most murders which were investigated. .... circumstantial evidence, if clear, was more convincing than the evidence of eye-witnesses, for the latter were liable to make a mistake."*

His Lordship occasionally spoke in low tones for he was addressing the jury just down to his right but Gough understandably wished to hear what was being said of him. The prisoner then "stretched forward" with his hands on the dock railings "in order to catch the words" much to the annoyance, no doubt, of his jailer who would rather Gough sit back in his seat.

His Lordship then *"proceeded at great length to review the evidence which had been placed before the jury on the part of the prosecution, and commented on the result of the cross examination...for the defence. The evidence of the chief witnesses was most carefully reviewed, and especially that of Miss Johnson, which.....the defence asked them either to disbelieve or not act upon. They had heard her evidence, and saw her to be an intelligent woman, who knew what she was talking about. They saw her not flurried in cross-examination, not disparaged in any of her statements but very clear and precise, (It really formed the vital part of the case, and it was evident from what she saw that the prisoner had just come under a terrible temptation - under the influence of a horrible lust. When Miss Johnson came out with a broom-handle the man disappeared, but if he had gone towards Chesterfield she would have seen him, and if he had gone towards Brimington there were people in the road who would have seen him; the probability being that he was behind the high hedge already* mentioned.) ... they had to say whether there were any grounds on which they would be justified in not placing confidence in her statements. It appears the judge has already made up his mind as to Gough's innocence! Assuming that the prisoner committed the crime, the most natural thing for him to do, being well-known in the neighbourhood, was to go his ordinary round, to divert suspicion. It was suggested that the prisoner went away gathering rags and bones while the cart was at the end of Johnson's lane, and it was said that he had 70lbs. of rags and bones at night. But it must be remembered that that was at night after he had been selling his toys. When the witness Cantrell saw the cart she distinctly declared that there were no rags in it, and the prisoner himself said to Mrs Neale, whose attention appeared to be drawn to the state of the cart, that he had not got many rags, as he had not come far. It was for the jury to say which of the two theories set up was the right one. As regarded the evidence of Holmes, His Lordship observed that all.... the defence could say against and in disparagement of his evidence was that the case had been talked about, and that Holmes somehow or other got it into his head that this conversation had taken place, and was either mistaken in his idea or was deceiving the jury. They had heard Holmes' evidence, let them see what conclusion it brought them to. Holmes had *been a friend of the prisoner, and His Lordship asked why on earth he should come before them to take away Gough's life.* (No doubt Alfred Gough was wondering the same thing!)

Having dealt with the evidence following that of Holmes the judge thought it unnecessary to comment further. He had suggested to the jury his views on various points and the facts from both sides.

"The responsibility now rested with the jury, and he would leave them to it. They had discussed the case most thoroughly; they had paid to it all the attention it deserved, all the attention that it was necessary to give to it. If all the facts set up on the part of the prosecution were established satisfactorily, and there was no evidence on the part of the prisoner to disprove or qualify them, then they had to say whether those facts led them to the conclusion that the man at the bar committed the murder.

If they came to that conclusion the consequences were not what they (the jury) were responsible for, (That would be for the judge to worry about) *they must do their duty. But, if they did not come to that conclusion, he asked them, as reasonable men, to give the prisoner the benefit of the doubt and say he was not guilty."*

His Lordship took one and a half hours to sum up the case. It was now ten past one. The twelve men of the jury rose to file out of the court through their own door behind the judges' bench. It was still common for some juries to reach their verdict without leaving the jury box but this jury had their own little room to go to. Not that there would be any home comforts there except at the judge's discretion. In the first half of the nineteenth century there would be no fire lit, although it was November, no food or even a drink until the verdict was reached. Alexander Pope quoted "wretches hang that jurymen may dine!"

Not that this jury was in danger of it, it only being Thursday, but at an Assizes it had been the practice that if the jury had not reached a verdict by the time the judge was ready to leave to go on to the next Assize town on his itinerary he could have them placed in a cart following on behind him. If by the time he reached the next county border and the jury had not come to a verdict they would be "shot into a ditch!" This "carting" was rare in the nineteenth century but the threat was still used to Oxford jurors in 1848. Modern day judges may well consider such a revival long overdue!

After the jury's door was closed His Lordship sent Gough back down to the cells and then rose himself. There was nothing more to do but wait. The court itself however remained crowded. The general public were not going to give up their seats or standing positions at this crucial stage. Superintendent Carline gave a smile and some words of encouragement to William Windle and for a time they spoke of how the proceedings had gone with Mr Middleton. This was an important trial for the young solicitor to deal with and important London barristers too! How was he faring with them?.....

Five past two. Word was sent to His Lordship that the jury were ready to come back into court with a verdict. The usher went off to call the case on in the hall area and find the barristers to come in and take their places. When all were assembled the judge entered and all stood until he was seated. The nod was given for Alfred Gough to ascend that staircase just one more time and take his seat. The jury then filed back into court. Their deliberations had taken less than an hour. Alfred was motioned to stand which he did and resting his crossed hands on the dock in front of him he gazed at the jury. Unlike today the names of the twelve jurymen were once again read out.

The clerk of the court then asked the foreman of the jury if they were all agreed on their verdict? Their spokesman replied "Yes".

"Do you find the prisoner, Alfred Gough, guilty or not guilty?"

At this point one could have heard a pin drop.

"Guilty, sir."

The clerk then addressed himself to Alfred- *"Alfred Gough, you were arraigned upon a charge of wilful murder, and upon that arraignment you put yourself upon your country. Have you anything to say why you should not die according to law, and why sentence of death should not be passed upon you?"*

Alfred shook his head and in a low voice too soft for even some of the reporters to hear said *"No, sir."*

"Amid breathless silence", the judge whose black cap was beside him addressed the prisoner:-

"Alfred Gough, it is no part of my duty to address to you words of complaint or words for reproach at the terrible crimes that you unquestionably committed upon Eleanor Windle, but I believe it is my duty to warn you to be prepared for the fate that inevitably awaits you. You must be prepared to die. I shall hold out to you no hope of mercy here.

From the middle of the century, even when the death sentence was passed, petitions for clemency could be brought before the authorities. It has been estimated that only about one in ten who were sentenced to death actually faced the noose. Sentences could be commuted to life instead. This process would mean a wait of some weeks for the defendant to know his/her fate but the judge is already indicating that this will not happen here.

You have yielded to one terrible, to one diabolical temptation; do not yield to another; do not harden your heart, but look now for mercy where alone mercy can be extended to you. I now (placing on the black cap) proceed to pass upon you the sentence of the law, which is- that you be taken hence to the place whence you came, and thence to the place of execution, that you be there hung by the neck until you shall be dead, that your body be afterwards buried within the precincts of the prison in which you shall have been last confined before your conviction, and may the Lord have mercy upon your soul."

A "profound silence prevailed in the court whilst the sentence" was delivered and all the time Gough stood erect, his eyes fixed on the judge calmly listening to his fate with no show of excitement or emotion. When all had been said Gough simply unclasped his hands, took one last "rapid glance" at His Lordship and the jury, turned around and followed a warder down the stairs and back to the court cells. Once Gough had left, the room soon emptied. The court staff then were busying themselves in readiness to call on the next case. There was no time to ponder on Gough's fate there was still work to be done. The jury that convicted Gough would possibly be needed for two more trials in which Mr Weightman was defence counsel to both defendants and then His Lordship had four sentences to deal with where the prisoners had pleaded guilty on the Tuesday and all to be dealt with before the end of the day.

Superintendent Carline and "his small army of witnesses" made their way back to the railway station in what was left of the afternoon daylight. A message was sent by telegraph back to Chesterfield and its environs with the anticipated news of the verdict. It was all over. It was hard to believe but now it was time to try and get back to a more normal existence without having to think about Gough. The trial had settled that. There was not going to be any pardon for him. The judge had made that very clear. His days on earth were numbered.

When Gough left the court he could not have complained that he did not get a fair hearing. According to "NOTES FROM THE CROOKED STEEPLE"- the jury were gentlemen of Leicestershire rather than Derbyshire and therefore "knowing less about the case beforehand, were less likely to be influenced by outside considerations, and more likely to be guided strictly by the evidence". The judge had provided him with a very skilled barrister and "ample opportunity" and time were given for the defence to be fully stated. "Surely more consideration could not have been shown to anyone, and that it was extended to a wretch who was a disgrace to humanity"!

In the early nineteenth century it was thought that someone's inner nature and character could be explained away by observing the body, especially the face (but not its expression) and head. This now considered pseudo-science was known as physiognomy. It was largely discredited by the time of Gough's trial but it still was obviously a curiosity to the newspaper readers. A "gentleman" physiognomist who apparently had an opportunity of observing Gough's features found characteristics in common with "the type of men who come under the hands of the executioner"! "The face is of more than ordinary width, and the projection of the skull above the ears denotes great destructiveness, severity and sternness of disposition. The forehead is square and well shaped, which, with his wide mouth and firm-set lips, shows great determination of purpose. The lips are thick and indicate an amative (amorous) and sensual disposition, and the alimentative (nourishing) faculties are well developed". Does this mean Alfred likes his food?!

The down to earth journalist of The Derby and Chesterfield Reporter dismisses the justification of "any of those semi-scientific speculations in which many of our contemporaries delight to indulge at such times. Gough was undoubtedly a man of a gross, animal temperament"!

A sexologist, Henry Havelock Ellis writing in the 1890's described the sex offender's body as having in all likelihood an asymmetrical face with malformed ears and nose, a large lower jaw with imperfect teeth, eyes of blue though they could also be different coloured, a lot of hair - fair, especially red, irregularities in the genital area, be possibly epileptic and have a fondness for drink. Alcohol could cause degeneration in these offenders but it could also be a symptom of degeneracy itself, its "poison" letting "loose the individual's natural or morbid impulses."

24. Sketch of Alfred Gough from the Illustrated Police News 3rd September 1881

Gough had been variously described as having small, hazel eyes, a thin nose, rather prominent chin and brown hair. Drink, according to Gough himself, was his downfall but whether his other physical attributes matched in any way to a sex offender is not possible to judge. However, a famous trial lawyer, Clarence Seward Darrow, in the early decades of the twentieth century, wrote that all men contained "the beast" within them under certain environmental conditions. It is uncanny how close Gough fits the conditions' criteria:- having little money, generally no family, being poorly fed and clothed, possessing few if any attractions and having a remote occupation where satisfaction of the sexual appetite was almost impossible. Gough was in the army in India and Afghanistan and it could well have been there that instinct took over from the mores and conventions of how to behave. It was reported that unmarried soldiers resorted to the local brothels. And at any one time one in ten of the army were hospitalised due to venereal disease! From the mid-1870's medical men considered life in a tropical climate as debilitating both physically and morally. Anyone subjected to heat-stroke or heat-exhaustion could suffer "serious effects on the brain and nervous system" and this coupled with the taking of alcohol might well affect someone in such a way that rational control was "disrupted". "It may very likely be accepted as a fact that" Gough "drank a great deal more than was good for him on the morning of the crime; but we cannot perceive, from the evidence, any ground for justifying the supposition that alcohol on this particular day found Gough a comparatively blameless being, and forthwith converted him into a ferocious and unrelenting devil." Defendants had been known to use this argument at their trials but not Alfred. "However much rum he may have consumed on the day in question, the culprit was, when seen soon after the perpetration of the crime, in the possession of his mental faculties."

When Gough was returned to the court cell "he partook of some dinner." Even a death sentence would not put Gough off his food! Superintendent Carline would not have been surprised. He always said that Gough ate and slept well from the moment he was arrested!

In the evening, "under a strong escort of warders" Gough along with five other prisoners was taken back to the prison in Derby. These five prisoners were facing sentences of between 6 and 18 months imprisonment with hard labour. Five other prisoners were released and it is assumed they had to find their own way back home to Derbyshire.

Now Alfred Gough became a mere number to the prison authorities. He had left Derby as a remand prisoner but came back a convict and it is presumed was processed as any other convict. Yet as a condemned man, special rules applied and the governor, Captain Farquharson, himself, as opposed to a warder for the other prisoners, may have searched Alfred for items "dangerous or inexpedient to leave in his possession" which were confiscated immediately. A tepid bath was next on the agenda before being examined by Dr Wright Baker, the prison medical officer. The doctor made a note of each prisoner's height, weight, physical description and distinguishing marks for the records. Alfred's clothes were not returned to him. He, like the other five prisoners with him was issued with prison garb instead. Their own clothes, if hygienically fit, would be retained if a short sentence was being served otherwise destruction took place and a new set of clothes would be provided on release. The search and removal of his own clothes would have made Alfred fret as he had a dear and secret treasure hidden away which Superintendent Carline had allowed him to keep. Neither had it been found when he first entered the gaol in September. Carefully pinned in the lining of his trousers were a few letters or rather fragments of letters which when found he earnestly begged to keep. Amongst them was the last letter, worn and fragile that he had received from his mother before she died. Personal possessions were forbidden in prison so it is to be assumed the governor gave this permission for Gough to keep them. After all he was not going to be with them long.

Arriving back in Chesterfield that evening, to Superintendent Carline's relief, there were very few people at the station to view the return of all the witnesses and the infamous handcart. As he stepped down from the carriage he could see a bit of a commotion to the rear of the train. The handcart was being lifted out of the guardsvan and who had offered to wheel the cart back to Marsden Street lock-up? None other than "Mansfield Tom"! If Gough had known this he would have been beside himself with anger. The Sheffield Daily Telegraph claimed that if Tom had been "of a commercial turn of mind" he "might have transacted a brisk and profitable business by the sale of either flag, paper, bag, or anything connected with the barrow, as the main mementoes were at a high premium and souvenirs of the tragedy eagerly sought for." What probably stopped Tom was the close proximity of three police officers and Superintendent Carline keeping a watchful eye on him! But notwithstanding this the newspaper claimed "The paper was clutched at, and anything of a movable character taken away." This desire for souvenirs did not just occur in Chesterfield. Even some of the members of the jury in Leicester asked if they might keep the plans "which had been submitted to them of the localities of the outrage and the murder?" Surprisingly, permission was given which resulted in the maps being divided amongst the jury "without any regard to the connection of the parts"!

Back in Brimington a hearty welcome and congratulations were awaiting William Windle, Alice, (his now only remaining daughter) other relatives and friends. The Sheffield Daily Telegraph, one of the few voices who championed Miss Johnson throughout the weeks prior to the trial even claimed that the locals' opinion of her had changed in great measure from anger to admiration because of the complimentary remarks the judge had given to her for the manner in which she had given her evidence. This may be true but Miss Johnson did not live out her days in Brimington! At the height of the murmurings against Miss Johnson on the 25th August The Sheffield Daily Telegraph reported "She is not the coward she has been accused of being." "She has a fair amount of courage; for at one time when a sweep entered her house by the chimney in the absence of her brother, she attacked him with a heavy weapon and drove him ignominiously off the premises"!

On Saturday, The Derbyshire Courier wanted to remind its readership after all the sensationalism of Gough's trial to spare a thought for Mr and Mrs Windle. *"The parents of the murdered child deserve the sympathy of all. It must have been a hard trial for them. For loving parents to lose a child by the natural course of disease is hard enough to bear; but to have one taken away in such a manner as this, must be heartrending."*

CHAPTER SIXTEEN

FRIDAY 4th NOVEMBER 1881

THE CONDEMNED CELL

Gough woke to the sound of the prison bell but he was not alone. There in the corner was one of the warders that would be in constant attendance upon him day and night until his last hour. The authorities were to make sure Gough left this earth when they wanted him to and not before! He had been escorted the previous night to the "condemned cell" after listening to the list of rules and regulations read out by a warder. A list so long that after all the excitement of the day it was promptly forgotten by all the new intake. The condemned cell had been home to only two previous murderers- Albert Robinson hung earlier in the year and another child murderer, John Wakefield, who died the previous summer. The original condemned cell was deemed to be inconvenient and "not to afford sufficient control over the movements of the prisoner." Consequently the cell Gough now occupied was larger and "somewhat spacious" having two windows that lit the room well, a little table and a chair for himself. From the warders' point of view as regards security this cell had a "better means of approach than the old one." It was possibly situated in the male "C" wing as it was reported as being "near the Gaol Infirmary in the inner circle". It would not have been "B" wing where the chapel was situated for there he probably would not have had to cross the bridge leading to the chapel and it is known Gough did but that is the only other wing close to the Infirmary. Sadly only the frontage of the prison remains today.

Alfred would be pleasantly surprised with his meal time arrangements for now as a condemned man he was on a more liberal and superior diet than that allowed to the other prisoners. An improvement from the poor fare he received whilst on remand. His appearance was to improve in consequence according to the newspapers but his sister was of another opinion.

Sir James Charles Mathew still in his lodgings at Leicester, as court business had not finished with Gough, wrote a quick line to the Secretary of State today informing him that Gough had been found guilty and he had passed the death sentence upon him. "I see no reason why sentence should not be carried out". In order to justify this he had directed that his own notes that he had taken during the trial and used to refer to in his summing up should be copied and then forwarded to the Home Secretary.

Meanwhile in the outside world The Sheffield and Rotherham Independent after Gough's trial reported that the "intense interest" in the case was not due to cleverness on the part of Gough but to the "mystery" which surrounded how or where the murder actually occurred and the "total indifference" of Gough as to his fate. "The mystery has not even yet been wholly cleared up". It was now the goal of the newspaper editors to be the first to get the scoop on Gough's confession before the noose went around his neck! Rumours were being circulated – in the course of an interview with his sister, Gough had confessed his guilt and promised to give a detailed account of the murder!—"without foundation"! "Pure fabrication"! "The authorities of the gaol assert most positively that he has not made any confession and that the statement is a concoction"! The Sheffield Daily Telegraph of 8th November completely rubbished this article published in a "contemporary" newspaper. The race for the elusive confession was still on.

CHAPTER SEVENTEEN

SATURDAY 5th NOVEMBER 1881

GOUGH'S EARLY POLICE CAREER AND ARMY LIFE

If Gough was now in a reflective mood whilst awaiting his end would he have realised that as a police constable fourteen years earlier to the day it appears to the world that there was a change in his behaviour and not to the good? Guy Fawkes Night, 1867 and The Constables' Conduct Book records Alfred as being drunk on duty and accordingly fined 2/6d. A month later on two occasions at the end of the year he was absent from his beat. On the first occasion it was one hour fifteen minutes and on the second- forty minutes for which he was fined another half crown. Two days later, New Year's Day, 1868 and Alfred was drunk again on duty. Another 2/6d fine! Was this just the seasonal revels of a young man or was there something else that was troubling him? The Derbyshire Times reported that his drinking was due to "a disappointment in love". He had "formed an attachment" to a young woman in Leeds but "was deceived." This could not be verified. But alternatively could it have had something to do with his mother? Either way a paramilitary style police force had strict rules to follow and did not tolerate this kind of behaviour. Constable Gough appeared to settle down again but 8 months later on 19th August he collected another half crown fine for being absent from his beat and under the influence, yet again, of liquor.

Two months pass but once again on 20th October Alfred was fined another 2/6d for being absent from his beat on two occasions. Could his mother taking a new husband only two days later have had something to do with his behaviour? He had always been the "man" of the house since he could not remember when. His mother had chosen to follow him to Leeds rather than stay with his sister in Nottingham. Why after all these years of them being together should his mother need someone else in her life? For Alfred this was difficult to comprehend. The Derbyshire Courier reported that he was devotedly attached to his mother and she in turn took great pride in him and spoiled him. He was reported as being a "homely youth" giving the "minimum of trouble" as a schoolboy. Still, although he may not have approved of this step his mother was taking he did go to the ceremony and was a witness to the marriage at Leeds Parish Church. It is possible that the bridegroom's family were equally disappointed with the match for the other witness to the marriage was not a member of the Duffield family at all but the registrar himself.

Catherine Gough was now 50 years old. She perhaps saw that her son would not always be with her. He would one day find himself a bride. Her new husband was a 70 year old widower. Thomas was a Yorkshire man born and bred, by trade, a blacksmith, living in Headingley, Leeds. He had had a long marriage with his first wife Ann and had at least 3 sons and a daughter. But Ann had died the summer of 1867 at the age of 74, the children had grown-up and left home and Thomas suddenly felt alone. He needed a woman to look after his needs and Catherine fitted the bill. Whether his mother's marriage was the trigger or whether Gough had (as some newspapers reported) a love-affair gone wrong but a mere six days after the wedding Alfred had left the police force and was on a train to Liverpool bound to enlist in the 17th Foot Regiment.

28th October, 1868 at the age of 23 Alfred struck the first blow to his mother's heart. The shame of him enlisting voluntarily! People would think he had a reason to disappear, was he a "bad lot" after all because that is what was commonly thought? How was she to live this down? Did the thought now make him reach for her precious letter?

He had spent the initial few months of his first year in the army in Ireland with the II Battalion, on hand for the Irish elections, but by April of 1869 the battalion sailed south to the Channel Islands. Gough was in one of three companies that were billeted in Alderney, North East of Guernsey and West of the French coast near Cherbourg. Here he was to stay until the summer of 1870 where according to "A History of the Services of the 17th (The Leicestershire) Regiment (1688-1910)" by E.A.H. Webb the II Battalion left the Islands for Aldershot about the 26th July. The first half of 1870 was not a good year for Alfred. For some reason he just went off the rails. It seemed to begin the day after his first anniversary in the army when he lost a day's pay of 1/2d for being absent without leave. The 7th March he was fined 7/6d for drunkenness- that is over six days' pay! After that things just seemed to escalate! From the quarter, 1st April to 30th June Gough received less than half his pay and a pound was to be recovered from him for drunkenness. "The Payment Book of II Battalion" records Gough as spending 18 days in confinement from 15th May- 1st June of which 6 of these days were in the hospital and then the following day he began a spell of 29 days in the cells! The next quarter's pay records Gough as only receiving 58 of his 77 days' pay on account of him still being in the cells from the 1st July until the 18th. That is a total of more than 2 months in prison or confinement. The 19th July he was in confinement and the following day before a court martial! It would be no surprise to find that 16th September he was "transferred to 1/17". He was one of 90 men each being swapped between the "1st and 2nd Regiment". Alfred is then paid up until 29th November under the auspices of the "Depot 1/17 Regiment" "to join the service companies". It was reported in the local newspapers that Gough left for India 30th November 1870. "The Times" does actually report that on that date a "large body of troops" from Manchester and "Aldershott" "embarked at the Royal Arsenal on board the screw steamer City of Brussels for Calcutta via the Suez Canal. The troops consisted of Capt. White, Lieut. Bertie, three sergeants, 176(175 according to the Army Embarkation Book WO25/3506) rank and file, 11 women, and 29 children of the 1st Battalion 17th Regiment from Aldershott, to join the service companies in India …altogether, 11 officers, 365 non-commissioned officers and men, 20 women and 43 children."

It is with this knowledge that one can get more of an insight into the letter Alfred's mother sends to him. Alfred had obviously written to her regarding his problems and his lack of money which is why she refers to her financial situation and the hope that his behaviour may improve!

"Headingley, Nov. 24, 1870.

"My dear Son,--I received your kind and welcome letter, and was very glad to hear you were well. I hope you will be a good boy. I am sorry you are going, I was in hopes you would not go until after Christmas. But, my dear, perhaps it is all for the best. My dear, I hope and trust you will get safe over the seas. I hope you will put your trust in God, and pray that you may get safe and send you health. I hope you will be able to stand the heat. If you can you will get on better there, and your time will be out soon. My dear son, I am sorry I have no money to send you, but I get nothing now, for I have given up the shop. But I hope my boy I shall be better off some time. I live in hopes I shall see better days. You must be sure and write to me before you get to India if you can. Wittam wrote to his mother some time before he got home; do the same if you can. If it should happen that you do not get there I hope someone will let me know. But my dear, we must trust in Providence. Be a good boy, and take care of yourself as well as you can. May the Lord bless you and prosper you. Be steady, and save money if you can towards buying yourself off. All send their love to you. Good bye, and God bless you. From your affectionate

"MOTHER."

Clearly the letter of a doting parent- hoping he would be a good boy, sorry he was leaving before Christmas, hoping he will be able to stand the heat; sorry she has no money to send him, asking him to write even before he reaches India but if he doesn't make it to his destination will someone please let her know? A letter typical of a worried mother whose son means a great deal to her. Six days after this letter was written Alfred's battalion set sail for India. For his mother, like so many, news of the posting to India was considered a virtual death sentence for her only son. Carefully, Alfred refolded the delicate paper and returned the letter back to where it had always been secreted ever since he had received it. The letter had been on many journeys with him. What he could not have known was that this was to become his mother's last epistle to him! It was said by friends that his mother on hearing the news of Alfred's departure pined away for her beloved son and died of a broken heart. Within 4 months of Alfred's leaving Catherine was dead and he was half a world away!

Now assigned to the 1st Battalion, his first billeting in April 1871 was in North India, right in the middle of the country at Lucknow. Fourteen years previously Lucknow had been the scene of fierce fighting caught up in the Indian Mutiny. Hundreds of rebels had been killed and the city looted. So much so that it never recovered its former glory. Alfred spent over two and a half years in Lucknow. Generally, settling down well to the army life. There is only one mention of a lapse: - prison in April of 1872 which may have coincided with the anniversary of his mother's death. But, on the other hand he had three mentions of good conduct, acted as a "guard on two occasions and in September of 1873 was recorded as "bungalow orderly". (This could be where the story of him being a "batman" has arisen.)

29th November 1873 saw Gough leaving Lucknow with his battalion of some 800-1000 men for a destination that would not be reached for some 3 months. They mustered in Delhi in December but were heading onwards- North West to the borders of Afghanistan near to the eastern end of the Khyber Pass. On 2nd March 1874 the battalion had reached their journey's end or was it world's end? –Peshawur- having covered 896 miles! It was described as "probably one of the most unhealthy places in the world", "a most unpleasant area, with a trying climate and a semi desert mountainous terrain.

406

25. Photograph of 1st Battalion, 17th Foot Regiment at Lucknow, India. Is Alfred Gough somewhere in this picture?! By courtesy of the Royal Leicestershire Regiment Museum Trustees

Regular troops tended to regard it virtually as a penal colony, and service there was unpopular." (The Indian Army1822-1922- T. A. Heathcote) Gough spent over a year in Peshawur at the cantonment (military camp) 2 miles West of the city but during the unbearable heat of the summer months of May-September the army headquarters, two of the battalion's companies and those who were ill withdrew to the hilltop sanatorium at Cherat. A settlement 30 miles South-East of Peshawur and some 4,500' above sea level (higher than the highest mountain in the British Isles) where the day and evening temperatures were more bearable. Peshawur inspired "a sort of terror for the English soldier from its proverbial unhealthiness" Its summers could reach temperatures of over 100 degrees Fahrenheit (40C)!

Once again in the month of April Gough found himself in prison but was performing guard duty by the end of the year. The latter months of 1874 found the battalion besieged by the ague (a fever or malaria) and a deadly fever- a malady peculiar to the Peshawur Valley. It was alleviated by the practice of the battalion leaving the garrison and camping and marching and marching throughout the district until the disease naturally died out. This drill had also occurred at Lucknow in the previous year just before the battalion set off for Peshawur when cholera, (an ever recurring disease in India) broke out killing over a hundred men. Unbeknown at this time this method worked because it took the soldiers away from the unhygienic conditions in the garrisons though money was being spent at this time on improvements. "The British soldier was both an expensive item to obtain and an invaluable one to use. It was only good economics to take care of him when he was there!"- T. A. Heathcote. However the infected water, lack of sanitation and the ever present swarms of flies accompanying the transport animals still made their mark on the health of the British. Opthalmia (an infectious inflammation of the eyes) and small-pox made themselves known to the soldiers at various times too. Alfred's "fresh complexion" of 1868 gave way at some stage to a bout of small-pox according to the 1881 description of his face. It is possible that one of the four spells in hospital was for this condition.

During his time at Peshawur there were constant skirmishes along the border with the tribesmen in that region. But these were mainly dealt with by the Sikhs and Punjabis who made up the Punjab Frontier Force. These Indian regiments classed themselves as the corps d'elite. Yet the British soldier still classed himself as superior to the Indian soldier. For every one British regiment there would be 2-3 Indian regiments but the men did not tend to mix as Indian officers had no authority over British soldiers. Since the Indian Mutiny co-operation between the two sides had dwindled and the British soldiers really only had contact with the Indian servants employed in menial tasks in the garrison. However Alfred must have tried to make contact with the locals as he claimed to know Hindustani.

Gough spent the first 4 months of 1875 still quartered in Peshawur but respite from the summer heat came by being sent to the high land of Cherat during May and June. In July one of his rostered duties was that of a "bungalow orderly" and by the end of the year he was on "cookhouse duty"! This was not a punishment but rather a regular duty the men had to perform.

1876 started with Gough in hospital but he recovered and by March the regiment was on the move South East to Rawal Pindi over 100 miles away and then onwards North East heading for the Murree Hills where the battalion was stationed in four of the main gullies of the hills. Gough was in Kuldanna. The region at 7516' in parts meant the climate was much more to the soldiers' liking. Pleasant summers and cold, snowy winters. "Magnificent views over forest-clad hill-sides into deep valleys studded with villages and cultivated fields."

For Gough this would have been a short stay. He would not get to see the snow clad hills in winter for the Muster Book simply states "Embarked for England 6.4.76". His time in the army in India was over. He was to return home nearly an inch taller but where was home? His beloved mother was dead. He must have had mixed feelings as to what was to lie ahead for him. Would seeing his sister be part of his plan? He certainly had not planned for his current predicament! He had not planned for his life to be so public either and yet unbeknown to Alfred the letters he had written to his sister before the trial in October were now released to the press.

CHAPTER EIGHTEEN

TUESDAY 8ᵀᴴ NOVEMBER 1881

UNFINISHED BUSINESS FOR THE JUDGE

His Lordship Judge Mathew was now ensconced in the judges' lodgings at Nottingham presiding over the serious cases for that particular area. However he still had some unfinished business to attend to from his time at Leicester the week before. His own notes, the "Notes of Evidence", had now been copied for him and he needed to send them on to Sir W. V Harcourt, the Home Secretary which he duly did. There was to be no reprieve for Gough.

CHAPTER NINETEEN

THURSDAY 10TH NOVEMBER 1881

GOUGH'S LETTER TO HIS SISTER, ANN.

Alfred wrote to his sister for the first time after the trial dating it 9th November (Wednesday). This may have been with encouragement from the chaplain and governor who both visited him now on a daily basis. No doubt they felt he needed to put his affairs in order and time was running out. He deplored the great trouble he had brought upon himself but asked Ann and Thomas to visit him one last time so that he could say his farewells.

"My Dear Sister and Brother
(the usual niceties follow including the concern as to the recipients' health)*this leaves me middling in health but only i feel weak with Being so long on low diet Awaiting My trial but i have a better diet but it is not for long As the Lord as willied it my dear sister i never thought i Should have come to this auful end to be sentenced to death it is fearful thing to look at it but God's will be dun you would have heard of it by the papers i shall have to make the best of it now and trust in the almighty God that is above us. Try and come and se me by a week on Saturday next as i expect i have only a week on Monday to live* (Alfred was correct in his assumption and in fact as this letter was being read the Under

Sheriff was composing his own letter to the Home Office informing them that the Sheriff had fixed the date of Gough's execution for 8 o'clock in the morning on Monday 21st November) *So try and come next Week some time for the last time in this world i have some things I want to give to you to keep for your unfortunate Brother oh had i but of died out in India before coming to this disgrace God Help me i hope he will for this wicked Sinner i have been a wicked sinner for years but i hope that God will for Give me i will rite nother letter dear ann and tom kiss the children for me and may God Bless them and keep them from all arm and keep them from drink dear Ann and Tom dont let them taste Drink at all they will be better without it dont forget what i say no more from your Affectionate Loving Brother*

"ALFRED GOUGH."

 To reinforce the request the Governor, Captain Farquharson, sent Mr and Mrs Tollington a "courteous note" informing them that if they wished to see Alfred he would obtain them the "necessary permission to do so." This would have been by order of a Visiting Justice.

 When Thomas had finished reading the two letters to his wife there was a sharp intake of breath. They wanted to move on from the whole incident but they could not deny Alfred his last wishes. They knew if they refused it would only haunt them but perhaps they also thought money could be made out of this awful situation! Thomas took pen to paper and wrote to the Governor. Thank you for your kind letter… it would be convenient for us to be at the prison on Tuesday if an order could be obtained for that day. Thomas also replied to Alfred's missive stating when they would hope to visit and- "I hope when we are with you, you will tell us all about it." This gave Alfred something to think about! The Governor replied once more to Thomas- the order would be ready for them as desired. The meeting was set.

CHAPTER TWENTY

FRIDAY 11th NOVEMBER 1881

GOUGH'S LETTERS AGAIN APPEARING IN PRINT!

The Sheffield and Rotherham Independent printed yesterday's letter from Alfred to the Tollingtons today! In his letter he urges his sister and brother in law to keep their children away from drink and lo and behold, curiously the newspaper reports that in his cell Alfred "occasionally laments most bitterly that he ever gave way to drink. He has repeatedly exclaimed, "But for the drink I should not have been here." On one occasion, when apparently absorbed in thought, he muttered, "If she had only interfered she might have saved the child's life and mine too." He was evidently living over again the terrible events of that eventful Saturday; and had someone but stepped in to have broken the spell of the overpowering temptation that was upon him, the life of the child at least, he felt, might have been saved, and he would have been meted out a less awful punishment. Whether he is right in his statement, that he was actually seen conducting himself improperly with the deceased, it is impossible to say; no evidence to that effect has been given. It is a remarkable fact (allegedly) that neither in his letters nor in any other way has he been known to deny his guilt; but his conduct and his exclamations –more particularly of late – have been clearly admissions of it. There is no doubt that the burden of it is now pressing more and more heavily upon his conscience, and that before many days he will make a full and frank admission of his crime." Ever that elusive scoop is being chased!

In ignorance of all this Alfred wrote once more to his sister and brother:-

"i received your kind and welcome letter and pleased to hear from you i ham gitting on as well as can be expected in such a trouble   they are as kind to me as can be   i have a Couple of Stamps but you can send me two or three more Please. Oh if i had but got married and Settled down i Should have been a different man now but it was not to be (It appears young Mr Scott, the lodging house keeper in Sheffield, was mistaken. He had claimed that Alfred had been married but his wife died whilst he was in the army. This, thought Scott, was corroborated by him having seen several letters belonging to Gough commencing "My dear husband" and believing they had been written from Leeds.)   hear i must now conclude this time so Good night and God Bless you All   your Affectionate Loving Brother   Kiss the Children for me and God Bless them for ever   i wish i was Looking at them now."

The Derbyshire Times reported that whilst Gough was staying with his sister's family in Nottingham "the children were exceedingly fond of their uncle, who always had a cheery word for them, and sought to amuse them by every means in his power". This may well have been so for in the same report the journalist is still describing Gough as "so inhuman a being" and it is doubtful that the newspaper would be so disposed to show Gough in a good light if it was not the case.

Alfred had written another letter at this time to a "former friend of his". How this got into the newspaper can only be guessed!?

"i know you will feal Greatly for me   it will be a gret trouble to you but bear up as well as you can   i ham very sorry to think i ham in such a sad trouble but it carnt be helpt   i never thought i should of come to such a sad thing as i have   My Poor Dear Mother took it to heart When i (en) listed but this is fearfull i live in hopes that God will give me his Blessing and save my soul."

CHAPTER TWENTY ONE

SATURDAY 12TH NOVEMBER 1881

SUPERINTENDENT CARLINE'S THOUGHTS ON GOUGH

Superintendent Carline was sat at his desk upstairs in his office at Marsden Street police station. He was reading yet more column inches on Gough even though the trial had concluded more than a week ago. Here the local paper was actually repeating what one of the Sheffield newspapers had reported the previous Monday and which article had already been rubbished by another paper the following day! Still Gough sold newspapers! Reading on, Elijah noted Alfred was portrayed as a "most remarkable criminal", "not once known to have shown a sign of fear", "a reckless want of anxiety" when in public, "had made up his mind to die from the beginning" Some of this he might concur with but when Elijah read:-"The only thing that he really dreaded was the public gaze, and he is known to have stated that nothing troubled him so much as his removal from one place to another. The eyes of his fellows seemed to pierce him, and he could not bear the torture." What rubbish! The Superintendent could read no further. Where were they getting their information? The Courier itself stated that the above was said to be "a pure fabrication". It was! Thought Elijah. "But we have reason to believe that the substance of the paragraph is perfectly correct." No it was not. Elijah knew from first-hand experience that each time he and Sergeant Radford took Gough through the streets of Chesterfield in a cab and the populace were "howling" after him what was Gough doing? He was whistling and singing! He cared "not one jot" about the situation! However, the

421

Superintendent, ever the professional would not divulge any of this information regarding Gough until years after the event and only after his own death.

CHAPTER TWENTY TWO

MONDAY 14TH NOVEMBER 1881

LIFE IN THE CONDEMNED CELL.

Since he had entered the condemned cell ten days ago Gough had never been left alone. A warder sat in constant attendance but Gough conversed little with them. Mr Wright Baker the prison medical officer (surgeon) called in every day allowing Gough tobacco to smoke a pipe whilst taking his daily exercise in the prison yard but accompanied by minders —no other prisoners were permitted to be present. He took his improved meals regularly which he enjoyed "greedily" and slept well and "soundly" giving little trouble to his warders. Years later Superintendent Carline spoke to the press regarding his observations of the phenomenon of sleeping, eating and murderers. *"They always slept and* ate *well right up to the time they were hanged." "I used to think when I read an account of an execution and saw it repeatedly stated that the murderer had passed a good night even on the eve of being hanged that reporters were having* (telling untruths, as in "having you on" or "pulling your leg") *the public, but I have since found it quite true, and if I ever met a man charged with murder who could not eat and sleep well, I should begin to think there was a mistake and we had not got the right man. I never knew Gough lose a night's rest from the time we arrested him."*!

Alfred was still allowed out of his cell to attend the morning chapel services which he did throughout his time left but because of the high bridge that had to be crossed from the main prison building to the chapel he was handcuffed to two warders in order to prevent him from throwing himself off the bridge. Once in the chapel a pew was allotted to all three of them. Since Gough's first day as a condemned man the Reverend Henry Moore, the old Irish prison chaplain, had come to see him privately in his cell twice a day and would continue to do so until the last day. He was there to "appeal" and "warn" Gough. His spiritual needs had to be attended to. The Sheffield and Rotherham Independent claimed that Gough "listened with marked respect and attention, and gradually his cold and callous behaviour is forsaking him and he is becoming more serious and more reserved. He has not once been heard to question the justice of his sentence; neither has he entertained the slightest hope that any effort will be made to obtain a reprieve for him. He went to Leicester expecting to be found guilty and to be sentenced to death; and he has felt the full significance of the judge's warning that he was not to expect any mitigation of his punishment." This piece was written on Friday 11th November. Exactly a week later The Derby and Chesterfield Reporter had a more jaundiced view! *"We are given to understand that the rather maudlin attempts made by a contemporary to show that Gough is seriously concerned in his mind at the doom which awaits him, are totally devoid of foundation."*! He receives spiritual counsel with the *"same indifference"*. *"Betrays no emotion."* Worrying more about his own comforts *"eating and sleeping with extraordinary heartiness and composure."* This local paper is not prepared to consider Gough as having a conscience at this stage!

CHAPTER TWENTY THREE

TUESDAY 15TH NOVEMBER 1881

THE FINAL INTERVIEW

With a heavy heart, Ann and Thomas Tollington arrived at the prison gates around 11 o'clock in the morning. A warder acted as guide and escorted them through the arch and across the cobbled courtyard to the main building directly ahead where the Governor was to be waiting in his office. The warder knocked. The Tollingtons entered. They stated their names and the purpose of their visit and when the Governor was satisfied as to their identity he himself led them towards the condemned cell. En route Ann must have glanced out of a window for she could see only Alfred out in the exercise yard accompanied by two warders. He was handcuffed and surprisingly smoking a pipe. No other prisoners were allowed out in the yard whilst a condemned man was exercising. Mrs Tollington must have made some remark to the Governor. Alfred and his escort were called and returned to the cell where Gough and his warders, in a few minutes, were joined by the Governor and two reluctant visitors. The key was turned in the lock and all were ensconced in the condemned cell. Immediately Alfred went up to his brother-in-law and "very heartily" shook him by the hand. Ann had come in last but when her brother saw her "he embraced her with much emotion". Eventually all sat down as best they could.

The newspapers commented on how differently things were at Derby gaol in comparison to Armley prison at Leeds. There, the condemned man "was literally thrust into an "inner prison", relatives who went to see him were only

427

allowed to speak to him through a massive iron grating; and on no account were they allowed to shake hands with him or touch him." The Governor held with none of those severe restrictions at Derby. Mr and Mrs Tollington were permitted to be "as much with him (Alfred) in a sense as though they were in their own room at Nottingham"!

The Sheffield and Rotherham Independent and The Derbyshire Times both report this interview exactly word for word so it is obviously the same reporter who covered the story. How he got the information and from who is another matter? However it was reported on 21st November that the regulations of the Prison Commissioners prevent gaol officials from providing any information to the Press with regard to the habits of a convict in their charge. Yet the reporter claims he can vouch for his information being accurate even though it was "obtained from other sources". There can only be one other source and that is the Tollingtons themselves or friends they may have spoken to.

"He (Alfred) asked them how they were, and said he was very glad to see them. While this greeting had been going on the brother and sister had been closely scrutinising the convict, and they expressed themselves as shocked at his changed appearance.(It had been four weeks since Ann last visited her brother) He looked so thin and so pale- not half the man he was when he left their home two years ago. In answer to Mr. Tollington, he said he was better than he had been, "thanks," added he, "to the kind treatment I am receiving from everyone here."By this time he was much more composed than either of his relatives, and seeing their distress he said, "I never thought you would have to come to a place like this about me."They replied that such a thought had ever been as far from them as from him. "I have no doubt, "he answered. "It *is* a bad job; but it cannot be helped now;" and he spoke in a tone that convinced them he was entirely resigned to his fate, and had no hope whatever of escaping from it."

Thomas had a letter for Alfred from, in our eyes, the mysterious aunt. It implored him to make a full confession of his guilt and to seek forgiveness without delay. This is what Thomas hinted as to its contents. Alfred took it and very quietly stated "I will write my aunt a reply." Thomas had remembered to bring some more postage stamps in case Alfred wished to write again and handed them over.

"There is one thing," said Mr. Tollington, "I want particularly to ask you; and I hope you will tell me the whole truth about it."

"What is it?" asked Gough, looking him steadfastly in the face.

"I want you to tell me plainly, did you commit this crime for which you have to suffer?"

Gough rose from his chair, went to a little table in another part of the cell, and took from under the Bible he had been using a letter. Handing it to his brother he said, his voice quivering with emotion, "You have my answer there."

"I want to read that letter," interposed one of the warders and he took it from Mr. Tollington (who had hardly laid hands on it!) and read it aloud.

"IN THAT LETTER THE CONVICT MAKES A FULL CONFESSION OF HIS GUILT".

How annoying is that? Could the reading public not have had a snippet of the contents?! The news story merely claims that Gough "states simply, and without entering into details, that he murdered the little girl"

"The warder having read the letter, passed it to the Governor, who took possession of it, and said it should be forwarded to Mr Tollington in due course; but whether he will retain it until after the execution was not clearly understood."

It seems Thomas was not satisfied, however, with this written confession and proceeded to ask Alfred some more direct questions.

"Where did you do it?" asked Mr Tollington.

"I did it," he replied, "in the lane where I was seen with her. It is a bad job."

"How could you do such a thing?" he was asked.

He replied. "I had no intention of doing it. The child followed me up the lane, and having committed myself, I became reckless, and did the job!"

"And is it true that you had the body of the child in the cart at the time you went to the Miners' Arms, at Brimington Common, for that glass of beer?"

"Yes, it is true," he made answer. "The body was in the sack, and the children were playing round it."

Mr Tollington remarked, "It was surprising that you should have left your cart in that way?"

"Yes," he said, "it was mysterious that I should have done such a thing; but I felt so reckless that I did not care what became of me."

"It has been stated in the papers," pursued his brother, "that you had had fourteen cups of rum that day; is that true?"

"Oh!" he exclaimed, with much earnestness, "I had a lot of drink that day; a lot of drink! I went out in the morning without my breakfast, intending to go to Clay Cross. I started for there, but, unfortunately for me, I changed my mind, and turned back. If I had gone to Clay Cross I should never have come here. It is a bad job, and I must now make the best of it!"

In answer to further questions, he said he turned back from Clay Cross; went drinking from one public house to another; and having nothing to eat he got into such a state that he hardly knew what he did. He repeated that one of the witnesses saw him with the child in the lane, and he again alleged that she saw much more than she had told. Alfred is referring here to Miss Johnson but the newspaper comes to her defence stating that as she is "nearsighted" she might not have witnessed all Gough thought she had seen.

"Is it true ," asked Mr. Tollington "that you had a conversation on that Saturday evening with Mansfield Tom?"............

Gough showed considerable feeling at the mention of that name, and said "I declare positively that I never knew him, and never spoke to the man in my life. I cannot think how he could make up such a lie. It was too bad of him to try and swear a man's life away like that."

Gough continued that if he could have laid his hands on Mansfield Tom "he would have crushed him up"!

"You see," said the relatives, "what a terrible disgrace you have brought upon us all by what you have done."

"I know that," he quickly retorted, "but you can't help it. It was not your fault. You can't help what I have done."

"And then," they continued, "there is the sorrow you have brought upon that poor family at Brimington."

"Yes," he said in a very subdued tone, "I am very sorry for them- very sorry; but it can't be helped now."

At this point in time a warder entered the cell with Gough's dinner. It was now mid-day and the prison routine was paramount. Replying to the questions of how he was treated and did he have any complaints? Gough replied, "I could not be treated with greater kindness than I am by the Governor and everybody; and I am very thankful for it." He now had plenty of good food and even more to his liking the prison doctor, Mr Wright Baker had ordered that he should have a pint of beer a day! This on top of a tobacco allowance too.

Alfred's handcart meant a great deal to him and since the trial he had frequently stated that he wished his sister and brother-in-law should have it. At that time it was back in Chesterfield but the flags and windmills had long gone gleaned by the morbidly curious seeking mementoes. He again spoke of his wish that they should have it but they declined it on the grounds that there were "too many painful associations for them to wish to possess it". The Sheffield and Rotherham Independent stated that it would probably be sold and there was already a purchaser "very wishful to have it".

Although there was no attempt made to shorten the interview by the Governor or warders and "no restraint was placed upon their free conversation" still the parties themselves felt it inadvisable to prolong their meeting and Ann and Thomas made ready to leave. However, Alfred first had something he wanted to give to his sister. "A little packet, containing all the worldly treasures he possessed. Utterly valueless to a stranger, but prized beyond anything on earth by him." A small leather purse fastened by a steel clasp and within it a penknife (though this must have been confiscated by the Governor as "dangerous or inexpedient to leave in his possession" when he returned to the prison as a convict. It is presumed Alfred had made it known to Captain Farquharson that he was intending to give away all his possessions to his sister on this last visit.). The purse also contained three paper packets, on two of which Alfred had written something:- "Our dear mother's hair; take care of it", "Our dear aunt's hair".**"These locks of hair he had carried with him while a soldier, and in all his wanderings since."** To Mullingar in Ireland, his first posting after enlisting being paid a pound for his trouble. (He was 23 years old then but most of the 43 recruits were just youngsters, there had only been six older than himself!) Afterwards his battalion decamped to the Channel Islands, then on to Aldershot and finally India. After a spell in the barracks at Monmouthshire his time back in England was spent mainly in Yorkshire, Nottingham and fatefully and finally Chesterfield. Gough's third packet contained the locks of his own hair for his aunt and sister. His "special request" to Ann was that she should keep all the locks for his sake, "and the sake of those to whom they referred."

Since he had been incarcerated in the Chesterfield Police Station Alfred had kept, very carefully, in his possession a small-sized copy of the "British Revival Hymn Book". He loved singing and the book "dirtied by much use" contained the songs and solos of the Salvation Army. It had been given to him by someone whilst in the lock-up. Whether it could have been a fellow prisoner, a person from the Salvation Army itself or someone who had access to the cells is not known. It certainly would not have been a member of the public and Gough had no friends wanting to see him. Indeed no one was to have had access to Carline's prisoner. Alfred was known for always singing and had learned some of the hymns contained within the book repeating them "over and over many times a day". Indeed, "at an earlier stage of his imprisonment, he was never tired of repeating its songs" but of late understandably the joy had somewhat left him. Inside the book Alfred had written "You never did speak to me at all till we met on the road." It was reported "to what or to whom it referred is not at all clear" and no theory is given. However, Alfred could have been referring to Mansfield Tom, the incident, real or imaginary, playing on his mind or if it was in a religious context he may have been referring to Paul's conversion on the road to Damascus and applying this to himself. He certainly was spending more time with the Irish Chaplain, Reverend Moore.

Alfred's final offering for his sister to keep safe were his precious delicate letters on the outside of which he had written "Keep thease for our dear Mothers Sake". Written by his beloved mother "and other persons" who obviously had meant a great deal to him at one time in his life. "**They are literally worn into pieces, and so stained as to be almost illegible.**" To finally part with these after all his years of carrying them safely on his travels must have been a wrench, bringing home to him that this was the last time he would set eyes on someone that knew and had loved him and that on his sister's departure she would have with her all his worldly possessions such that they were. Alfred now stood up to say his farewells. He managed to maintain his composure whilst speaking to his brother in law, Tom but when he turned to his sister it was too much. Alfred "broke down utterly and sobbed like a child." Brother and sister's farewells "were choked with sobs". It was for Thomas to guide his distraught wife out of the cell leaving Alfred "overwhelmed with grief."

CHAPTER TWENTY FOUR

WEDNESDAY 16th NOVEMBER 1881

THE PUBLICATION OF GOUGH'S LETTERS BY THE PRESS

Tuesday's final meeting between Alfred and his sister appeared in The Sheffield and Rotherham Independent which also reported that Gough's letters to his sister and brother in law written, before the trial, in October "with a few excisions of matters of a strictly private character" had been published by them. "For obvious reasons, the names of these friends and their residence were not given at the time." This was at the request of Ann and Thomas who keenly felt the disgrace that an only brother had brought upon the family. "Although they had no intention of then and there disowning him, and refusing him their counsel and sympathy, they did desire to remain as far as possible, undiscovered to the world." However The Derbyshire Times had also published these letters but had revealed the name of Mrs Tollington and that she resided in Nottingham more than a week past in their 5th November issue! The Sheffield paper claims the leaking of this confidential information was done much to the annoyance of Mr and Mrs Tollington and so they were publishing their full address now "in order to say that they express their indignation at the crime that has been committed as strongly as anyone; and to say further that they sympathise very deeply with the parents of the unfortunate little girl."

Notwithstanding the Tollingtons wanting to keep a low profile in this sorry affair it was not beyond them to allow the journalist of The Sheffield and Rotherham Independent access to the bundle of letters that Alfred had given into his sister's safekeeping only the previous day! There in black and white is the last letter his mother wrote to him along with another letter written it was thought by a lost love. Apparently these two letters were chosen as examples of the character of the others in the bundle. The newspaper journalist states that this second letter **"written in a female hand"** was probably some person to whom Alfred **"once paid his addresses"**. A **"fair friend"**, the name is withheld, who had disappointed him, and left him to go to America. How the journalist would know that is anybody's guess! No address is given on the letter. Is this information provided by Ann or is it just artistic license on the part of the journalist? None of the other newspapers seem to have used this story. This is the reason why Alfred never married. **"Having been "jilted" once, he was determined not to run the risk of being treated in the same way again."**

Alfred had returned from India and Afghanistan the 12th May 1876. This particular letter was dated 28th August 1876. How it ever reached Alfred can only be surmised but possibly he received it via the army postal system though how fast delivery was is not known. Where he was billeted during the rest of 1876 is not known either but in 1877 he had a short stay in Newport Monmouthshire before his connection with the 17th Foot Regiment terminated. The paper was edged in black indicating the announcement of a death. It appears to be written with some affection but whether it was someone he had known in Leeds before enlisting (and if that was the case she would be someone in her mid-20's at least by this date) or someone he had met whilst in the army. If that is the case it could be a girl from Ireland, Aldershot or Alderney.

"My dear Alfred, i reseved (received) your very kind letter and was glad to hear from you love, you will think Me long before i rite to you but I think of you (even) if i did not rite   My Dear i have had a deal of truble since i have loste my Dear father on the 19th ov this month i do feel lost with dought (without) him and it is a big truble to Me. My Dear Alfred i do feel low i wish you are near Me to chir (cheer) Me up i dont know what to do but it is God will and it cant be un done   he whent very happy   i hope you are very well as i cant say i ham at present   i feel as if my heart would break at present   My Dear Alfret you said each day is bringing you nearer me   i shall be pleased when the time come   i onely wish t was (k) now love if the(you) thinks as much as i do it wont be long   but i know he dose   i long to see that happy day   i live in hopes of it when we shall have hours walk if God spars hus   we must trust in him he do e all thing fore hours good if We can only think so My Dear love you Must excuse me not riting to you be fore as you know what fore   i think i have no More to say at present My love so i must conclude with My very best love to you   Aunt send her best love to you and she is glad you are well as she is very well to   good night and God bless you from your

"M____."

Did Alfred ever meet "M"? If he did then there was no successful outcome. If she was in America he never made it. Perhaps, after a time, with all Gough's moving around the country after he had left the army her letters never found their way to him! Each may have thought the other had lost interest. Could this be one of the contributing factors for Alfred's decline? He had come back to England almost rootless-his beloved mother was dead so what was there for him in Leeds? He tried living with his sister in Nottingham but that did not last long. His whole life he had been moving from one place to another.

CHAPTER TWENTY FIVE

THURSDAY 17th NOVEMBER 1881

GOUGH'S HANDCART

Today, Mr and Mrs Tollington received, to their home, an anonymous letter. Obviously someone, known only as "L.M.," had read about their feelings regarding the handcart. As they had also had their address printed in the paper there was now the possibility of anyone writing to them directly. This person suggested the cart's destruction to which Ann and Thomas replied the following day. The letter was published in The Derbyshire Times:-

"Mr and Mrs Tollington sincerely thank the writer "L. M." for the kind sympathy expressed in the letter they received on Thursday, and wish to state they entirely coincide with the views it contained as to the disposal of the hand-cart, and that they have to-day requested Superintendent Carline, of the Chesterfield police, in whose possession it is, to have it destroyed at once, as they desire, like the writer, that nothing shall remain to remind the public of the crime of their unfortunate brother, who, they are assured, deeply regrets the position in which he has placed himself, and the disgrace he has brought upon his family. In this, their greatest distress they look to One above from whom only that comfort which they so much need can be obtained."

CHAPTER TWENTY SIX

FRIDAY 18th NOVEMBER 1881

WILLIAM MARWOOD

26. Photograph of William Marwood, the executioner.

The Sheffield and Rotherham Independent today reported a new character that was about to enter centre stage in Gough's miserable saga.

"Marwood will arrive in Derby to-morrow (Saturday) afternoon, though he might easily reach there on Sunday from his home at Horncastle." Who is Marwood? A 61 year old former cobbler from Lincolnshire who only nine years previously managed to persuade the Governor of Lincoln prison to let him have a go at hanging someone! He had been experimenting for some time with regard to the length of the rope in relation to the weight of the person being hung in order to cause instant death. It was not unknown for the person hung to be completely decapitated. William Marwood was credited with the so-called "long drop" technique although executioners in Ireland had already started this method some years previously. The "short drop" method of hanging meant death came slower by strangulation whereas Marwood's method was to break the neck instantly and whilst unconscious the prisoner would die of asphyxia. Luckily for Marwood his first hanging was a success and on the back of it he was being engaged by other Governors and Sheriffs throughout the country. In a mere three years he was rated as the number one hangman though he himself preferred to be called an "executioner".

It was now, according to The Derby and Chesterfield Reporter, that Gough "seemed to realise his position more fully than he had hitherto done". Several times that day, and the next, Alfred allegedly fell on his knees to pray! "The old dogged spirit was from this time seen no more. He was heard to express the wish that he could have another chance of life, in order to show how differently he would act." However, approvingly Gough did not show "any of that unctuous, demonstrative kind of repentance which many of our notorious criminals are wont to garnish the chronicles of the condemned cell"! "Not unfrequently" it was reported, that Alfred "qualified the admission of his guilt and the expression of his sorrow, by such axioms as "What's done can't be helped," and "It's over now, and there's no use talking about it".

CHAPTER TWENTY SEVEN

SATURDAY 19TH NOVEMBER 1881

CARLINE'S DESTRUCTION OF THE HANDCART

Superintendent Carline was sat upstairs in his office in Marsden Street re-reading the letter he had received from Mr and Mrs Tollington the previous day. He also had another letter lying on his desk that had been recently written to him by Gough. Elijah was given the task, by Alfred, to sell the cart and hand the proceeds over to his sister. Now, Ann was wanting the cart destroyed. It was an easy decision for Elijah to make. If the handcart was kept it would probably go on display somewhere for the morbidly curious to pay their pennies and "gawp" at. Elijah called down to Sergeant Radford to give the order for some of the young constables to finally start breaking up "Eleanor's bier".

Elijah took pen to paper and curtly replied to the Tollingtons:-

Madam, -- In compliance with your request I have had the hand-cart broken up and completely destroyed to-day. I think you have acted wisely to do away with it altogether. — Yours respectfully,

E. Carline, Superintendent.

Elijah was not impressed with the Tollingtons. He had kept up with the newspaper reports of Gough in prison and could not fail to notice that Gough's letters to his sister "always appeared in the daily papers the day after they were sent on to her." As fast as she got them she was selling them to the Sheffield press and probably not just the letters addressed to her! When Elijah wrote to Gough about his suspicions is not known but it would have been after Alfred's final meeting with his sister on the Tuesday where Gough was still talking about leaving the cart to her. Reading the private letters of Alfred's mother and sweetheart in the Sheffield newspaper on the Wednesday for all to see may well have prompted Elijah to write at that point. He may or may not have liked Alfred Gough but he still thought of him as a human being who had some right to privacy in his final days. Elijah must have sent the letter either Thursday or Friday but before he received the Tollingtons' letter to destroy the handcart. He obviously told Gough about his sister's carryings-on but had not mentioned the destruction of the cart.

Saturday came and went but there was no sign of Marwood!

CHAPTER TWENTY EIGHT

SUNDAY 20ᵀᴴ NOVEMBER 1881

MARWOOD FINALLY ARRIVES

Gough wrote to Superintendent Carline this morning. The news of his sister selling his letters to the press was deeply troubling to him and he "was very much displeased". He thought he could have relied on his family to respect his wishes but he was wrong. Had he have known what was to become of his own letters he would not have written them. He could only rely on himself and "the only friend he had in the world"—Superintendent Elijah Carline! Whether Elijah welcomed this friendship is doubtful but Elijah was a man who made friends amongst all classes. Alfred's letter asked Elijah "to sell his handcart for £1-10-0 out of which he was to send 15/- to his aunt and to drink his health with the other 15/-"!

Gough also, according to The Derby Mercury, requested that the Governor should destroy the confession he had written to his brother-in-law, Thomas Tollington which at present was in Captain Farquharson's possession. Apparently on either the Thursday or Friday Thomas, "or someone for him" wrote to the prison authorities asking for "any further letters Gough might have written". All Gough would say was that "he did not wish to make any further communication as his time was so short"!

Sunday in the prison always meant two chapel services that day to which Gough and his escort attended. For the previous few days, however, special prayers had already been said for him by his fellow inmates at Alfred's own request and because the size of the chapel would not accommodate all inmates together the Chaplain had recently been holding two services daily. The form of prayer being used was the ordinary Morning Service of the Church of England. The Reverend Moore was there officiating as usual. The sermons he was to preach today obviously had a special reference to the impending execution but the prison chapel was not the only religious institution referring to this matter. Several of the local Derby churches were offering up prayers for "the doomed man". The Reverend *"took his text from a passage in the lesson for the day, "Then shall the dust return to the earth as it was, and the spirit shall return unto God who gave it." Ecclesiastes XII, 7. He referred to the solemn lesson to be drawn from the chapter, and remarked upon its singular appropriateness as the lesson for the day, dealing as it did with the necessity of preparing for the inevitable end of all that is mortal in man. In the course of an eloquent sermon, he urged upon his hearers the truth conveyed in the last verse of the lesson, "For God shall bring every work into judgement, with every secret thing, whether it be good or whether it be evil.""* Alfred joined in the devotions with intense interest for Gough had been approached by Reverend Moore before the services that day to see if he would like to choose the psalms and hymns. After all, since his imprisonment, it was reported that Alfred "devoted a large portion of his time to the study of the Bible". This is not so surprising for the Bible had always been available in his cell as in other prisoners' cells throughout his time at Derby. It would be unusual if he had not picked it up to read to relieve the boredom of his incarceration if nothing else. It was widely reported that Gough loved singing. He had a "powerful, melodious voice, although he does not always keep to the tune" and it seemed he had "also evinced a fondness for singing the hymns of the Salvation Army." One of the hymns he chose for that day was "the well-known penitential psalm (51st) *Miserere Mei Deus* – "Have mercy upon me, O God, according to thy loving kindness: according unto the multitude of thy tender mercies blot out my transgressions."

In the late afternoon, after such a beautiful blue sky day, the final service which Gough would attend on this earth was again conducted, in fading light this time, by Reverend Moore. He took as his text *"the 15th verse of the 1st chapter of the first epistle to Timothy, "this is a faithful saying, and worthy of all acceptation, that Christ Jesus came into the world to save sinners"* ("of whom I am chief."It is surprising The Derbyshire Times did not give the full quote as it is so apt.) *Gough listened attentively to both sermons, and seemed much impressed by the words of the preacher."* Four thirty, the service had concluded and the sun had set for the last time on Alfred's life. Handcuffed to his warders, he made his way back to the cell. When the door closed upon him this time he would not be let out again until "he is led forth for execution."

Marwood, contrary to the expectations of the prison authorities and their probable annoyance, finally arrived in Derby by the Great Northern train just before 4 o'clock in the afternoon. It had been a beautiful day- one of those Indian Summer days and Marwood possibly tarried far too long in Nottingham. He had spent the previous evening there with friends whereas all in Derby were expecting him to have come from home! When his duty was over he was heading straight back to Nottingham. Making his way for the fourth time to the gaol it was almost dark and according to the Sheffield and Rotherham Independent Marwood was to report first to the Under-Sheriff, Mr B. Scott Currey and then proceed to the gaol where he was supposed to "inspect the arrangements for the execution, and make all necessary preparations for the ceremony on Monday morning". Because of the fading light Marwood may not have called in to the Under-Sheriff. The inspection of the scaffold was awaiting him. It had been erected a few days previously to test and then by Saturday it had all been taken down again but since then as it took little time to put it all together it was now erected and waiting for Marwood's approval and would not be taken down until Gough was dead. According to The Sheffield and Rotherham Independent the gallows **"will be rather different from that used on the last occasion, in consequence of a slight mishap which then occurred, but which did not become known at the time."** Intriguing! All Marwood had to do was just bring his rope. A length with a thickness of some five eighths of an inch. The one he had used on his last occasion at Derby Gaol. The one where there was a slight mishap! He would need to do his calculations but it was expected to be a drop of eight feet. A large hole for Gough's body to fall into had also been dug.

When Marwood had finished his tasks he went to the lodging that was provided for him within the prison. He was not expected to go from the precincts until after the hanging and he may even have attended the final evening chapel service that Gough was to attend. Although this was reported it is doubtful he arrived in time for chapel but he may well have looked out for Gough and his two warders making their way back to the condemned cell along the corridors. Did he want to size Alfred up from a distance?!

Later that evening Gough received his regular visitor Reverend Moore who stayed with him until a late hour. The chaplain reported that Alfred's behaviour of late "could not have been nicer". Gough spent the time reading the Bible, ("a great source of comfort to him during the past few days" according to The Hull Packet and East Riding Times!) praying and writing. The reverend sought *"to bring him to a sense of the deplorable fate which awaited him."* Gough had thanked Reverend Moore for his kindness on more than one occasion. Alfred was appreciative of the chaplain's attentions to a sinner but Alfred was not bitter regarding the sentence passed upon him. It was completely justifiable. The Derbyshire Times felt that there was reason to believe Gough would die penitent but whether those in Chesterfield were of a forgiving mood was doubtful.

CHAPTER TWENTY NINE

MONDAY 21st NOVEMBER

THE HANGING

It was not until 3 o'clock in the morning that Alfred finally retired to his bed. Why sleep now when he would have eternal sleep in a few short hours? He had many thoughts crowding his mind, memories and "what-ifs" but he was calm. This was how it should all end. He slept, but only fitfully, until 6 o'clock when he was woken to take his final breakfast of tea, bread and butter. No doubt Superintendent Carline would smile at this. Gough was still eating even now! Glancing at the windows it was still dark outside but people were astir. Precautions had or were being taken **"to prevent any of the prisoners, or persons coming to the gaol on business, from witnessing the execution. Those who have occupied cells overlooking the gallows will be removed to other parts of the gaol, and a hoarding has been put up at the end of the yard, which is near the entrance to the prison."**

Gough's prison uniform was today taken from him and swapped for the clothes he originally wore on first entering the gaol as a remand prisoner- "though they appear more ragged than formally". His oft mended corduroy trousers, his cotton shirt that came above his faded green coat, his small red and black scarf that he would tie around his neck and even his well worn brown hat that he was wearing the day he was arrested. These were all handed over to him to put on.

At 7am a rather damp Reverend Moore, for the weather was "wet and tempestuous", entered the condemned cell once more for the very last time. He had kept vigil with

Alfred the night before for which Alfred was grateful but the old clergyman was beginning to feel his age with all these to-ings and fro-ings. He was now to spend the rest of the allotted time in prayer with Alfred but not before Alfred had first given to him a "document" written the previous night.

Outside the prison gates were a group of half a dozen men waiting admittance- rain sodden newspaper reporters. It was initially thought on the Friday that Mr Sumner, the High Sheriff would only give permission for one reporter to attend the execution as initiated by his predecessor and the Derby press had already chosen one of their number- Mr Dinnis of The Gazette for the task. However, it appears Mr Dickinson from one of the Chesterfield newspapers was also given permission by the High Sheriff along with four others. It was now about 7.30 and dawn, (such as it was in this miserable, wet weather,) was just breaking, though it still seemed dark. Whilst the reporters were waiting groups of locals were beginning to congregate outside the prison walls, on the square. Apparently Derby acquired more curious people than other places as the scaffold was placed against the outer wall and the "drop" could be "plainly heard" from outside!

The six reporters were finally admitted by a "janitor" who spoke in gruff tones to them- "Are you all coming at once?" Yes, they were. It is presumed the reporters were directed to the waiting room on the right just inside the gates until they were needed rather than have them wander about inside the perimeter of the gaol.

A few minutes later Mr B. Scott-Currey, the Under-Sheriff, Mr W. B. Delacombe, his chief officer and Mr J. Wright Baker, the gaol surgeon arrived at the gates to be admitted.

At quarter to eight the prison bell began its doleful tolling and all the time people were gathering outside. The sound of the bell was the signal for the Under-Sheriff and his officer to proceed to the condemned cell situated over on the opposite side of the prison to that where the scaffold was erected near the prison infirmary in the inner circle. It was their duty to "demand" from the Governor "the body of Alfred Gough for execution"!

Five minutes after the Under-Sheriff had set off to the condemned cell the members of the press were collected by a warder who conducted them to the scene of execution. The Derby Mercury takes up the story- **"with startling abruptness"** the reporters **"were brought face to face with the gallows- which looked more than ordinarily hideous in itself and its surroundings. Turning to the right through a narrow door in the hoarding which screened the yard from the approach to the central building, the press representatives found themselves in what is known as the outer patrol- a circular lane paved with flags (flagstones), and bounded on one side by the gloomy prison walls, and on the other by the gaol buildings. Lying at the foot of the outer wall is a level platform about two feet high covered with grass, the burial ground of men previously executed."** Six simple stones bore the name of each grave's occupant, the date of execution and the crime for which they were punished. **"At the end of this plot of grass, and standing two or three feet above it, was the floor of the scaffold, the base boarded towards the grass, and the side next the pavement covered with a cloth. Above the platform, standing up bare and repulsive, were**

three iron bars, looking exactly like the horizontal bar of a gymnasium, save that from the cross bar was hanging a stout hempen rope." (The same rope used for the last hanging at Derby Gaol.)

"A few yards further on in the circular yard and hidden from the gallows by its bend, was the pinioning place, a recess in the gaol buildings. At ten minutes to eight it was tenanted by one person only- Marwood, the executioner—a little wizened old man, with a fresh complexion and pleasant face, who greeted a passing warder with a polite "Good morning to you." " There he was waiting for the procession that had now left the condemned cell on its somewhat "roundabout" and "circuitous" route to reach a door which lead into the outer portal and Marwood. Alfred, the model prisoner, walked slowly and steadily with warders to his front and back. Behind these walked the Governor, the prison doctor, Reverend Moore, the Under-Sheriff and his officer. It was here when Alfred came face to face with the hangman that the press obtained a clear view of the condemned culprit – "very pale" and "wan" though " firm and steadfast" just like he had been at his trial. He was bareheaded carrying his old brown hat in his hands revealing his usual unkempt hair and beard. On halting Gough passed his hat to a warder and "quite composed, walked into the presence of his executioner" waiting to begin his work.

It is typical of the press that after all the vitriol that Gough had had heaped upon him and no doubt a fair amount of lies written about him that the reporter for The Derby Mercury wrote- **"He was anything but the ferocious**

looking person some of the papers have stated him to be. His high and sloping forehead and parted lips gave him the look of a kindly dispositioned man, and with better clothing on than the faded green coat and frequently mended corduroy trousers which he wore, his appearance would have been that of a respectable artisan, rather than of a rag gatherer." Even the local Chesterfield paper- The Derbyshire Times wrote on this day that *"looking at his photograph in which he is wearing the uniform of the 17th Foot Gough appears a fine, good-looking man, and every inch the embodiment of what he has been -a true soldier"* and in a later column of the same newspaper *"from his* (Gough's) *conduct throughout there is no doubt if he had been educated he would have been an intelligent and respectable man"*!

Reverend Moore commenced in a subdued voice to recite from the Burial Service for the dead whilst Marwood proceeded to pinion Gough. There had been a stool placed close by for Gough to use whilst the operation took place but he dispensed with it preferring to stand erect submitting to all that Marwood was to do – a strong strap was fastened about his waist, his arms were tied, his hands and wrists were also fastened and the top part of his shirt and his small scarf were torn away to reveal his bare neck. And all the while Gough looked heavenward "feebly articulating what Marwood and those close to him believe to be a prayer for strength to bear the approaching ordeal and likewise for forgiveness". Before the short march to the gallows and his final resting place Gough was offered a drink (presumably brandy) from a small phial by one of the warders. It was put to his lips and Gough eagerly drained its contents then without faltering the procession began *"Gough marching with a step firm as if he had but been at drill in the barrack yard in the distant Indies"*. **"At the head.......two stalwart warders, then come the officials (each carrying black wands) and the chaplain-who still reads portions of the Burial Service –and these are followed by the condemned man between several warders and the executioner the representatives of the Press bringing up the rear, all heads being uncovered."** Just a few yards and the gallows were in view. One reporter states Gough "did not hesitate but moved forward" the other claimed Gough gave "a very slight but perceptible start" which was "apparent in his frame. But this is all the sign of fear-if fear it be- that he gives" for without the slightest assistance which the two warders on either side of him were prepared to offer he ascended the steps leading to the scaffold. On the platform Gough cast "one last imploring, piteous glance" at those around him but said not a word though his lips were moving. He took his place under the rope and looked upward. Marwood stepped forward to fasten Alfred's legs together. The white cap was then placed over his face without so much as a murmur. Finally the noose was placed over Alfred's head by one who had had much practice in these things and equally quickly and skilfully Marwood drew the noose tight. The two warders who had accompanied Gough onto the gallows' platform took a step back. Could Gough feel that their closeness had gone? But there was the Reverend still praying for him- "Man that is born of a woman hath but a short time to live,"…..then nothing! Marwood had drawn back the bolt and Gough, all 11stone 10 pounds of him, disappeared from view with a "dull heavy thud."There was a silence in the watchers whilst Doctor Wright Baker stepped forward to lift the white cap to check that Alfred Gough was indeed dead. Death had been instantaneous. Eleanor Windle's murder had been avenged! The eight foot drop calculated against Gough's weight provided him with a speedy death rather than a struggle. Some in Brimington would say he had too easy a death! The demise of Gough was a sign to hoist the black flag over the prison some two minutes later for those who had gathered outside. The groups had spoken in loud whispers to while away the time but at the appointed hour all fell silent as the clock struck. The Derby Mercury claimed there were nearly a thousand persons in the vicinity by 8 o'clock whereas The Derbyshire Times considered the numbers to be only several hundred *"mostly of the lower class"*. The constant drizzling rain being a factor that kept others away who had previously attended the executions held within the walls of the prison. The policemen stationed outside the prison had little to do for there would be no demonstration to save Gough from the noose. Indeed The Derby and Chesterfield Reporter stated- "from first to last, we have not heard of a single attempt being made to get up a manifestation of sympathy with regard to him. As a rule, some such effort is made." However, all felt that it was a just decision and when the crowds knew that Gough was indeed dead they melted away back to their own lives. Did they know that Alfred's body would hang where it was for a further hour before being cut down?

"The officials having cast a glance at the body suspended from the scaffold proceeded to Capt. Farquharson's rooms where the formal declarations were made out." This was a notification signed by the officials - the Under-Sheriff, the Chaplain, Governor and Sheriff's officer, - that the sentence had been carried out in their presence. The surgeon completed his certificate to state he had examined Gough and found him dead. These two documents coupled with the findings of the Inquisition (the inquest) that was to take place shortly were to be sent to the Home Office by Mr Delacombe, the Sheriff's officer. A further notification displaying to all that Gough was dead was posted outside the prison gates.

At 9.30 a.m. the 38 year old, Mr William Harvey Whiston, a solicitor, opened the formal coroner's inquest within the prison in the Prison committee-room (Gough's body having now been taken down). This was the usual procedure. A jury was present and Mr Benjamin F Peacock, a 44 year old publican of The Wheel Inn was the foreman. The Derby and Chesterfield Reporter stated that *"The Coroner, in opening the proceedings, said this inquest was held under the Capital Punishment Amendment Act, 1868, which abolished public executions. Unfortunately the number of executions in the town had lately been unusually frequent, and most of the jury would therefore be pretty well acquainted with the course that had to be taken. Before 1868 when executions were public, it was not necessary to hold an inquest, but when they were made private it was considered advisable to hold such inquiries, in order that the public might be satisfied that the right man had been hung. The jury were then sworn and proceeded to view the body of the deceased. It had been placed in a coffin, which lay in a shed near to the scene of the execution."* The only witness that needed to be called was the governor. *"The Derby and Chesterfield Reporter" claimed that Captain Farquharson stated- "I am the Governor of Her Majesty's Prison at Derby. The body just viewed by the jury is that of Alfred Gough. I produce the record sheet bearing the date of his reception, conviction and execution. He was an inmate of this prison on a charge of murdering Eleanor Windle at Brimington on the 20th August. He was sentenced at Leicester Assizes to be executed on the 2nd November. Sentence of death has been duly carried into effect this morning, within the walls of this prison. I was present at the execution. Gough was 34 years of age, and was unmarried. He was described as a hawker by trade."*

The Coroner said that was really all the evidence and if the jury were satisfied with it, it would be their duty to return a verdict in accordance with it. The jury at once found that Alfred Gough had been duly executed this morning within the prison walls, and in accordance with law."

Now that Marwood could retrieve his rope from the gallows he was off and on his way back to Nottingham. He seemed to be a bit of a character. "According to a Sheffield contemporary, to whose inventiveness the public owe many unusual and fantastic stories," (Personally this does not fill me with confidence as to the veracity of his reporting!) "Marwood, the executioner, is very fond of Nottingham and after leaving Derby.....held a kind of reception among his numerous admirers.......No sooner was it known that Marwood with his ominous black bundle in hand, was making his way towards Lower Parliament street than the hue and cry was raised, and ere he stepped into the Hope and Anchor, one of his favourite houses of resort in Nottingham, he had a crowd of persons about him. Turning round when he had got onto the steps leading into the old-fashioned hostelry kept by an ex-warder of the gaol, Marwood took off his hat and politely bowed to those present. Now and again Marwood would rise and bow to the crowd of people in the street, accompanying the bow with the ejaculation, "God bless you all". Having safely deposited his bundle in the corner nearest his seat, Marwood was soon "at home" among the occupants of the bar, all of whom kept up an incessant chatter with the hangman, who would now laugh at some jest, or assume a serious aspect when a solemn subject was introduced. Of course everybody had a question to ask. First and foremost he was asked how Gough had died, and this brought forth the reply that "he died very firm," and "like a soldier." "Did he as he said he should, die like a Christian?" asked one. "He did." Was Mr. Marwood in favour of reprieves? Yes, Mr. Marwood was if they were brought about by Divine aid............Marwood informed his audience that the rope with which Gough had been hanged was two and three-eighths of an inch in circumference..........Although willing to converse, Marwood would not let his black bundle be tampered with, nor would he allow his friends to see the rope he had that morning used."

Meanwhile whilst Marwood was laughing and joking during the day Alfred was being buried in "the only vacant space which is now left" within the raised patch of grass by the prison wall. Buried "in the usual manner," for murderers, "his coffin being filled with quick lime". It was possibly thought that this would aid decomposition of the body whereas the opposite appears to be true.

The last letter from Gough was published by the newspapers – the document that was given to Reverend Moore early that morning. The chaplain was given permission to let it be printed and it was corrected rather than recorded in Gough's own style:-

Sir – (To the Minister) – I now take my pen in my hand to write a few lines to you to thank you for being so good and kind to me, poor unfortunate prisoner, who has committed such a fearful, wicked crime. I hope the Lord will forgive me for it. I am very sorry for it; if I had a hundred lives I would give them to call that poor, sweet, innocent, little girl back to life; but it cannot be. But the Lord has taken her soul to Heaven to be with the angels of glory, in that bright and happy land above, where there is no sorrow, but all is bliss and happiness; to which I hope my Lord and Saviour will lift me up, and wash all my wicked sins away, and make me as white as snow, and to sing the praises of Jesus Christ our Lord and Saviour for ever and ever, amen. Good-bye and God bless you, sir, for being so kind to me, a poor sinner. I shall soon be cold and in the dust, but hope to be forgiven and rise in glory at the last day. So no more, yours truly, ALFRED GOUGH. May God bless you, and the doctor for his kindness, and likewise the governor.

Alfred had frequently thanked the chaplain, the governor and the other officials for "their kindness and attention to him" and his last letter was to make sure this was reiterated.

However, The Derby and Chesterfield Reporter have one more scoop for the public's delight. Apparently, though unbelievably given Superintendent Carline's information to Alfred regarding his sister's use of the letters sent to her, Alfred wrote one more letter "on the prison correspondence form". "It is clearly written and apparently done in a firm, steady, clear hand". In the early hours of his final day Gough wrote:-

"My Dear Sister, - i now take my pen in hand to rite a fue lines to you. the last that i your unfortunate brother shall rite to you in this world- your unfortunate Brother that has been so unfortunate to let his sinful heart commit such a dreadful Crime. it is fearful to look back to. i ham very very sorry for it. if i had a hundred lives i whould o given them all to Call Back that Sweet little girl back to life. But God has taken her to heaven to Himself to be with the angels above ware all his Glory. and love. And i hope my Saviour will forgive me a poor Penitent Sinner for all my Sins. when you recive this letter i shall be no more. I shall be laid low in the dust

hoping God has for given me a poor Sinner for all my wicked Sins for they are of a great many and very black ones but I hope God as taken my soal to heaven before you get this my letter. Dear Sister i hope you will try your best and bring your children up in the fear of the Lord and may God bless them forever. Hear i must conclude with best love to you all.

"ALFRED"

Hymn Sung to-day

Sunday,

Here follows the hymn, "Just as I am" etc

Good by and God Bless you. i hope we shall all meet in heaven.

Gough's letter to the Tollingtons was actually enclosed within another letter from the prison governor, Captain Farquharson. His, like Superintendent Carline's letter to Alfred's sister and brother-in-law, was curt and to the point!

"Sir,-I enclose the last letter written by Alfred Gough to his sister. The former one which you saw when visiting him was yesterday destroyed at his request, and in his presence. No pressure whatever was put upon him as you suggest; he was simply informed of the fact that his letters to you were immediately published. His last days were much embittered by the knowledge that such use was made of his correspondence which he said was a

"shameful thing for a sister to do," and that it *" troubled him"* so much that he could not keep it out of his thoughts, which ought now to be set upon other things. - I am, sir, yours faithfully,

"C.E.FARQUARSON,

"Governor."

The Governor clearly had a low opinion of the goings- on of the Tollingtons. He refers to the letter he had received from them, or their representative, on the Thursday or Friday seeking Gough's confessional letter. That would have been worth something! They were obviously suggesting that the Governor was somehow coercing Gough into not passing on the letter and even forcing him to have it destroyed. The Governor refutes this. It was the information from Superintendent Carline regarding the Tollingtons' actions that had unsettled Gough and at a time when Gough should have been considering the salvation of his soul rather than considering why his family would let him down so.

Thomas Tollington is determined to have the last word and writes to the Governor on the very same day of Gough's execution.

"Sir, -We thank you for your letter and its inclosure received this evening. We are glad to learn that our suggestion was a mistaken one. The reason we allow the letters to be published was this, that their contents showed that our brother was a different man from

what he was supposed to be by a large portion of the community, thus correcting the largely prevailing wrong impression created by some of the newspaper reports in the earlier stages of the case. -

Yours respectfully,

"THOMAS TOLLINGTON."

Could this really have been the reason? It would have been laudable if true. However, if this was their thinking it would have been better if they had somehow conveyed this intention to Alfred. He readily appeared to be able to see the worst in them rather than give them the benefit of the doubt!

In two households the newspaper was put down after the final article regarding Alfred Gough was read. Superintendent Carline took it all in his stride, ever the professional. He had other cases to deal with and like most of the inhabitants in Chesterfield it was time to move on. The Windle family as one would expect from God-fearing folk found it altogether more difficult. William's two eldest sons moved away completely to Australia and the Newbold branch of the family seemed over time to completely forget about their Brimington kin. Yet the essence of Eleanor's story, though somewhat altered, has passed through the centuries in oral form within the females of one branch of the Windle family and the wonders of the computer age has brought the true story of little Eleanor Windle back to life.

POSTSCRIPT

This book came about as a result of wanting to know more about my ancestors. It started with a scribbled note written down by my teenage self in the 1960's. Quizzing my grandparents as to who was who and the stories they told of previous generations. A murder in the family was always an exciting tale. Of course it was not in our immediate family. Only by marriage were we connected to the unfortunate young lady. Or so it was thought! It was a tale to tell little girls to beware of strangers! Now move on half a century and the wonder of the internet has made family research so much easier. There to discover, eventually, Eleanor Windle. Only a name to begin with but by elimination she had to be the murder victim. Now I had a name and date Google found a paragraph on her. Wow, that was real progress. The bare bones of the story and within it something that made me shudder. My birthday was the same date as Eleanor's death!! I had to find out more. A trip to Chesterfield and the local studies library beckoned to trawl through the newspaper reports of the time. I was very familiar with the nineteenth century Derbyshire Times and was anticipating a paragraph or two on the murder. Little did I know of the flood gates of reportage that were to open and the deluge of facts that were to pour out! It was so exciting! I could see it all now. A docudrama on the silver screen! The information was so visually amazing you just could not make it up. The trouble was someone had to write it first! I stepped forward and with the aid of all those anonymous reporters now long dead but who told the story far better than I ever could we have reached the end of the story of Eleanor Windle, Alfred Gough and the able Superintendent Carline who in time became Deputy Chief Constable of Derbyshire.

My research has taken me to Sheffield, Harrogate, Derby, Buxton, Matlock, the National Archives in London and Leicester. I particularly want to thank Ms Tyler-Divine for allowing me access to the Castle where the Assizes were held for the trial of Alfred Gough. How could I have known that I was stepping back in time to see the actual courtroom layout and the dock where Alfred stood? We even ventured down to the cells. An eerie experience when there is only two of you in the building and the place is in such an abandoned state. (Future film crews take note!) I've been thrilled with all the snippets of information I have found which has helped put meat onto the bare bones of the reported stories and hopefully has corrected some reported wrongs.

Writing this book has always been a dilemma. I did so want it to be a thriller and pin the crime on someone else. I certainly have one or two candidates. However the historian in me won out. It is, after all my family that I am writing about, I am only going to write this book once and so I had to get it right to the best of my ability. However, if ever anyone wants to pick up the story and run with it as a novel feel free to do so.

BIBLIOGRAPHY

Buxton Museum and Art Gallery, Terrace Road, Buxton

General photographs relating to the Derbyshire police:-

DERSB: 2004.44.481 Derbys. Assizes at the crown court on St. Mary's Gate, Derby.

DERSB: 2004.44.543 Derbys. Constabulary Officers based at Chesterfield Division. Circa 1888

DERSB: 2004.44.786 Derbys. Constabulary Officers, 1880's/1890's- 3 Sgts., 1 Inspector, and 15 Constables

Chesterfield Library (Local Studies Department), New Beetwell St. ,Chesterfield

The Brimington Quarterly Messenger and Strange Tales from Humble Life No. 10 Oct.1878- No.23 Jan. 1882. Issued by the Brimington Tract Society- notes on churches, Sunday School, board schools, etc.

Brimington Methodist Church Nisi Dominus Frustra 1967 (History of Mount Zion, Bethel and Trinity on completion of new church)

Derbyshire Times -3rd October 1896 p.6 col.5- opening of new Wesleyan Chapel

"   "   26th November 1898-Death of Deputy Chief Constable Carline

Establishment of Derbyshire Constabulary- J. E. Heath. In Derbyshire Miscellany Vol. IX Part 1 Spring 1980 p. 19-22.

Keeping the Peace- law and order in the past in Derbys. - A beginners' guide (Derbyshire Record Office box file 22393)

Notes on some Derbyshire Toll Houses and Turnpike Roads- Robert Thornhill. In Derbyshire Miscellany Vol.IV No.4 Autumn 1968 p. 185-216 and Vol.V Part 4 Autumn 1970 p. 198-204

Derbyshire Miscellany Vol. VI Part 6 Autumn 1973 p.198-209- Joseph Scott (including map) L942.51

Turnpike Roads- Act of Parliament 5th July 1865- Brimington and Chesterfield to Brampton L625.7p 9101/20533

The Sheffield and Chesterfield to Derby Roads- Howard Smith L-David Wilmot388.1

Tupton Turnpike and Toll house   see Cuttings file (Star 29th May 1968) - David Wilmot. In Chesterfield and District Local History Society Newsletter June 2007 p.3-6

Derbyshire Turnpikes compiled by A.P.Munford and D. V. Fowkes   1972   L625.7 oversize (Derbyshire Record Office L10735)

Stanton and Staveley – A Business History – S.D.Chapman ch.3 (Woodhead-Faulkner 1981)

The Derby and Chesterfield Reporter   August- November 1881

The Derbyshire Times   August- November 1881.   All events well- documented

"   "   "   29th December 1935 p.20 Obituary and photo of Eleanor's mother-Harriett Windle

The Derbyshire Courier   August-November 1881. All events well- documented

25" Ordnance Survey Maps (3) 1876-1877 of Brimington – Chesterfield

Map of Derbyshire 1880 Ordnance Survey 1"-1mile (L912.4251 Acc.No.5290)

6" Ordnance Survey Map 1921   of Brimington

T.P. Wood's Almanac 1881.   L314.251

Derbyshire Record Office, Matlock

Q/5P   16/ 1-97 Calendar of Prisoners Aug.-Nov.1881 (Alfred Gough)

D3376/05   1/1 Derbyshire Constabulary Register 1857-1880   (Elijah Carline's police work record)

St Michael and All Angels Church, Brimington   M47 Vol. 2 Ann (Hannah) Windle 20.7. 73. Buried 22nd July 1873. Burial.

M47 Vol.8 William Windle 8. 9. 74. Marriage.

D770C/EA91   Methodist Infant School Log 1880-1882 (Eleanor Windle-a pupil here)

D177 A/PC   125- 135 Brimington Burial Board Records 1877-1947

D3A/TT111 Plan of Road and Tollhouse at Brimington 1876

D3 A/TT115 Rough Plan of Brimington Tollhouse and Garden

D3 A/TC 323-325 Correspondence on Purchase of Brimington Tollhouse by F.Fenton 1883-1884

Q/AB 1/ County Gaol, prisoners and building including:-

Q/AB 2/32   1929 Sale Catalogue of Derby Gaol + Plan of Derby Gaol in Vernon Street

D1500 Z/Z1   Letter regarding executioner's arrangements concerning a prisoner at Derby-refers to bringing the rope, etc. 1880

D2200 LOC P444 Plans of county building lock-ups including Chesterfield Lock-Up no.28 and 29

D2200/71   3-12, 14-15   Police stations and dwellings

Harrogate Library

Newspapers:-

"Harrogate Advertiser" Saturday 2nd November 1878

"Pateley Bridge and Nidderdale Herald" 1878. Reel number NP02016

Internet

http://archive.org/details/frederickswanwic00smituoft
The actual book "Frederick Swanwick-A Sketch" by J Frederick Smith printed for private circulation in 1888 has been made available on the Internet by The University of Toronto Library. Contains the magistrate's life story and two images of the man.

http://search.ancestry.co.uk   Use of 1881 census as starting point for finding the people referred to in this book. Following through to other census dates, birth, marriage and death records. England and Wales Criminal Registers 1791-1892, UK Medical Registers 1859-1959-(1879)

http://newspapers.bl.uk   There are many national newspapers covering the story on this site.

http://www.london-gazette.co.uk/issues -The London Gazette 2nd September 1881 p.4507-4508

http://www.bunker8.pwp.blueyonder —John Lea's criminology website of Courts and Prosecution in 19th Century England.

http://www.casebook.org/dissertations/rip-victoria - Casebook: Jack the Ripper. The Victorian Medico-Legal Autopsy. Part 1: Dissection in Pursuit of the Cause of Death by Karyo Magellan- useful bibliography in the footnotes.

http://www.oldbaileyonline.org/static/history.jsp- The Proceedings of the Old Bailey-London's Central Criminal Court 1674-1913.-useful glossary and background information on selective reporting of cases, rape, sexual offences etc. but really of an earlier period.

http://vcp.e2bn.org/justice/- Victorian Crime and Punishment —various useful headings on this website.

http://catsmeatshop.blogspot.com   (November 2010)   On remand at Holloway Gaol 1892

www.horncastlecivic.org.uk/worthies Horncastle Worthies: William Marwood- Executioner. Horncastle Civic Society

http://dsal.uchicago.edu/referencegazetteer Originally a late 19th century Imperial Gazetteer of India   Volumes 10 p.193 and 18 p.43 for descriptions of Cherat and Murree Hills area.

http://www.globalsecurity.org/military/world/pakistan
Peshawar Cantonment   Description of history of Peshawur

https://openlibrary.org/permanentrecordofqueenvictoria'sstatevisittoderby This is a book that can be read online. Page 159 contains the photograph of Captain Parry, the Chief Constable of Derbyshire.

Leeds Local and Family History Library

Leeds Mercury –Newspaper

Leicestershire, Leicester and Rutland Record Office, Wigston Magna

DE3736 (Box 6) Photos of Leicester Castle and 2 photos of Interior Rooms

22D63/78/1-3 Route description- Lucknow to Peshwar and route Muster Roll 1st Battalion 17th Foot Regiment (1873)

DE5834/17, 18, 19. Three photographs –partly in civilian clothes, partly in uniform- of men of the 1st Battalion, 17th Regiment at Peshawur

DE5834/16 Photograph of 1st Battalion, 17th Regiment at Lucknow

Spencers' Illustrated Leicester Almanac1880

www.leicester.gov.uk- Leicester City Council- Environment and Planning- background information to Leicester Castle and its environs

Local Studies Library in Matlock

"A Short History of the Derbyshire Constabulary" published 1981-5.

The National Archives

WO12/3492   General Muster Book of 2nd Battalion of 17th Foot Regiment (1868-1869)

WO12/3494   ( )   ( )   ( )   ( )   ( )
( )   ( )   (1870-1871)

WO12/3474   General Muster Book of 1st Battalion of 17th Foot Regiment (1871-1872)

WO12/3475   ( )   ( )   ( )   ( )   ( )
( )   ( )   (1872-1873)

WO12/3476   "   "   "   "   "
"   "   (1873-1874)

WO12/3477   "   "   "   "   "
"   "   (1874-1875)

WO12/3478   "   "   "   "   "
"   "   (1875-1876)

WO12/3479   "   "   "   "   "
"   "   (1876-1877)

WO25/3506   Army Embarkation records of 1870-1875

WO73/11   Army Monthly Returns for the year   1870

ASSI 12/14   The Midland Circuit: Indictment Files for 1881

ASSI 13/12   Criminal Depositions and Case Papers for 1881   This includes the map drawn up by Mr Roper of the murder scene in Brimington and shown in sections in this book at pages 24,37,44,83,93 and 160.

ASSI 11/33   The Midland Circuit Crown Minute Books (1873-1882)

HO144/89 (former reference A10204) Papers regarding trial and execution of Alfred Gough (1881):-
A10204/2,3,4,4a,5   Bundle of documents including a letter from His Lordship Judge Mathew to the Home Secretary, the judge's own trial notes + newspaper cutting of "Leicester Chronicle" 5th November 1881

Newspapers in General

The Times Tuesday 9th May 1876

"   "   Saturday 13th May 1876

The Derby Mercury   26th October 1881 (Issue 8702) - notice of Winter Assizes at Leicester re: witnesses

"   "   "   23rd November 1881 Execution of Gough

"   "   "   11th March 1857

"   "   "   3rd January 1872

The Sheffield and Rotherham Independent   9th May 1891, 11th May 1891-Announcements of Supt. Carline's promotion to Assistant Chief Constable.

The Sheffield and Rotherham Independent   16th March 1892-Derbyshire county police had no pay rise since 1873.

The Sheffield and Rotherham Independent   25th March 1892- Candidates for the post of Chief Constable of Derbyshire- Carline was barred as he was over 40 years of age.

Hull Packet and East Riding Times (Hull) 25th November 1881 Issue 5067 Execution of Gough

Reynold's Newspaper, London 28th August, 27th November 1881 Execution of Gough

Penny Illustrated Paper and Illustrated Times 27th August 1881 Issue 1050

The Pall Mall Gazette 22nd-23rd August 1881 (London)

Illustrated Police News 27th August, 3rd September 1881

(Numerous contemporary newspapers covered the murder of Eleanor Windle and Gough's execution throughout the land e.g. Leeds, Bristol, Glasgow, Birmingham, Liverpool, London, Aberdeen, Belfast, Manchester and Oxford.)

Sheffield Central Library (Local Studies Section), Surrey St. Sheffield

Newspapers:-

"The Sheffield and Rotherham Independent" August – November 1881

"The Sheffield Telegraph" August –November 1881

All the events well- documented.

West Yorkshire Archive Service at Wakefield

WYP/LE/A83/105 Constables' Conduct Book 1844-1867 p. 371 (Alfred Gough's police work record)

WYP/LE/A137/254 Register of Constables (Description of Gough on joining police force and previous employment

General Reference Books

A History of Brimington – Vernon Brelsford. Originally published 1937 and updated by Mandy Hicken 1989 Includes useful maps and photographs of the area.

English Criminal Justice in the 19th Century – David Bentley (The Hambledon Press 1998)

Police Uniform and Equipment –A.A.Clarke (Shire Publications Ltd.)1991

The New Police in 19th Century England (Crime, Conflict and Control) –David Taylor (Manchester University Press) 1997

A History of Police in England and Wales 900-1966 –T.A. Critchley (Constable and Co. Ltd 1967)

The Leeds Police 1836-1974 –written by members of the Research and Planning Dept. of the Leeds City Police, edited by Ewart W. Clay (E. J. Arnold and Son Ltd. Leeds)

The History of the West Riding Constabulary 1856-1968 – Barry Shaw M.A.I.E.of 16, Marlborough Drive, Tadcaster.

The Great British Bobby –Clive Emsley (Quercus)

The Victorian Policeman –Simon Dell (Shire Library Classics)

Prison Life in Victorian England –Michelle Higgs (Tempus Publishing Ltd.)

Practical Pathology –A Manual for Students and Practitioners-G Sims Woodhead (Young J. Pentland)

The Hangman's Record Vol. 1(1868-1899)--Steve Fielding

Rape. A History from 1860 to the Present – Joanna Bourke (Virago)

Child Sexual Abuse in Victorian England –Louise A. Jackson (Routledge1 2000)

Deadly Derbyshire 1700- 1900- Scott C. Lomax (Wharncliffe Books)

A History of the Services of the 17th (The Leicestershire) Regiment (1688-1910) - E.A.H.Webb (Vacher and Sons Ltd.)

The Indian Army 1822- 1922- T. A. Heathcote

The Army in India (A photographic record 1850-1914) published in association with The National Army Museum

Our Bones Are Scattered –Andrew Ward (The Cawnpore Massacres and the Indian Mutiny of 1857 (John Murray, Albemarle St.)

Sword of the Raj- The British Army in India, 1747-1947- Roger Beaumont (The Bobbs-Merrill Co. Inc., Indianapolis/New York)

Victorian News and Newspapers – Lucy Brown   (Clarendon Press Oxford 1985)

Papers for the Millions- The New Journalism in Britain, 1850's to 1914 edited by Joel H. Weiner (Greenwood Press 1988)

Directory and Topography of Sheffield 1862 p. 643 for Chesterfield

White's History, Gazetteer and Directory of Derbyshire and Sheffield 1857 p.486

White's History, Gazetteer and Directory of Derbyshire and Sheffield 1879

Wright's Directory of South Derbyshire 1874

Post Office Directory 1876 Derbyshire.

Kelly's Directory 1881 Derbyshire

" " 1891 Brimington Derbyshire

" " 1895 Derbyshire

Bulmer's History, Topography and Directory of Derbyshire 1895 re: Turnditch

A Brief History of Ringwood Hall- Sandra Struggles 2002 (A news-sheet of the now hotel-Ringwood Hall)

Family Skeletons- Ruth Paley and Simon Fowler (The National Archives 2005)

Chesterfield: Scenes from Yesterday (Borough of Chesterfield 1974)

Then and Now- Photographs of Chesterfield, past and present.-(Copyright Derek Jones and Dronfield Gazette Ltd, 1987)

A Dictionary of Medical and Related Terms for the Family Historian-Joan E. Grundy (Swansong Publications)

1	Map of Chesterfield Area, 1880		14
2	Map of Main Turnpike Road Leading to Brimington		24
3	Map of Johnson's Lane 1881		37
4	Map of Hoole's Plantation		44
5	Finding the Body in Hoole's Plantation (sketch)		46
6	Buck Inn, Chesterfield where Gough was Arrested (sketch)		51
7	Alfred Barnes, MP for Chesterfield and JP		62
8	Map of Brimington Area in 1881		83
9	Red Lion, Brimington where the Inquest was Held (sketch)		89
10	Map of Almond Place to the Tollbar		93
11	House Where the Child Lived (sketch)		116
12	Map of the Village Centre to the Miners' Arms		160
13	Mr Frederick Swanwick, JP		205
14	Captain Parry, Chief Constable of Derbyshire		208
15	Scott's Lodging House, Sheffield (sketch)		236
16	Only Remaining Section of Derby Gaol		252
17	Sir James Charles Matthew, Trial Judge		284
18	Leicester Castle Today		285
19	Contemporary Sketch of Leicester Castle		286
20	Prosecuting Counsel, Mr Chandos Leigh QC		310
21	The Child Follows the Pedlar (sketch)		315
22	Interior of Courtroom		344
23	Sketch of Charles Abney Hastings Brown		347
24	Sketch of Alfred Gough		392
25	1st Battalion, 17th Foot Regiment at Lucknow		407
26	William Marwood, the Executioner		443

LIST OF MAPS AND ILLUSTRATIONS

ACKNOWLEDGEMENTS

I would like to thank the archivists, their assistants and librarians who have given me assistance in finding the fascinating information held in their collections. By letter, phone, e-mail and in person I much appreciate the time they have given to me. The bibliography lists the many places I have either visited or made contact with. In particular I would like to thank Ms Tyler-Divine for the experience of a personally conducted tour of the courtrooms and cells at Leicester Castle where Alfred Gough was sentenced to death.

I am exceedingly grateful to Professor David Taylor, Emeritus Professor of History at the University of Huddersfield. He read my copious notes regarding the legal and penal procedures in 1881 and helped with the questions I posed. I am very obliged to him for his valuable time and thoughts.

Many thanks to Dr K. Laver for explaining my queries regarding the post mortem and Mr Robert Fleming for his aid regarding the 17th Foot Regiment.

Mrs Janet Jones cannot be forgotten for reading and critiquing my book in such a professional manner. Her enthusiasm was always an encouragement to delve deeper into the facts.

I want to record the generosity of spirit of Lorraine and Kev Edwards and Phil Mate —occupants of Almond Place who allowed into their homes a perfect stranger who said she was intending to write a book about the murder of Eleanor Windle! How many people today would show some one around their homes and lend books on old Brimington to a person who just turned up on their doorstep with a questionnaire?

Lastly, I would like to greatly thank my husband for all his computer wizardry in producing my book. It could not have been done without him! He also was my inspiration in that if he could write a book and publish it himself then so could I.

I have met so many people over the years of writing and research who have encouraged me in my efforts that if I have forgotten to mention anyone then apologies. It was not intentional.

NOTES REGARDING THE DIFFERING FONTS

The various print styles or fonts throughout the book relate to the articles published in the local newspapers of the day.

"Lucida Handwriting" print is used for the words of the reporters of either "The Derbyshire Times" or "The Derbyshire Courier". The two local papers of Chesterfield, the nearest town to where the incident took place.

"**Book Antiqua**" print is used for the Sheffield newspapers that actually got hold of the story some days earlier than their Chesterfield counterparts- "The Sheffield Telegraph" and "The Sheffield and Rotherham Independent".

"**Arial Black**" print is "The Derby Mercury".

Other newspapers will be referred to but the above four (apart from "The Derby Mercury") formed the basis of my information and the starting point to my research. It is regrettable that these nineteenth century newspaper hacks remain anonymous but I do acknowledge that it was solely their reporting that fired my enthusiasm to find out more.

Every effort was made to only use speech marks for the conversations reported at the time. However, if the odd phrase has crept in it is to be hoped it is in keeping with the feel of the situation and does not detract from the veracity of the story.

Made in the USA
Charleston, SC
31 October 2015